ALAN MOORE
OSCAR ZARATE

A SMALL KILLING

AVATAR™

Antony Johnston
Jaime Rodríguez
anatomy of a killing article

William Christensen
editor in chief

Mark Seifert
creative director

for Planeta De Agustini, SA Production
Chus Gomez
JuanJo McArro

AVATAR PRESS

9 Triumph Drive

Urbana, IL 61802

www.avatarpress.com

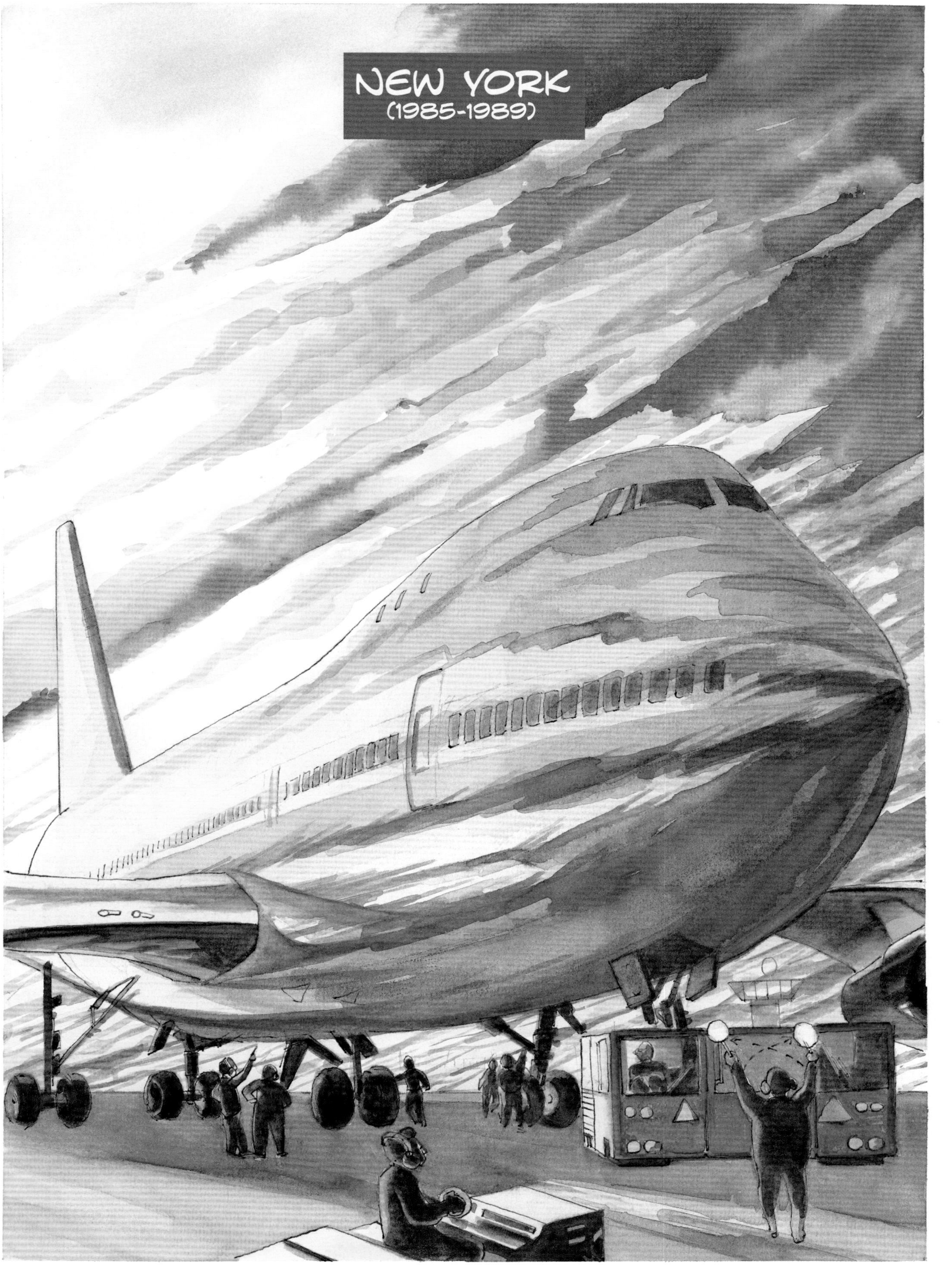
NEW YORK
(1985-1989)

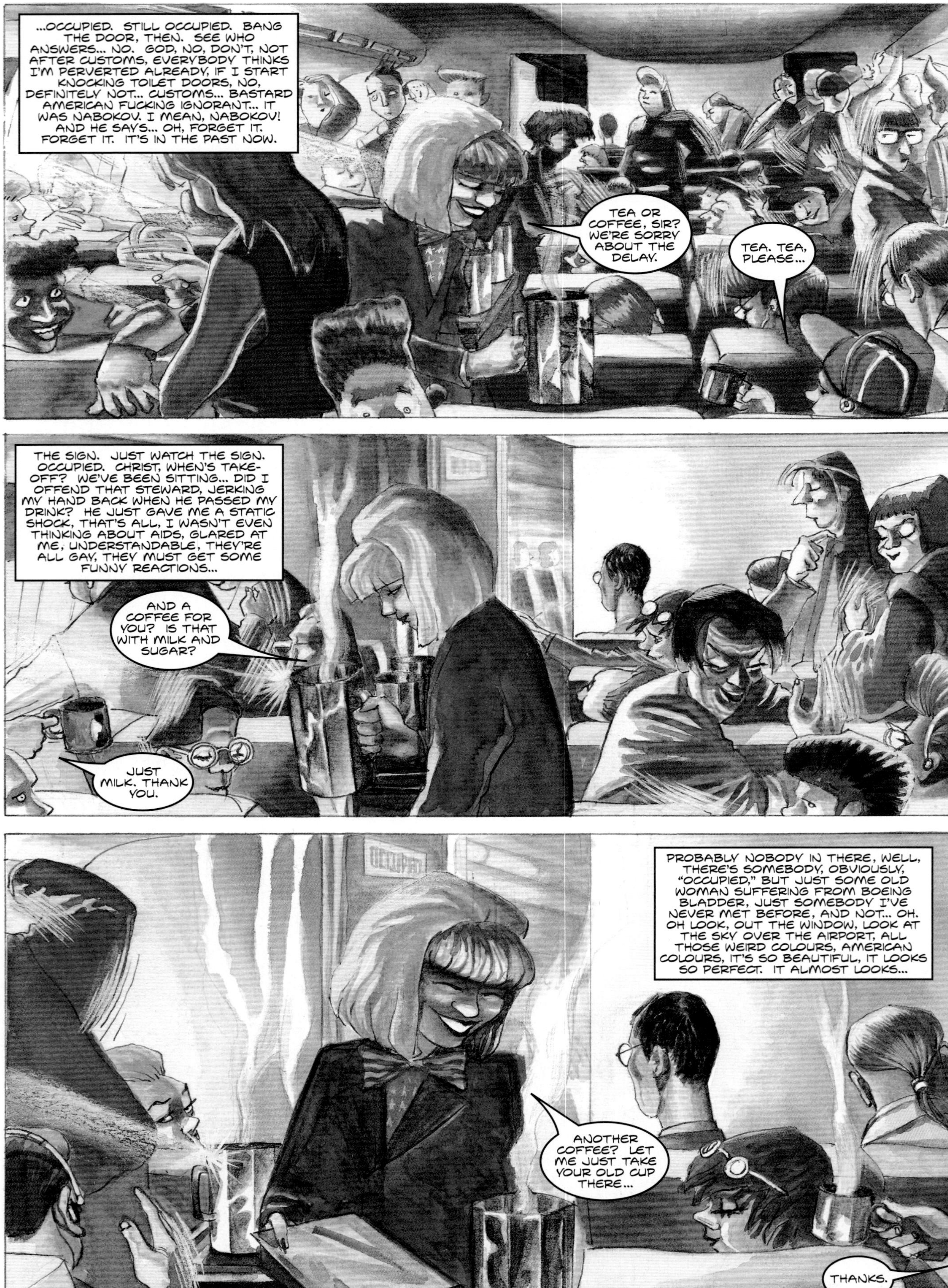
...OCCUPIED. STILL OCCUPIED. BANG THE DOOR, THEN. SEE WHO ANSWERS... NO. GOD, NO, DON'T, NOT AFTER CUSTOMS, EVERYBODY THINKS I'M PERVERTED ALREADY, IF I START KNOCKING TOILET DOORS, NO, DEFINITELY NOT... CUSTOMS... BASTARD AMERICAN FUCKING IGNORANT... IT WAS NABOKOV. I MEAN, NABOKOV! AND HE SAYS... OH, FORGET IT. FORGET IT. IT'S IN THE PAST NOW.
TEA OR COFFEE, SIR? WE'RE SORRY ABOUT THE DELAY.
TEA. TEA, PLEASE...
THE SIGN. JUST WATCH THE SIGN. OCCUPIED. CHRIST, WHEN'S TAKE-OFF? WE'VE BEEN SITTING... DID I OFFEND THAT STEWARD, JERKING MY HAND BACK WHEN HE PASSED MY DRINK? HE JUST GAVE ME A STATIC SHOCK, THAT'S ALL, I WASN'T EVEN THINKING ABOUT AIDS, GLARED AT ME, UNDERSTANDABLE, THEY'RE ALL GAY, THEY MUST GET SOME FUNNY REACTIONS...
AND A COFFEE FOR YOU? IS THAT WITH MILK AND SUGAR?
JUST MILK. THANK YOU.
PROBABLY NOBODY IN THERE, WELL, THERE'S SOMEBODY, OBVIOUSLY, "OCCUPIED," BUT JUST SOME OLD WOMAN SUFFERING FROM BOEING BLADDER, JUST SOMEBODY I'VE NEVER MET BEFORE, AND NOT... OH. OH LOOK, OUT THE WINDOW, LOOK AT THE SKY OVER THE AIRPORT, ALL THOSE WEIRD COLOURS, AMERICAN COLOURS, IT'S SO BEAUTIFUL, IT LOOKS SO PERFECT. IT ALMOST LOOKS...
ANOTHER COFFEE? LET ME JUST TAKE YOUR OLD CUP THERE...
THANKS.

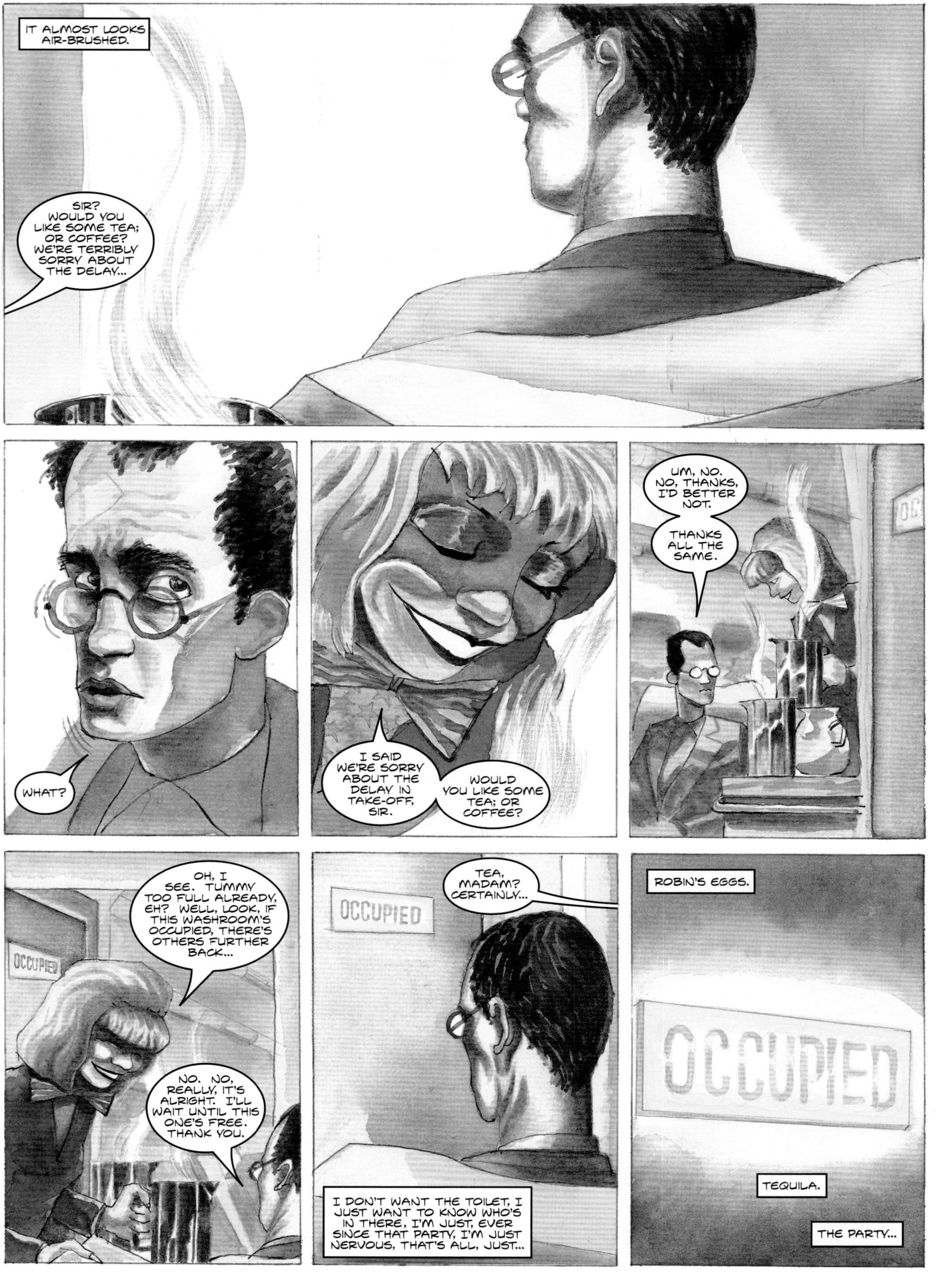
IT ALMOST LOOKS AIR-BRUSHED.
SIR? WOULD YOU LIKE SOME TEA; OR COFFEE? WE'RE TERRIBLY SORRY ABOUT THE DELAY...
WHAT?
I SAID WE'RE SORRY ABOUT THE DELAY IN TAKE-OFF, SIR.
WOULD YOU LIKE SOME TEA; OR COFFEE?
UM, NO. NO, THANKS, I'D BETTER NOT.
THANKS ALL THE SAME.
OH, I SEE. TUMMY TOO FULL ALREADY, EH? WELL, LOOK, IF THIS WASHROOM'S OCCUPIED, THERE'S OTHERS FURTHER BACK...
OCCUPIED
NO. NO, REALLY, IT'S ALRIGHT. I'LL WAIT UNTIL THIS ONE'S FREE. THANK YOU.
TEA, MADAM? CERTAINLY...
OCCUPIED
I DON'T WANT THE TOILET, I JUST WANT TO KNOW WHO'S IN THERE, I'M JUST, EVER SINCE THAT PARTY, I'M JUST NERVOUS, THAT'S ALL, JUST...
ROBIN'S EGGS.
OCCUPIED
TEQUILA.
THE PARTY...

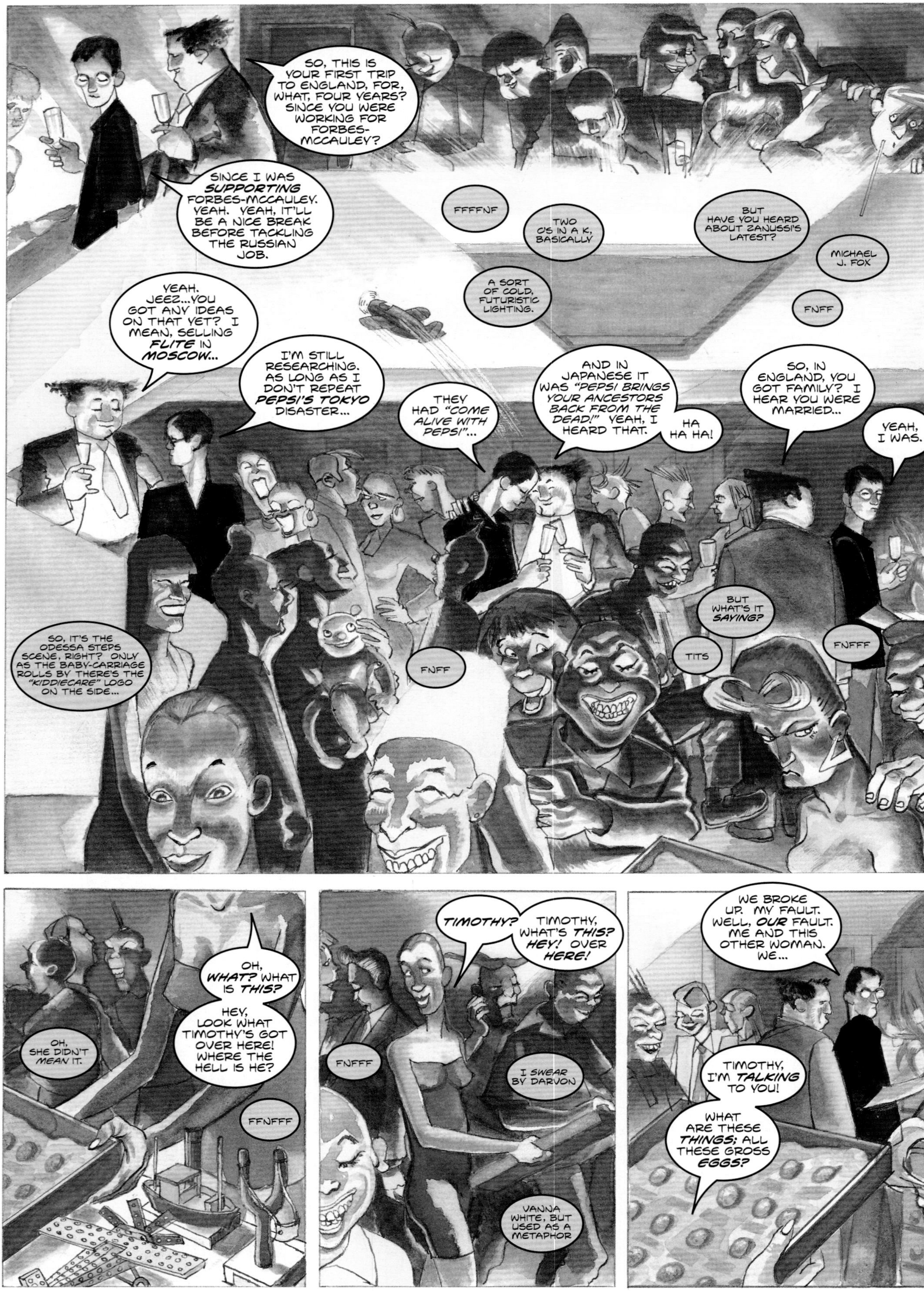
SO, THIS IS YOUR FIRST TRIP TO ENGLAND, FOR, WHAT, FOUR YEARS? SINCE YOU WERE WORKING FOR FORBES-MCCAULEY?
SINCE I WAS SUPPORTING FORBES-MCCAULEY. YEAH. YEAH, IT'LL BE A NICE BREAK BEFORE TACKLING THE RUSSIAN JOB.
FFFFNF
TWO O'S IN A K, BASICALLY
BUT HAVE YOU HEARD ABOUT ZANUSSI'S LATEST?
MICHAEL J. FOX
A SORT OF COLD, FUTURISTIC LIGHTING.
FNFF
YEAH. JEEZ...YOU GOT ANY IDEAS ON THAT YET? I MEAN, SELLING FLITE IN MOSCOW...
I'M STILL RESEARCHING. AS LONG AS I DON'T REPEAT PEPSI'S TOKYO DISASTER...
THEY HAD "COME ALIVE WITH PEPSI"...
AND IN JAPANESE IT WAS "PEPSI BRINGS YOUR ANCESTORS BACK FROM THE DEAD!" YEAH, I HEARD THAT.
HA HA HA!
SO, IN ENGLAND, YOU GOT FAMILY? I HEAR YOU WERE MARRIED...
YEAH, I WAS.
BUT WHAT'S IT SAYING?
SO, IT'S THE ODESSA STEPS SCENE, RIGHT? ONLY AS THE BABY-CARRIAGE ROLLS BY THERE'S THE "KIDDIECARE" LOGO ON THE SIDE...
FNFF
TITS
FNFFF
OH, WHAT? WHAT IS THIS?
HEY, LOOK WHAT TIMOTHY'S GOT OVER HERE! WHERE THE HELL IS HE?
OH, SHE DIDN'T MEAN IT.
FFNFFF
TIMOTHY?
TIMOTHY, WHAT'S THIS? HEY! OVER HERE!
FNFFF
I SWEAR BY DARVON
VANNA WHITE, BUT USED AS A METAPHOR
WE BROKE UP. MY FAULT. WELL, OUR FAULT. ME AND THIS OTHER WOMAN. WE...
TIMOTHY, I'M TALKING TO YOU!
WHAT ARE THESE THINGS; ALL THESE GROSS EGGS?

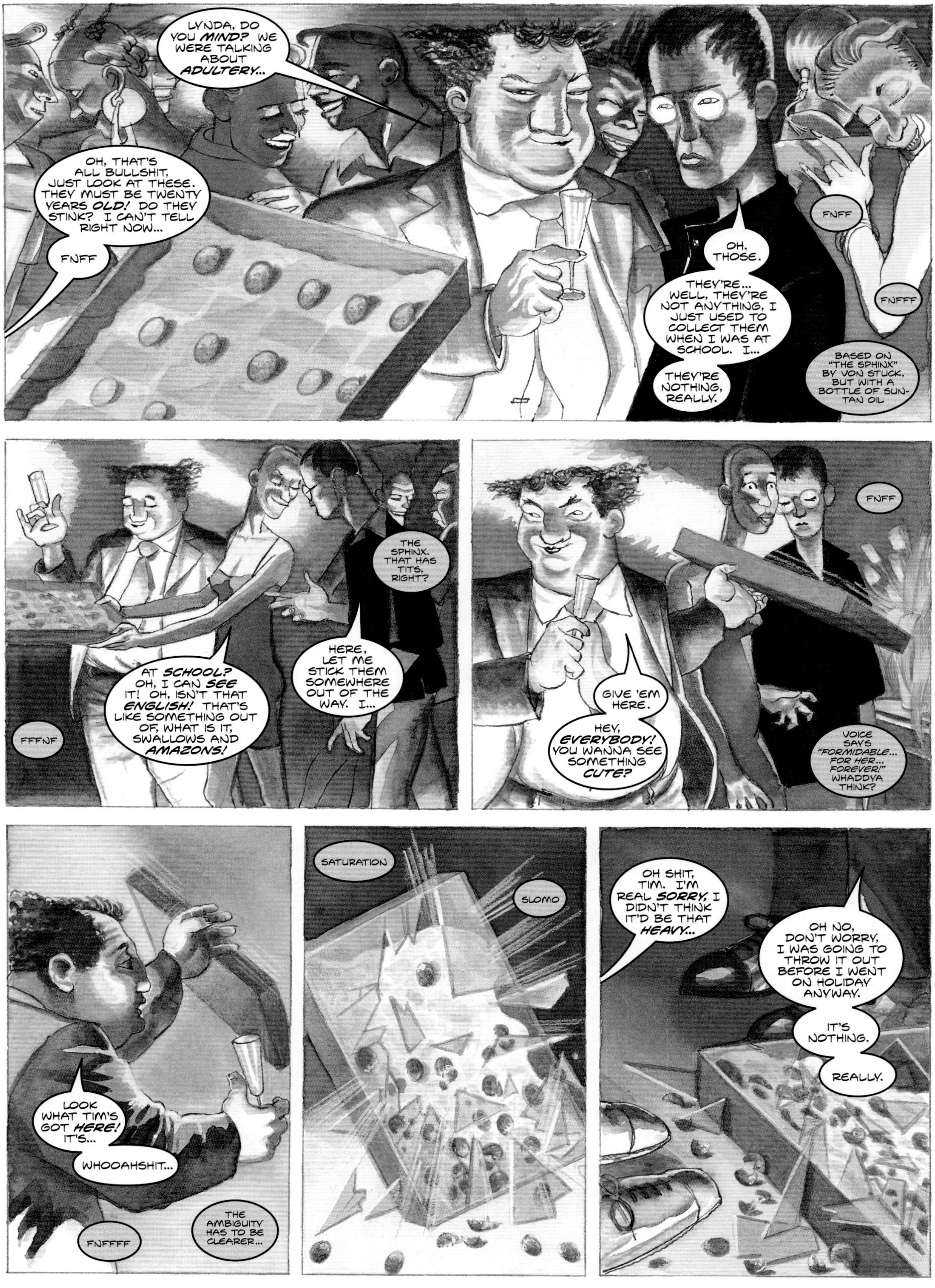
LYNDA, DO YOU MIND? WE WERE TALKING ABOUT ADULTERY...
OH, THAT'S ALL BULLSHIT, JUST LOOK AT THESE. THEY MUST BE TWENTY YEARS OLD! DO THEY STINK? I CAN'T TELL RIGHT NOW...
FNFF
OH. THOSE.
THEY'RE... WELL, THEY'RE NOT ANYTHING, I JUST USED TO COLLECT THEM WHEN I WAS AT SCHOOL. I...
THEY'RE NOTHING, REALLY.
FNFF
FNFFF
BASED ON "THE SPHINX" BY VON STUCK, BUT WITH A BOTTLE OF SUN-TAN OIL
AT SCHOOL? OH, I CAN SEE IT! OH, ISN'T THAT ENGLISH! THAT'S LIKE SOMETHING OUT OF, WHAT IS IT, SWALLOWS AND AMAZONS!
HERE, LET ME STICK THEM SOMEWHERE OUT OF THE WAY. I...
THE SPHINX. THAT HAS TITS, RIGHT?
FFFNF
GIVE 'EM HERE.
HEY, EVERYBODY! YOU WANNA SEE SOMETHING CUTE?
FNFF
VOICE SAYS "FORMIDABLE... FOR HER... FOREVER!" WHADDYA THINK?
LOOK WHAT TIM'S GOT HERE! IT'S...
WHOOAHSHIT...
FNFFFF
THE AMBIGUITY HAS TO BE CLEARER...
SATURATION
SLOMO
OH SHIT, TIM. I'M REAL SORRY, I DIDN'T THINK IT'D BE THAT HEAVY...
OH NO, DON'T WORRY, I WAS GOING TO THROW IT OUT BEFORE I WENT ON HOLIDAY ANYWAY.
IT'S NOTHING.
REALLY.

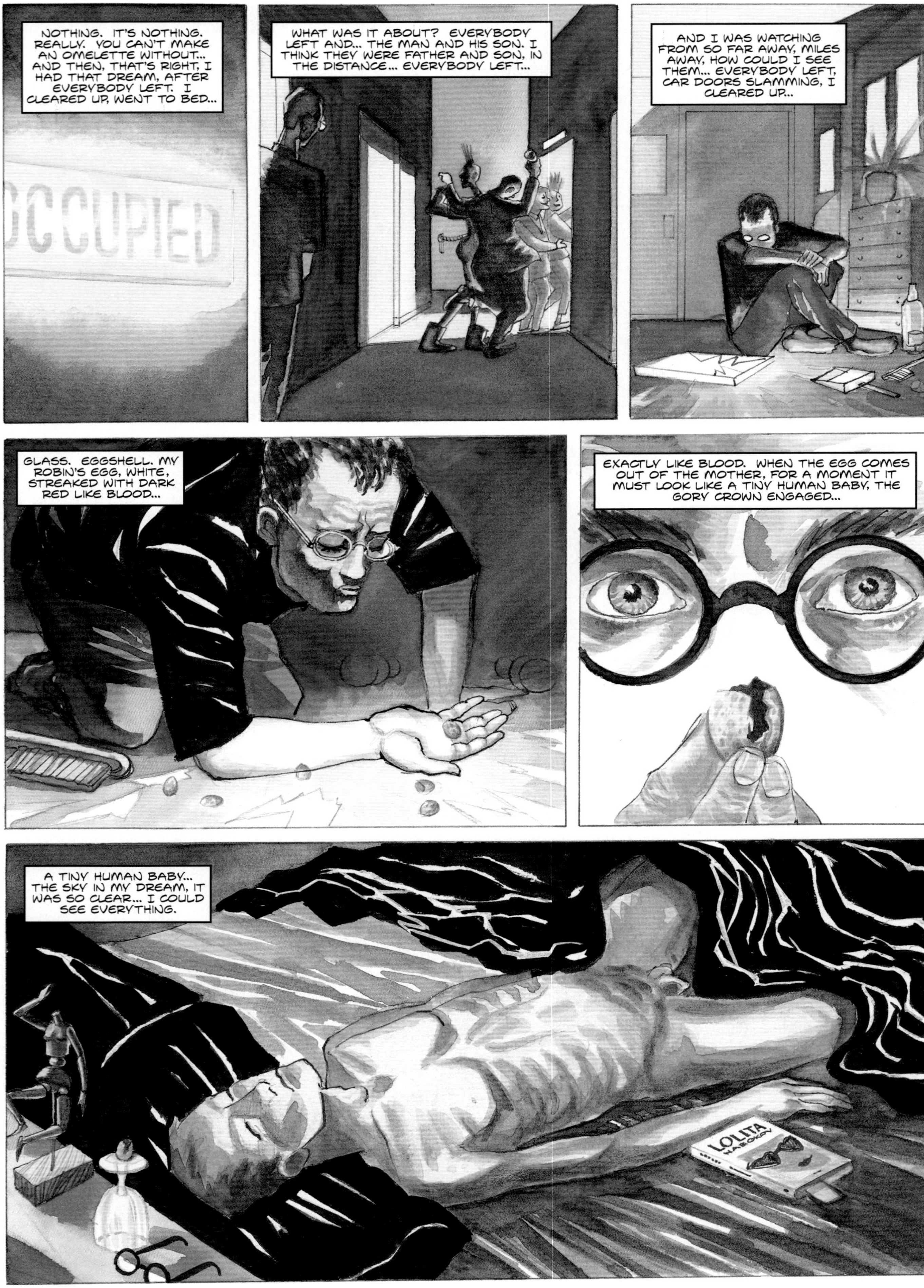
NOTHING. IT'S NOTHING. REALLY. YOU CAN'T MAKE AN OMELETTE WITHOUT... AND THEN, THAT'S RIGHT, I HAD THAT DREAM, AFTER EVERYBODY LEFT. I CLEARED UP, WENT TO BED...
OCCUPIED
WHAT WAS IT ABOUT? EVERYBODY LEFT AND... THE MAN AND HIS SON. I THINK THEY WERE FATHER AND SON, IN THE DISTANCE... EVERYBODY LEFT...
AND I WAS WATCHING FROM SO FAR AWAY, MILES AWAY, HOW COULD I SEE THEM... EVERYBODY LEFT, CAR DOORS SLAMMING, I CLEARED UP...
GLASS. EGGSHELL. MY ROBIN'S EGG, WHITE, STREAKED WITH DARK RED LIKE BLOOD...
EXACTLY LIKE BLOOD. WHEN THE EGG COMES OUT OF THE MOTHER, FOR A MOMENT IT MUST LOOK LIKE A TINY HUMAN BABY, THE GORY CROWN ENGAGED...
A TINY HUMAN BABY... THE SKY IN MY DREAM, IT WAS SO CLEAR... I COULD SEE EVERYTHING.
LOLITA
NABOKOV

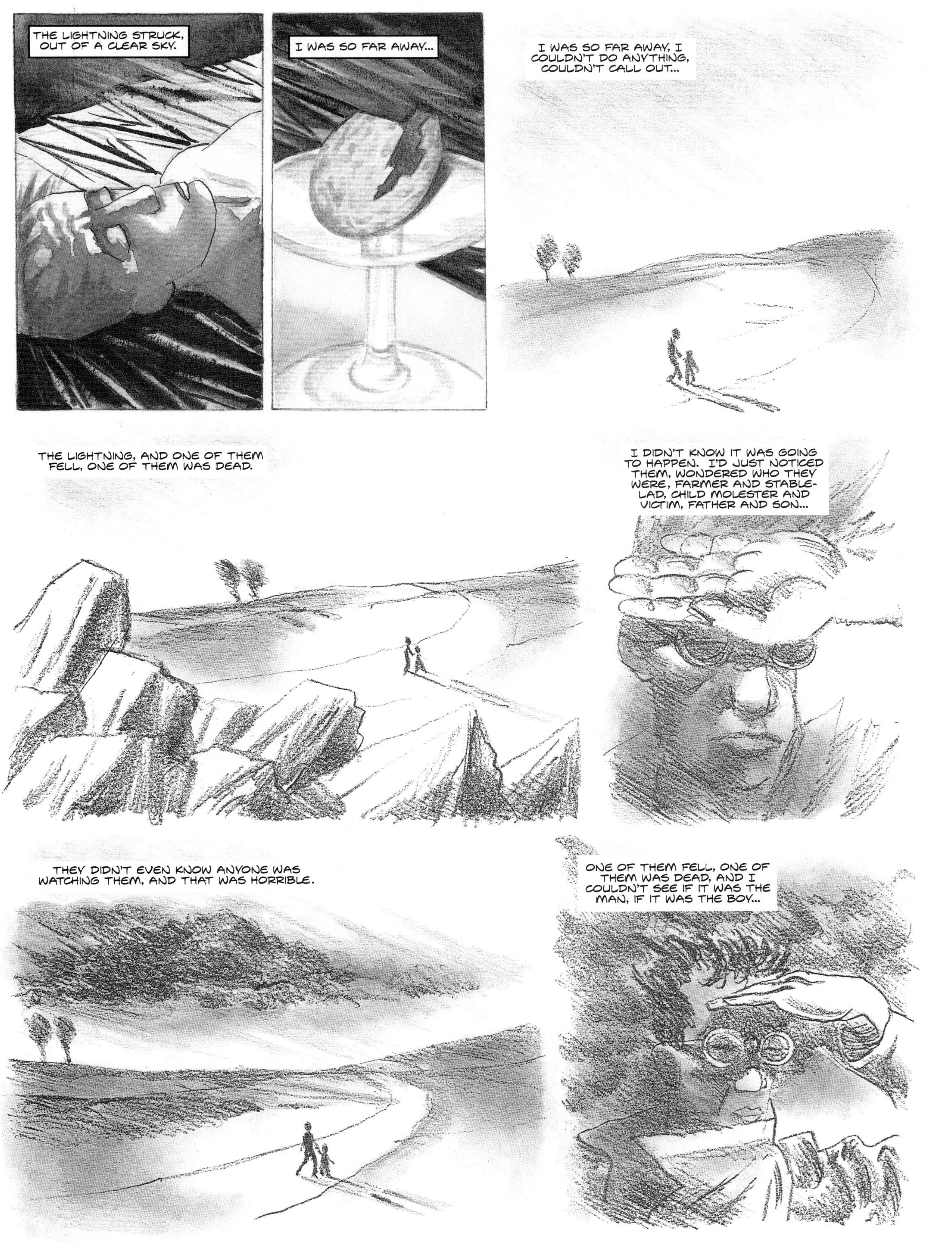
THE LIGHTNING STRUCK, OUT OF A CLEAR SKY.
I WAS SO FAR AWAY...
I WAS SO FAR AWAY, I COULDN'T DO ANYTHING, COULDN'T CALL OUT...
THE LIGHTNING, AND ONE OF THEM FELL, ONE OF THEM WAS DEAD.
I DIDN'T KNOW IT WAS GOING TO HAPPEN. I'D JUST NOTICED THEM, WONDERED WHO THEY WERE, FARMER AND STABLE-LAD, CHILD MOLESTER AND VICTIM, FATHER AND SON...
THEY DIDN'T EVEN KNOW ANYONE WAS WATCHING THEM, AND THAT WAS HORRIBLE.
ONE OF THEM FELL, ONE OF THEM WAS DEAD, AND I COULDN'T SEE IF IT WAS THE MAN, IF IT WAS THE BOY...

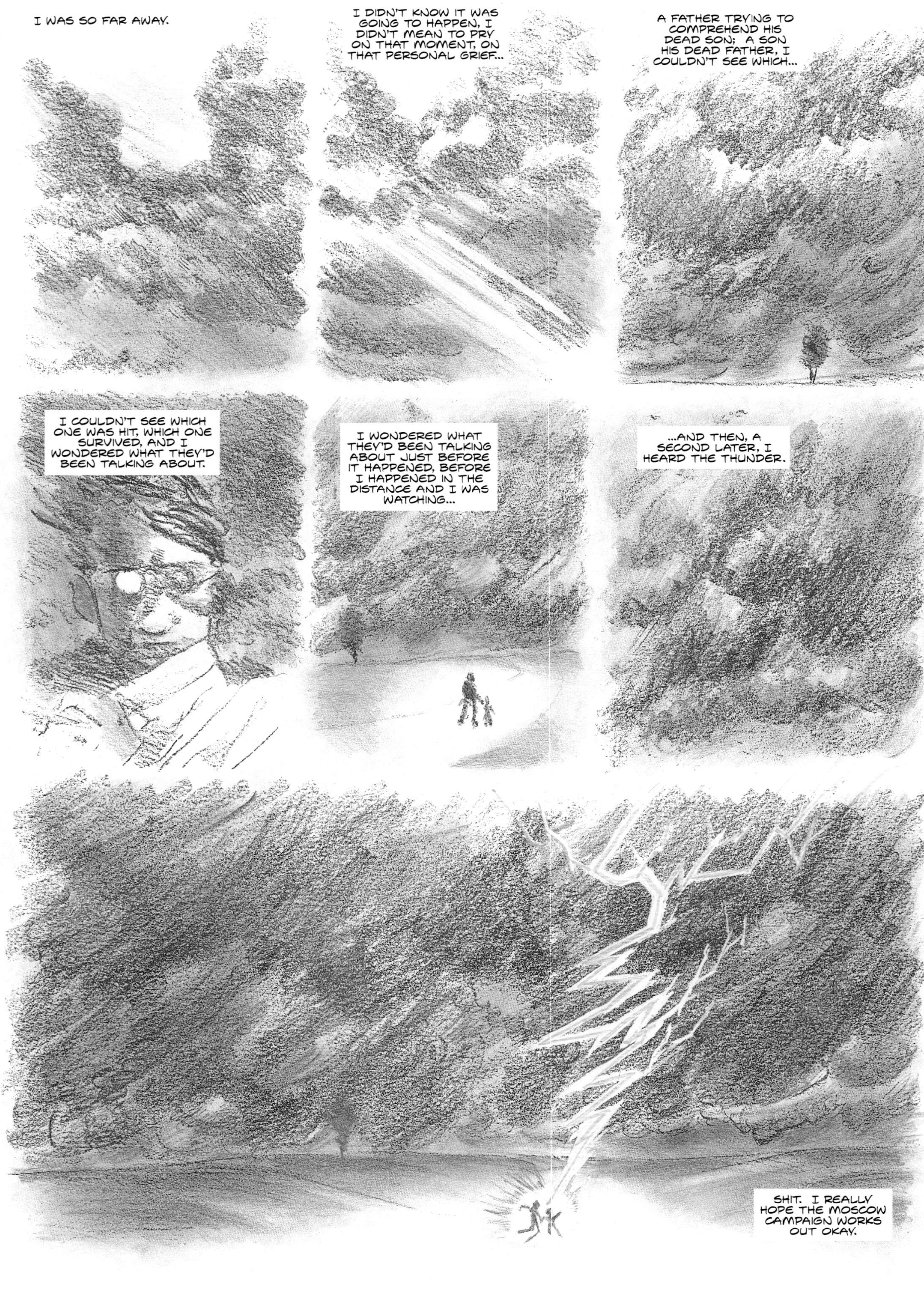
I WAS SO FAR AWAY.
I DIDN'T KNOW IT WAS GOING TO HAPPEN, I DIDN'T MEAN TO PRY ON THAT MOMENT, ON THAT PERSONAL GRIEF...
A FATHER TRYING TO COMPREHEND HIS DEAD SON; A SON HIS DEAD FATHER, I COULDN'T SEE WHICH...
I COULDN'T SEE WHICH ONE WAS HIT, WHICH ONE SURVIVED, AND I WONDERED WHAT THEY'D BEEN TALKING ABOUT.
I WONDERED WHAT THEY'D BEEN TALKING ABOUT JUST BEFORE IT HAPPENED, BEFORE I HAPPENED IN THE DISTANCE AND I WAS WATCHING...
...AND THEN, A SECOND LATER, I HEARD THE THUNDER.
SHIT. I REALLY HOPE THE MOSCOW CAMPAIGN WORKS OUT OKAY.

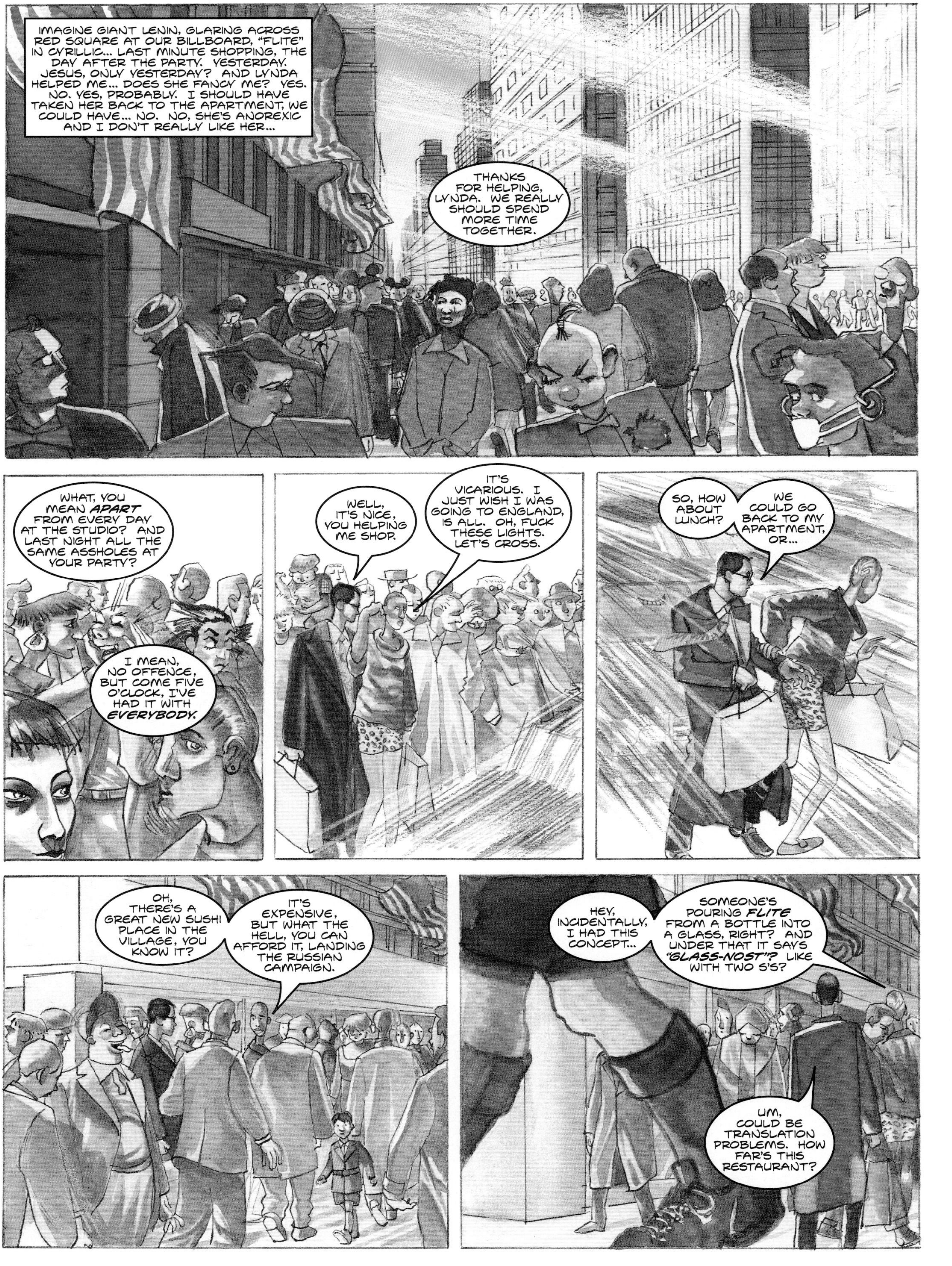
IMAGINE GIANT LENIN, GLARING ACROSS RED SQUARE AT OUR BILLBOARD, "FLITE" IN CYRILLIC... LAST MINUTE SHOPPING, THE DAY AFTER THE PARTY. YESTERDAY. JESUS, ONLY YESTERDAY? AND LYNDA HELPED ME... DOES SHE FANCY ME? YES. NO. YES, PROBABLY. I SHOULD HAVE TAKEN HER BACK TO THE APARTMENT, WE COULD HAVE... NO. NO, SHE'S ANOREXIC AND I DON'T REALLY LIKE HER...
THANKS FOR HELPING, LYNDA. WE REALLY SHOULD SPEND MORE TIME TOGETHER.
WHAT, YOU MEAN APART FROM EVERY DAY AT THE STUDIO? AND LAST NIGHT ALL THE SAME ASSHOLES AT YOUR PARTY?
I MEAN, NO OFFENCE, BUT COME FIVE O'CLOCK, I'VE HAD IT WITH EVERYBODY.
WELL, IT'S NICE, YOU HELPING ME SHOP.
IT'S VICARIOUS. I JUST WISH I WAS GOING TO ENGLAND, IS ALL. OH, FUCK THESE LIGHTS. LET'S CROSS.
SO, HOW ABOUT LUNCH?
WE COULD GO BACK TO MY APARTMENT, OR...
OH, THERE'S A GREAT NEW SUSHI PLACE IN THE VILLAGE, YOU KNOW IT?
IT'S EXPENSIVE, BUT WHAT THE HELL, YOU CAN AFFORD IT, LANDING THE RUSSIAN CAMPAIGN.
HEY, INCIDENTALLY, I HAD THIS CONCEPT...
SOMEONE'S POURING FLITE FROM A BOTTLE INTO A GLASS, RIGHT? AND UNDER THAT IT SAYS "GLASS-NOST"? LIKE WITH TWO S'S?
UM, COULD BE TRANSLATION PROBLEMS. HOW FAR'S THIS RESTAURANT?

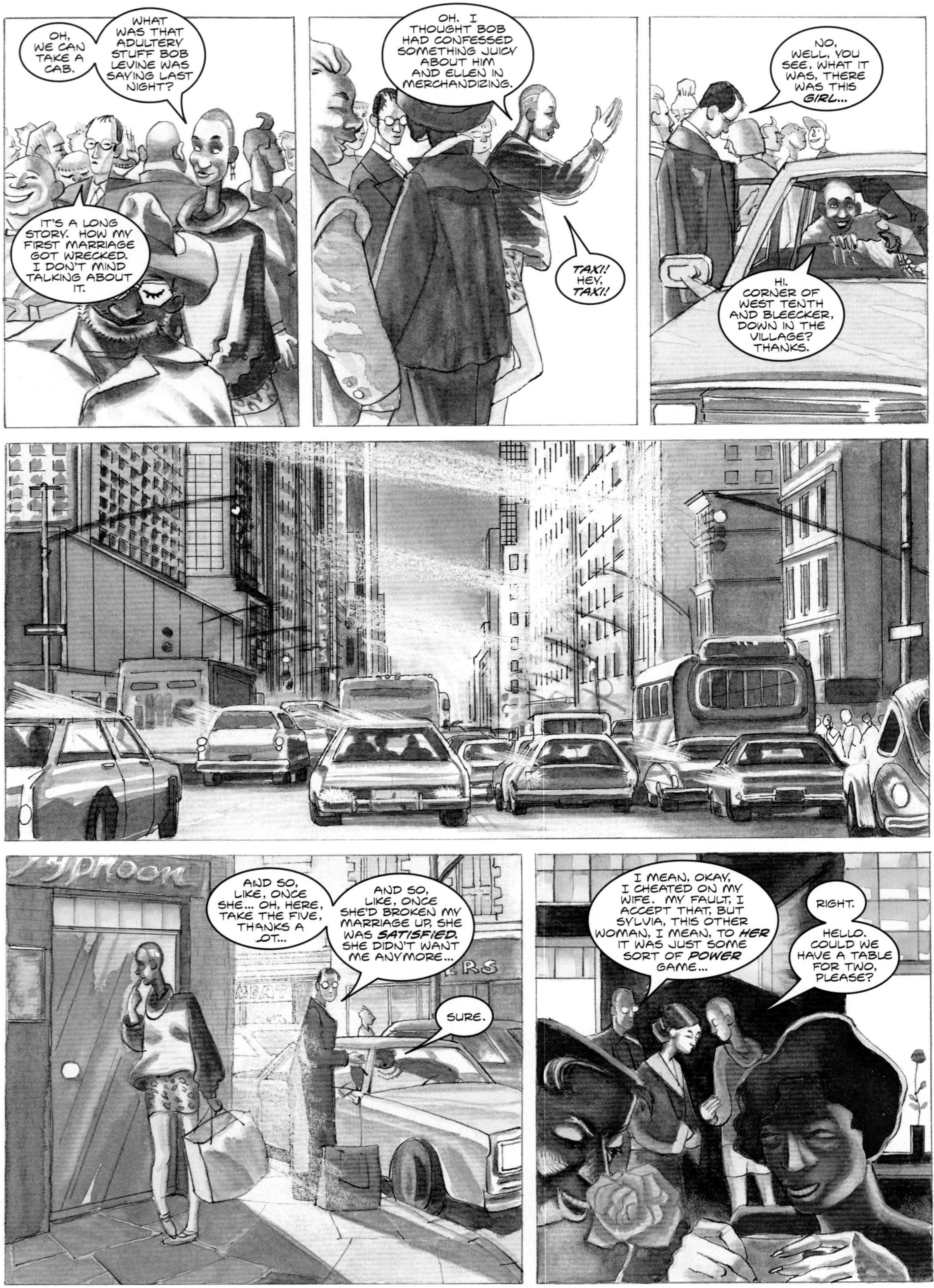
OH, WE CAN TAKE A CAB.
WHAT WAS THAT ADULTERY STUFF BOB LEVINE WAS SAYING LAST NIGHT?
IT'S A LONG STORY. HOW MY FIRST MARRIAGE GOT WRECKED. I DON'T MIND TALKING ABOUT IT.
OH. I THOUGHT BOB HAD CONFESSED SOMETHING JUICY ABOUT HIM AND ELLEN IN MERCHANDIZING.
TAXI! HEY, *TAXI!*
NO, WELL, YOU SEE, WHAT IT WAS, THERE WAS THIS *GIRL*...
HI. CORNER OF WEST TENTH AND BLEECKER, DOWN IN THE VILLAGE? THANKS.
AND SO, LIKE, ONCE SHE... OH, HERE, TAKE THE FIVE, THANKS A LOT...
AND SO, LIKE, ONCE SHE'D BROKEN MY MARRIAGE UP, SHE WAS *SATISFIED*. SHE DIDN'T WANT ME ANYMORE...
SURE.
I MEAN, OKAY, I CHEATED ON MY WIFE. MY FAULT, I ACCEPT THAT, BUT SYLVIA, THIS OTHER WOMAN, I MEAN, TO *HER* IT WAS JUST SOME SORT OF *POWER* GAME...
RIGHT.
HELLO. COULD WE HAVE A TABLE FOR TWO, PLEASE?

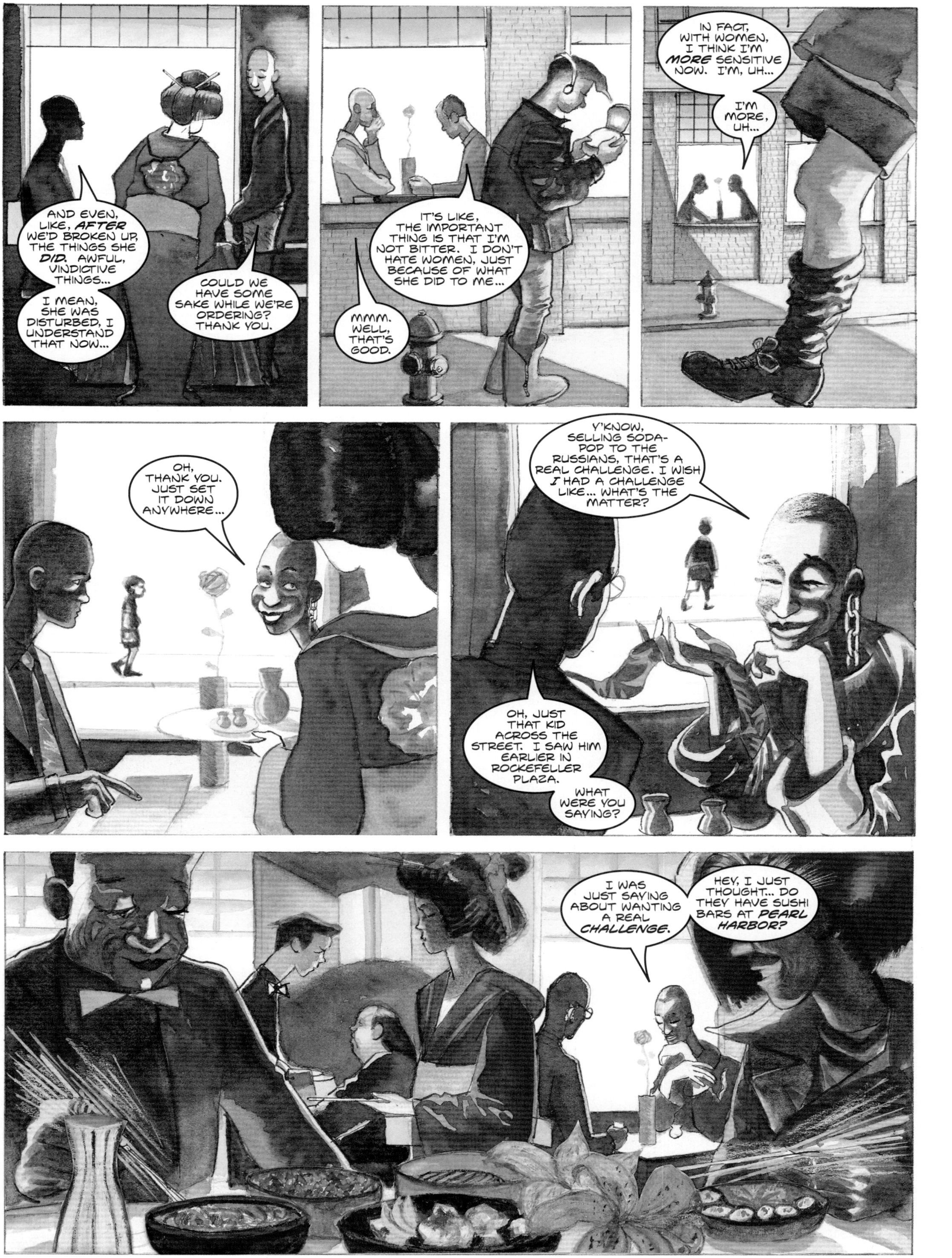
AND EVEN, LIKE, *AFTER* WE'D BROKEN UP, THE THINGS SHE *DID*. AWFUL, VINDICTIVE THINGS...
I MEAN, SHE WAS DISTURBED, I UNDERSTAND THAT NOW...
COULD WE HAVE SOME SAKE WHILE WE'RE ORDERING? THANK YOU.
IT'S LIKE, THE IMPORTANT THING IS THAT I'M NOT BITTER. I DON'T HATE WOMEN, JUST BECAUSE OF WHAT SHE DID TO ME...
MMM. WELL, THAT'S GOOD.
IN FACT, WITH WOMEN, I THINK I'M *MORE* SENSITIVE NOW. I'M, UH...
I'M MORE, UH...
OH, THANK YOU. JUST SET IT DOWN ANYWHERE...
Y'KNOW, SELLING SODA-POP TO THE RUSSIANS, THAT'S A REAL CHALLENGE. I WISH *I* HAD A CHALLENGE LIKE... WHAT'S THE MATTER?
OH, JUST THAT KID ACROSS THE STREET. I SAW HIM EARLIER IN ROCKEFELLER PLAZA.
WHAT WERE YOU SAYING?
I WAS JUST SAYING ABOUT WANTING A REAL *CHALLENGE*.
HEY, I JUST THOUGHT... DO THEY HAVE SUSHI BARS AT *PEARL HARBOR?*

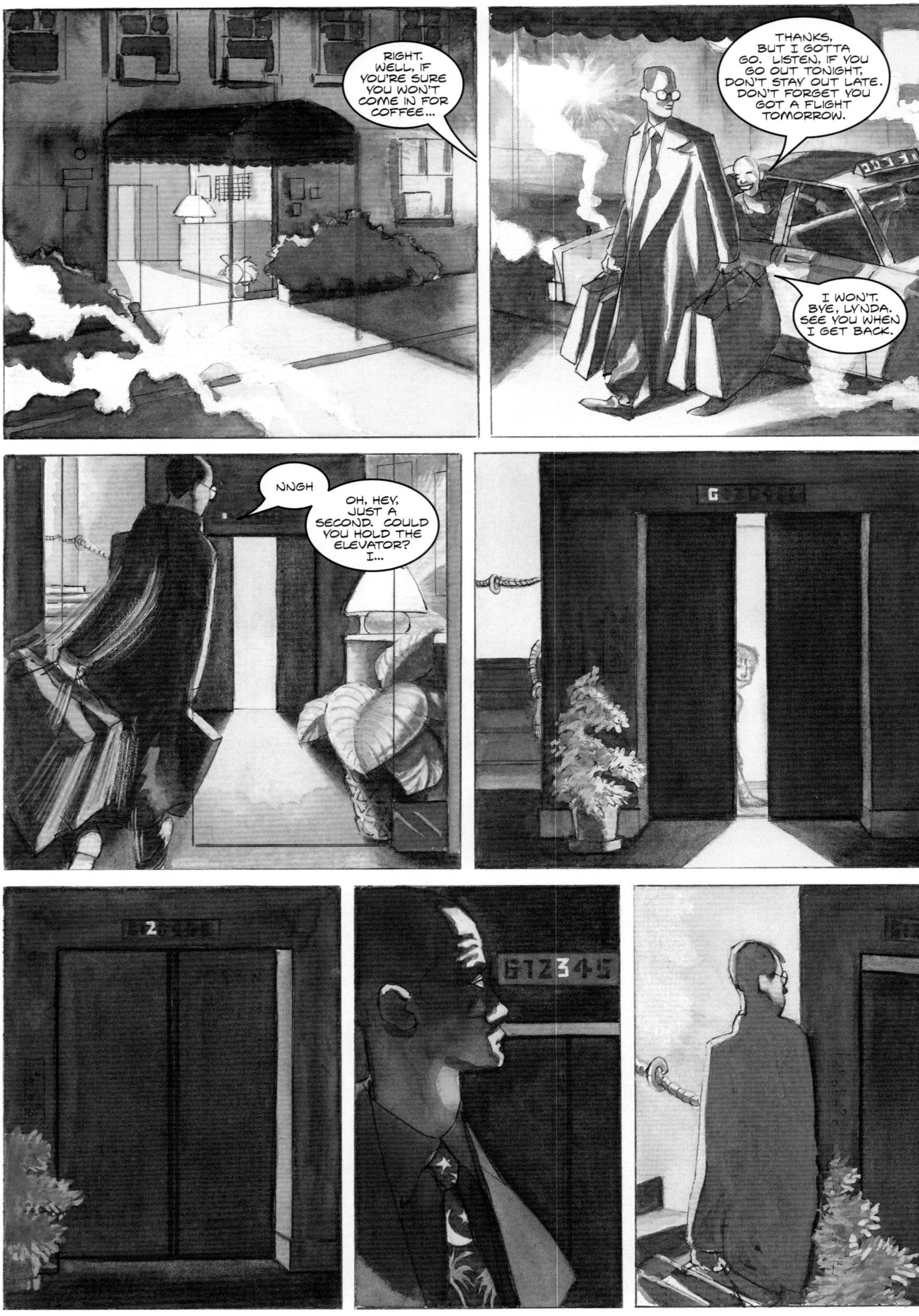
RIGHT. WELL, IF YOU'RE SURE YOU WON'T COME IN FOR COFFEE...
THANKS, BUT I GOTTA GO. LISTEN, IF YOU GO OUT TONIGHT, DON'T STAY OUT LATE. DON'T FORGET YOU GOT A FLIGHT TOMORROW.
I WON'T. BYE, LYNDA. SEE YOU WHEN I GET BACK.
NNGH
OH, HEY, JUST A SECOND. COULD YOU HOLD THE ELEVATOR? I...
G
2
G12345
4

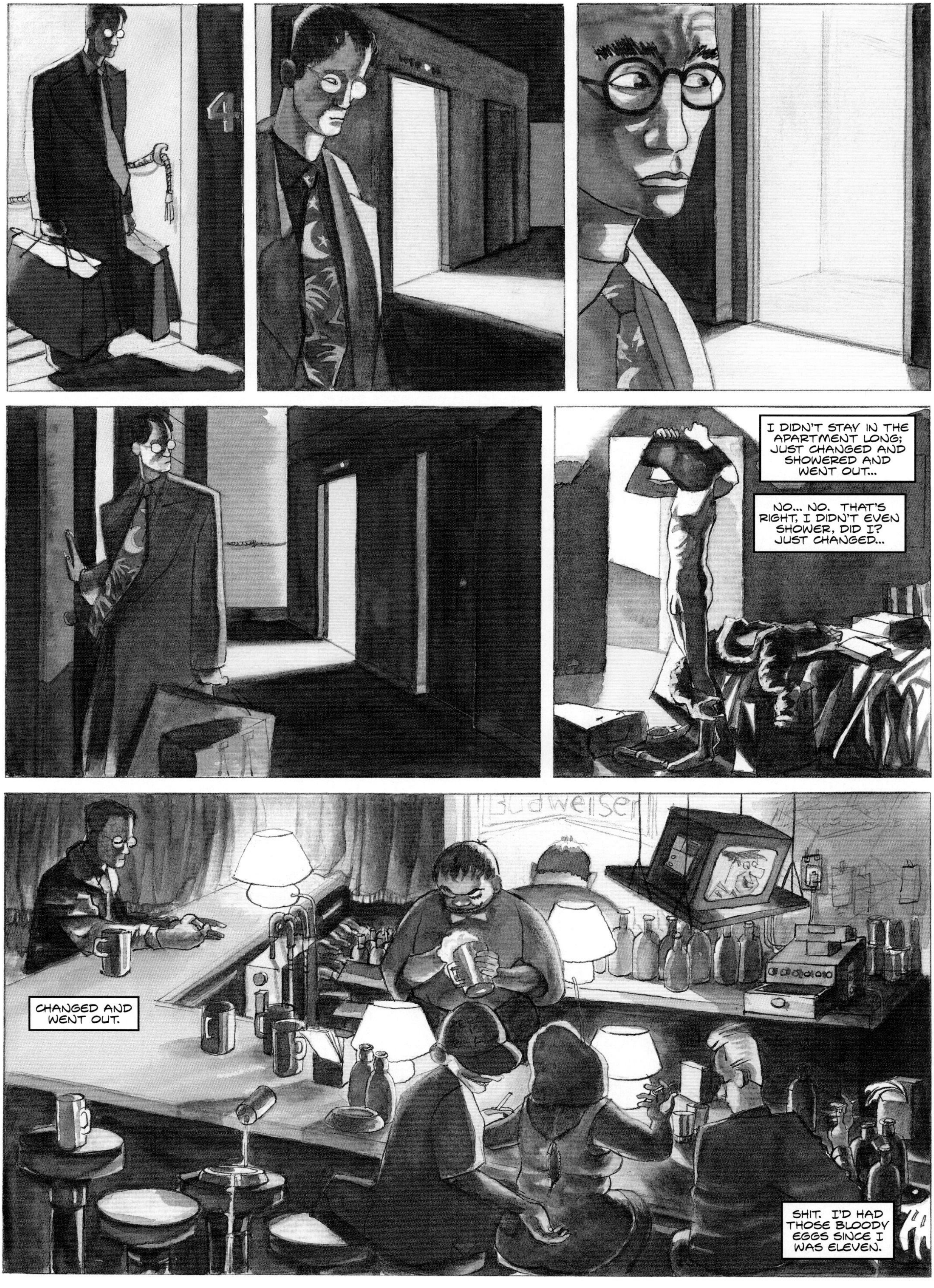
I DIDN'T STAY IN THE APARTMENT LONG; JUST CHANGED AND SHOWERED AND WENT OUT...
NO... NO. THAT'S RIGHT, I DIDN'T EVEN SHOWER, DID I? JUST CHANGED...
Budweiser
CHANGED AND WENT OUT.
SHIT. I'D HAD THOSE BLOODY EGGS SINCE I WAS ELEVEN.

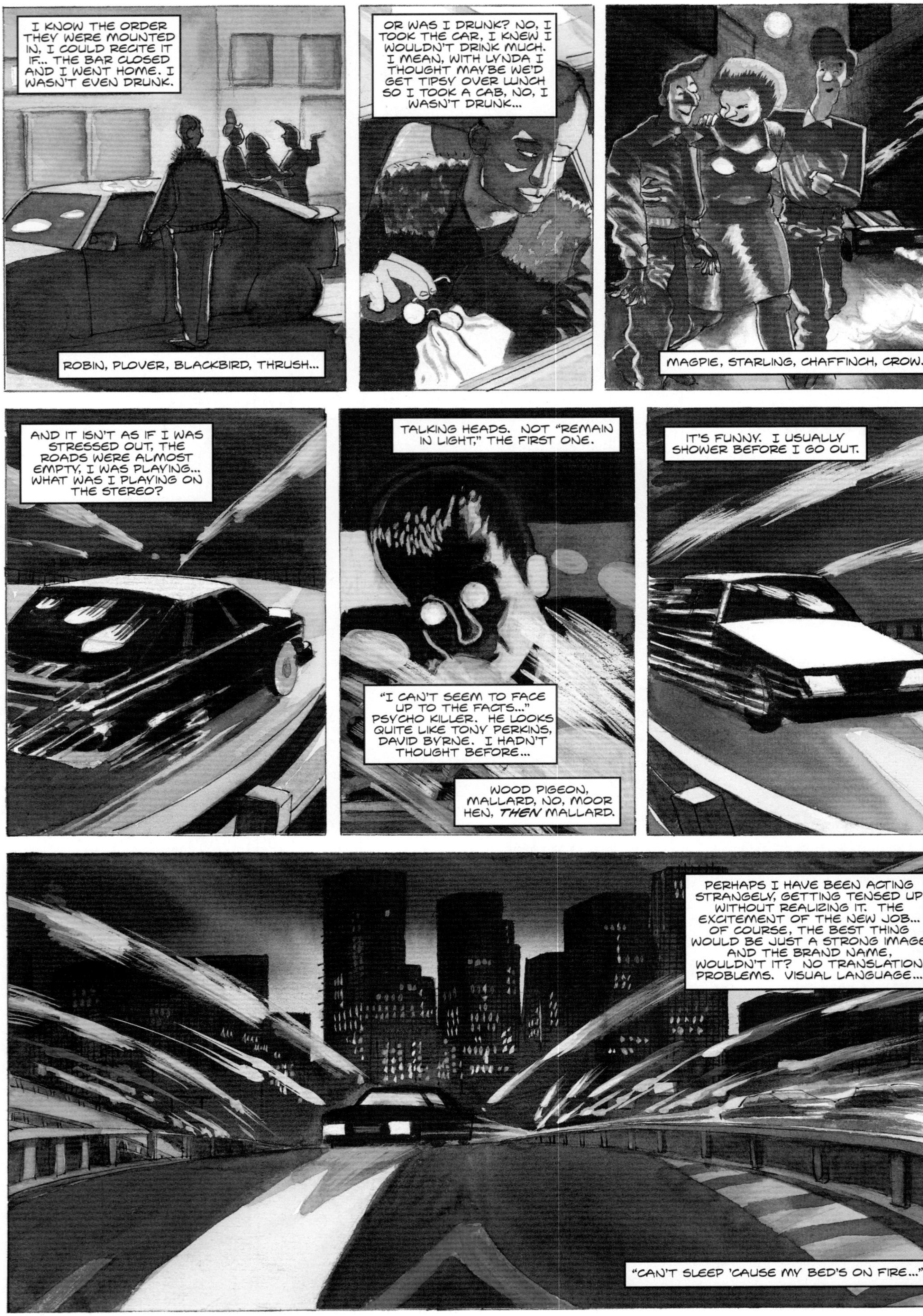
I KNOW THE ORDER THEY WERE MOUNTED IN, I COULD RECITE IT IF... THE BAR CLOSED AND I WENT HOME. I WASN'T EVEN DRUNK.
ROBIN, PLOVER, BLACKBIRD, THRUSH...
OR WAS I DRUNK? NO, I TOOK THE CAR, I KNEW I WOULDN'T DRINK MUCH. I MEAN, WITH LYNDA I THOUGHT MAYBE WE'D GET TIPSY OVER LUNCH SO I TOOK A CAB, NO, I WASN'T DRUNK...
MAGPIE, STARLING, CHAFFINCH, CROW...
AND IT ISN'T AS IF I WAS STRESSED OUT, THE ROADS WERE ALMOST EMPTY, I WAS PLAYING... WHAT WAS I PLAYING ON THE STEREO?
TALKING HEADS. NOT "REMAIN IN LIGHT," THE FIRST ONE.
"I CAN'T SEEM TO FACE UP TO THE FACTS..." PSYCHO KILLER. HE LOOKS QUITE LIKE TONY PERKINS, DAVID BYRNE. I HADN'T THOUGHT BEFORE...
WOOD PIGEON, MALLARD, NO, MOOR HEN, *THEN* MALLARD.
IT'S FUNNY. I USUALLY SHOWER BEFORE I GO OUT.
PERHAPS I HAVE BEEN ACTING STRANGELY, GETTING TENSED UP WITHOUT REALIZING IT. THE EXCITEMENT OF THE NEW JOB... OF COURSE, THE BEST THING WOULD BE JUST A STRONG IMAGE AND THE BRAND NAME, WOULDN'T IT? NO TRANSLATION PROBLEMS. VISUAL LANGUAGE...
"CAN'T SLEEP 'CAUSE MY BED'S ON FIRE..."

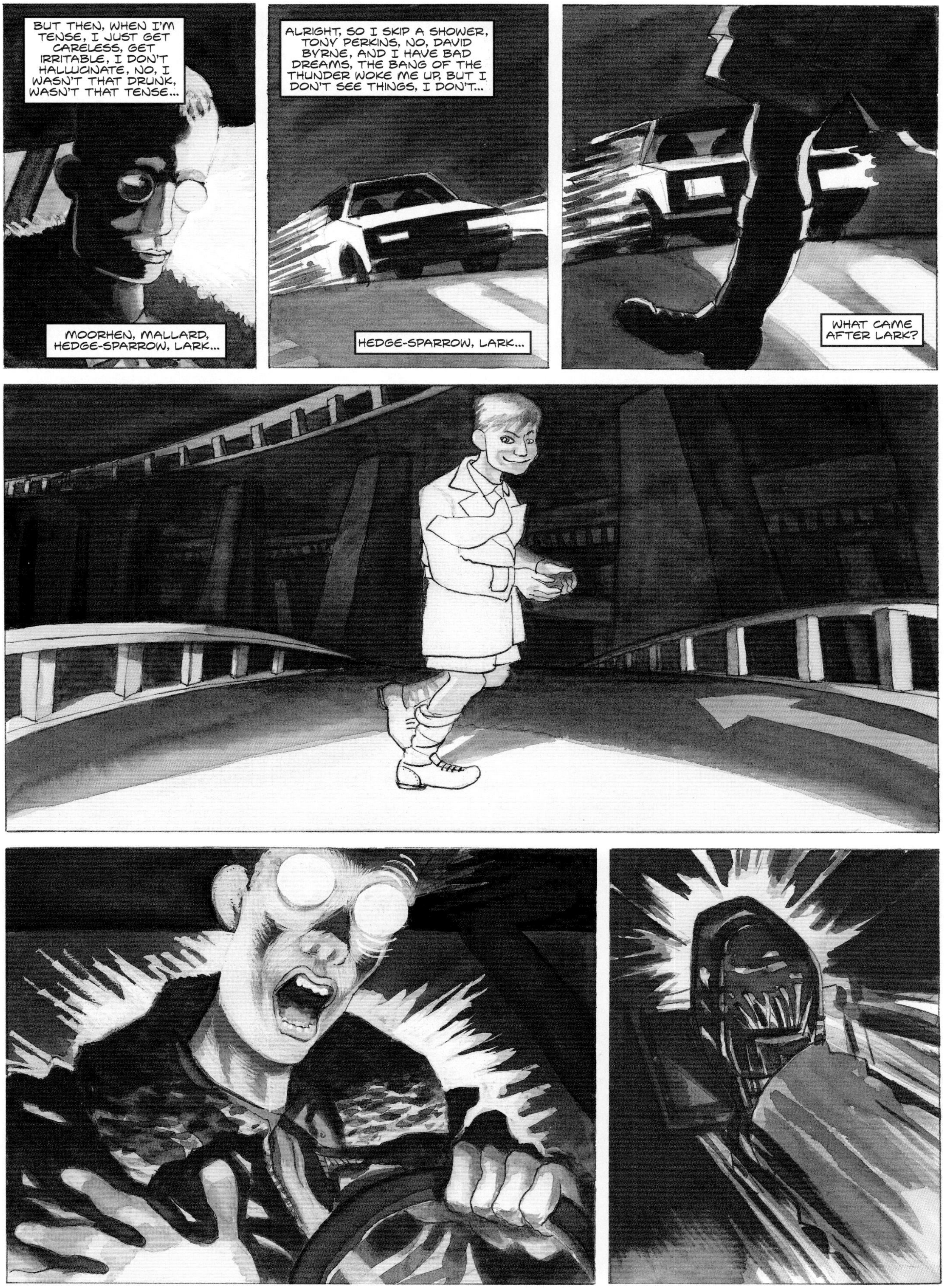
BUT THEN, WHEN I'M TENSE, I JUST GET CARELESS, GET IRRITABLE, I DON'T HALLUCINATE, NO, I WASN'T THAT DRUNK, WASN'T THAT TENSE...
MOORHEN, MALLARD, HEDGE-SPARROW, LARK...
ALRIGHT, SO I SKIP A SHOWER, TONY PERKINS, NO, DAVID BYRNE, AND I HAVE BAD DREAMS, THE BANG OF THE THUNDER WOKE ME UP, BUT I DON'T SEE THINGS, I DON'T...
HEDGE-SPARROW, LARK...
WHAT CAME AFTER LARK?

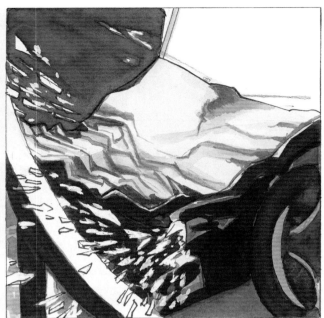

AAA!

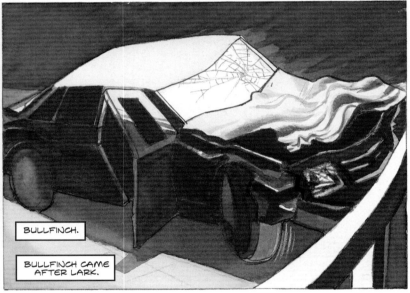

BULLFINCH.

BULLFINCH CAME
AFTER LARK.

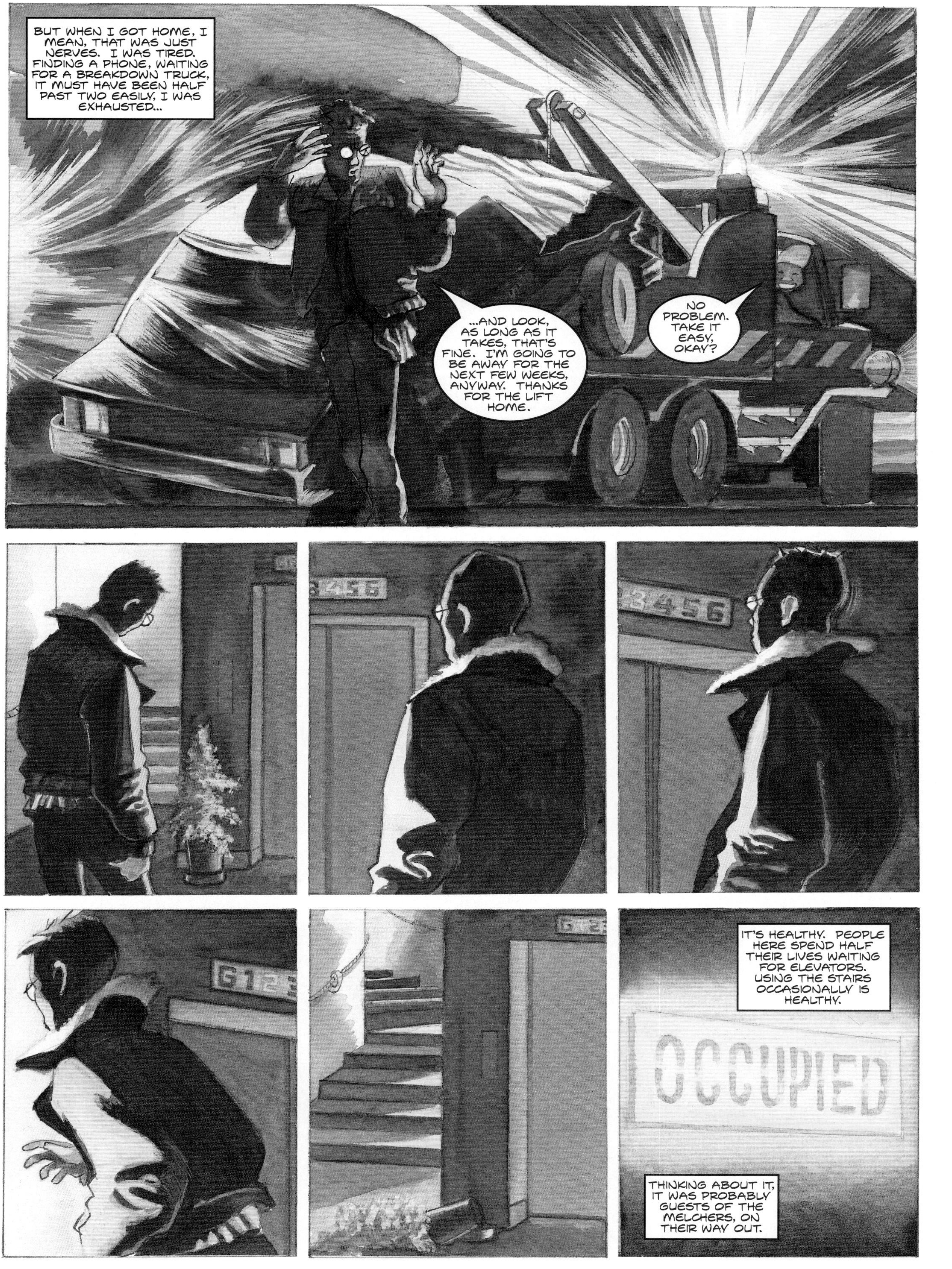
BUT WHEN I GOT HOME, I MEAN, THAT WAS JUST NERVES. I WAS TIRED. FINDING A PHONE, WAITING FOR A BREAKDOWN TRUCK, IT MUST HAVE BEEN HALF PAST TWO EASILY, I WAS EXHAUSTED...
...AND LOOK, AS LONG AS IT TAKES, THAT'S FINE. I'M GOING TO BE AWAY FOR THE NEXT FEW WEEKS, ANYWAY. THANKS FOR THE LIFT HOME.
NO PROBLEM. TAKE IT EASY, OKAY?
IT'S HEALTHY. PEOPLE HERE SPEND HALF THEIR LIVES WAITING FOR ELEVATORS. USING THE STAIRS OCCASIONALLY IS HEALTHY.
OCCUPIED
THINKING ABOUT IT, IT WAS PROBABLY GUESTS OF THE MELCHERS, ON THEIR WAY OUT.

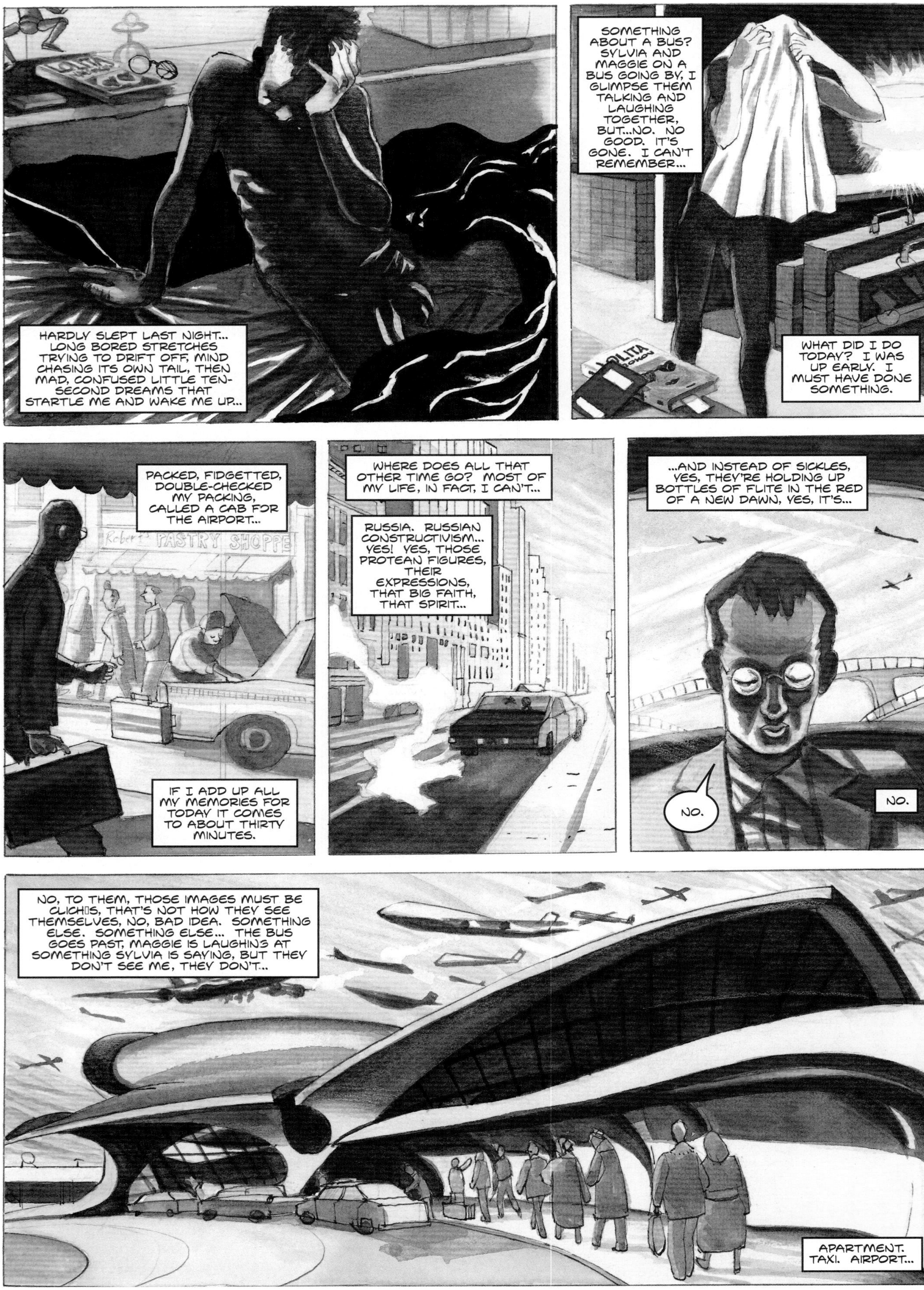
HARDLY SLEPT LAST NIGHT... LONG BORED STRETCHES TRYING TO DRIFT OFF, MIND CHASING ITS OWN TAIL, THEN MAD, CONFUSED LITTLE TEN-SECOND DREAMS THAT STARTLE ME AND WAKE ME UP...
SOMETHING ABOUT A BUS? SYLVIA AND MAGGIE ON A BUS GOING BY, I GLIMPSE THEM TALKING AND LAUGHING TOGETHER, BUT...NO. NO GOOD. IT'S GONE. I CAN'T REMEMBER...
LOLITA
WHAT DID I DO TODAY? I WAS UP EARLY. I MUST HAVE DONE SOMETHING.
PACKED, FIDGETTED, DOUBLE-CHECKED MY PACKING, CALLED A CAB FOR THE AIRPORT...
Robert's PASTRY SHOPPE
IF I ADD UP ALL MY MEMORIES FOR TODAY IT COMES TO ABOUT THIRTY MINUTES.
WHERE DOES ALL THAT OTHER TIME GO? MOST OF MY LIFE, IN FACT, I CAN'T...
RUSSIA. RUSSIAN CONSTRUCTIVISM... YES! YES, THOSE PROTEAN FIGURES, THEIR EXPRESSIONS, THAT BIG FAITH, THAT SPIRIT...
...AND INSTEAD OF SICKLES, YES, THEY'RE HOLDING UP BOTTLES OF FLITE IN THE RED OF A NEW DAWN, YES, IT'S...
NO.
NO.
NO, TO THEM, THOSE IMAGES MUST BE CLICH□S, THAT'S NOT HOW THEY SEE THEMSELVES, NO, BAD IDEA. SOMETHING ELSE. SOMETHING ELSE... THE BUS GOES PAST, MAGGIE IS LAUGHINS AT SOMETHING SYLVIA IS SAYING, BUT THEY DON'T SEE ME, THEY DON'T...
APARTMENT. TAXI. AIRPORT...

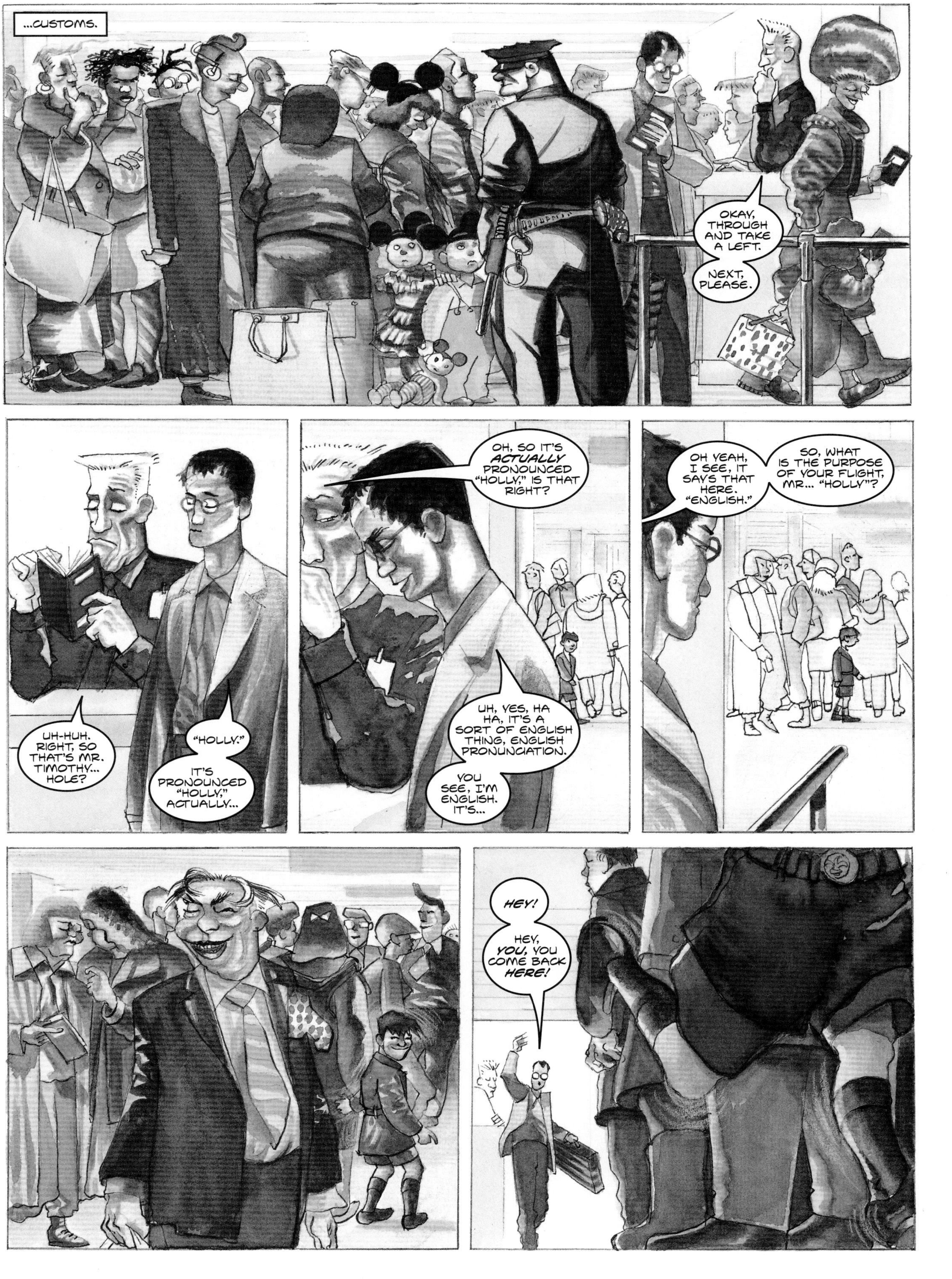
...CUSTOMS.
OKAY, THROUGH AND TAKE A LEFT.
NEXT, PLEASE.
UH-HUH. RIGHT, SO THAT'S MR. TIMOTHY... HOLE?
"HOLLY."
IT'S PRONOUNCED "HOLLY," ACTUALLY...
OH, SO IT'S *ACTUALLY* PRONOUNCED "HOLLY," IS THAT RIGHT?
UH, YES, HA HA, IT'S A SORT OF ENGLISH THING, ENGLISH PRONUNCIATION.
YOU SEE, I'M ENGLISH. IT'S...
OH YEAH, I SEE, IT SAYS THAT HERE. "ENGLISH."
SO, WHAT IS THE PURPOSE OF YOUR FLIGHT, MR... "HOLLY"?
HEY!
HEY, *YOU,* YOU COME BACK *HERE!*

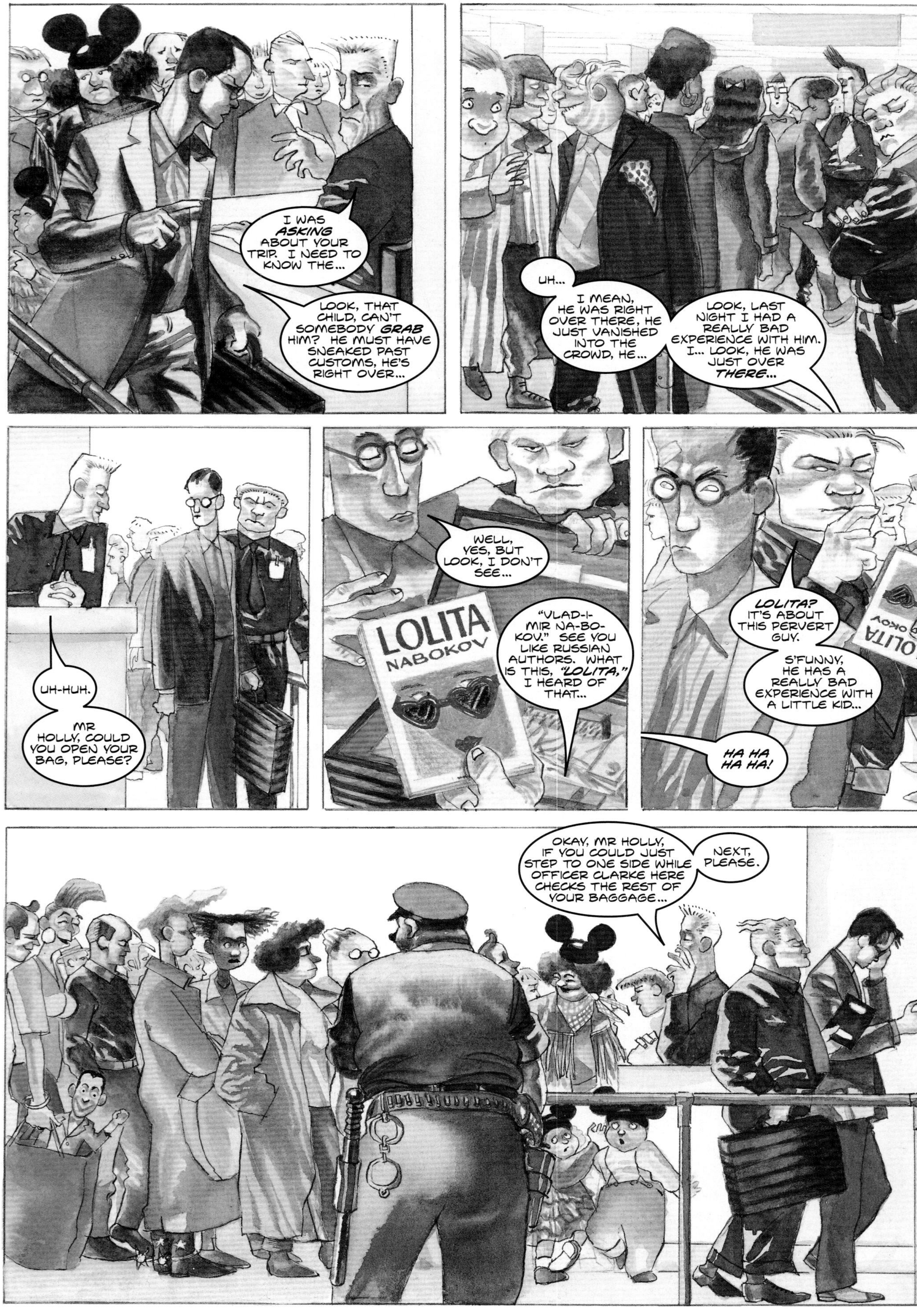
I WAS *ASKING* ABOUT YOUR TRIP. I NEED TO KNOW THE...
LOOK, THAT CHILD, CAN'T SOMEBODY *GRAB* HIM? HE MUST HAVE SNEAKED PAST CUSTOMS, HE'S RIGHT OVER...
UH...
I MEAN, HE WAS RIGHT OVER THERE, HE JUST VANISHED INTO THE CROWD, HE...
LOOK, LAST NIGHT I HAD A REALLY BAD EXPERIENCE WITH HIM. I... LOOK, HE WAS JUST OVER *THERE*...
UH-HUH.
MR HOLLY, COULD YOU OPEN YOUR BAG, PLEASE?
WELL, YES, BUT LOOK, I DON'T SEE...
LOLITA
NABOKOV
"VLAD-I-MIR NA-BO-KOV." SEE YOU LIKE RUSSIAN AUTHORS. WHAT IS THIS, *"LOLITA,"* I HEARD OF THAT...
LOLITA? IT'S ABOUT THIS PERVERT GUY.
S'FUNNY, HE HAS A REALLY BAD EXPERIENCE WITH A LITTLE KID...
HA HA HA HA!
OKAY, MR HOLLY, IF YOU COULD JUST STEP TO ONE SIDE WHILE OFFICER CLARKE HERE CHECKS THE REST OF YOUR BAGGAGE...
NEXT, PLEASE.

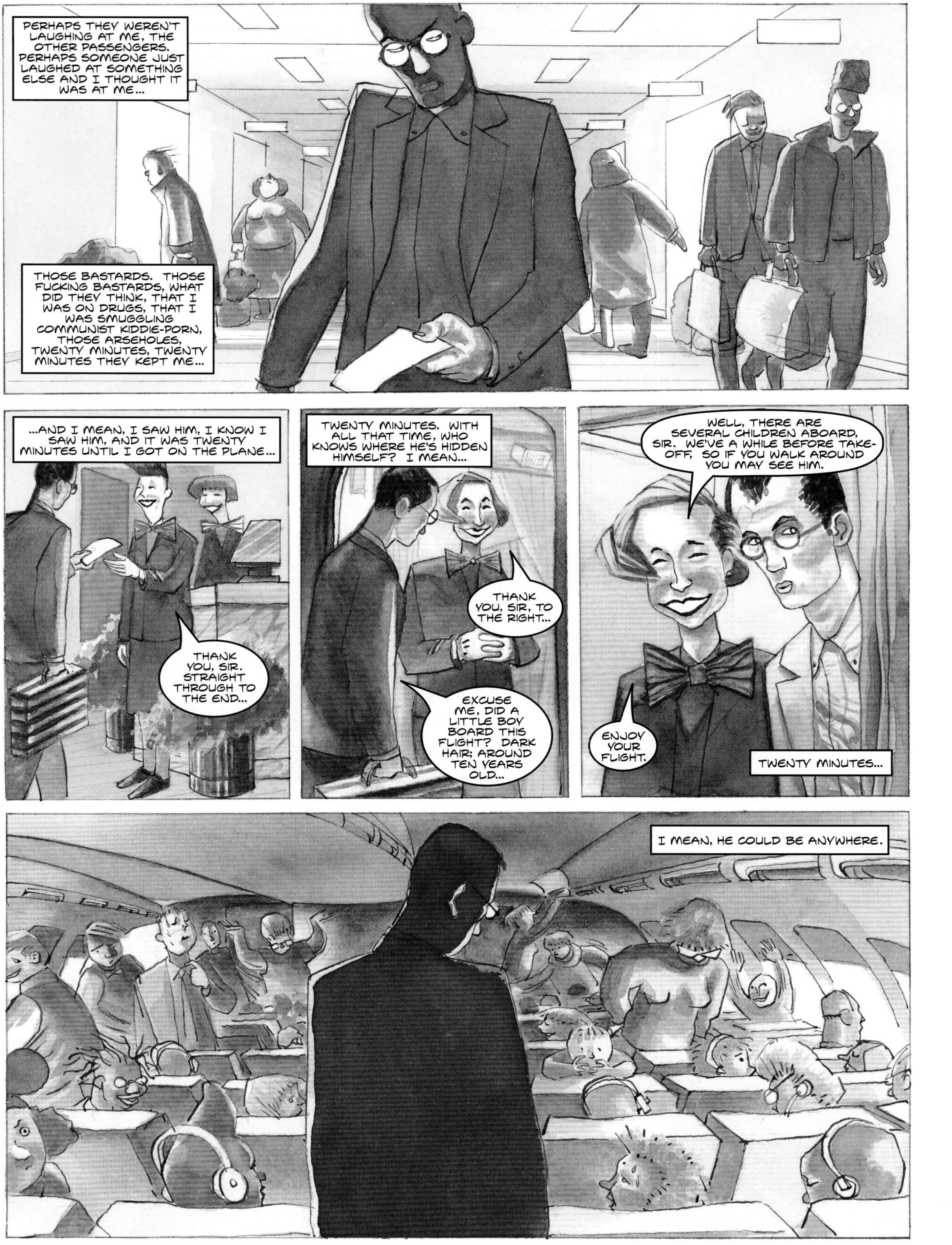
PERHAPS THEY WEREN'T LAUGHING AT ME, THE OTHER PASSENGERS. PERHAPS SOMEONE JUST LAUGHED AT SOMETHING ELSE AND I THOUGHT IT WAS AT ME...
THOSE BASTARDS. THOSE FUCKING BASTARDS, WHAT DID THEY THINK, THAT I WAS ON DRUGS, THAT I WAS SMUGGLING COMMUNIST KIDDIE-PORN, THOSE ARSEHOLES, TWENTY MINUTES, TWENTY MINUTES THEY KEPT ME...
...AND I MEAN, I SAW HIM, I KNOW I SAW HIM, AND IT WAS TWENTY MINUTES UNTIL I GOT ON THE PLANE...
THANK YOU, SIR. STRAIGHT THROUGH TO THE END...
TWENTY MINUTES. WITH ALL THAT TIME, WHO KNOWS WHERE HE'S HIDDEN HIMSELF? I MEAN...
THANK YOU, SIR, TO THE RIGHT...
EXCUSE ME, DID A LITTLE BOY BOARD THIS FLIGHT? DARK HAIR; AROUND TEN YEARS OLD...
WELL, THERE ARE SEVERAL CHILDREN ABOARD, SIR. WE'VE A WHILE BEFORE TAKE-OFF, SO IF YOU WALK AROUND YOU MAY SEE HIM.
ENJOY YOUR FLIGHT.
TWENTY MINUTES...
I MEAN, HE COULD BE ANYWHERE.

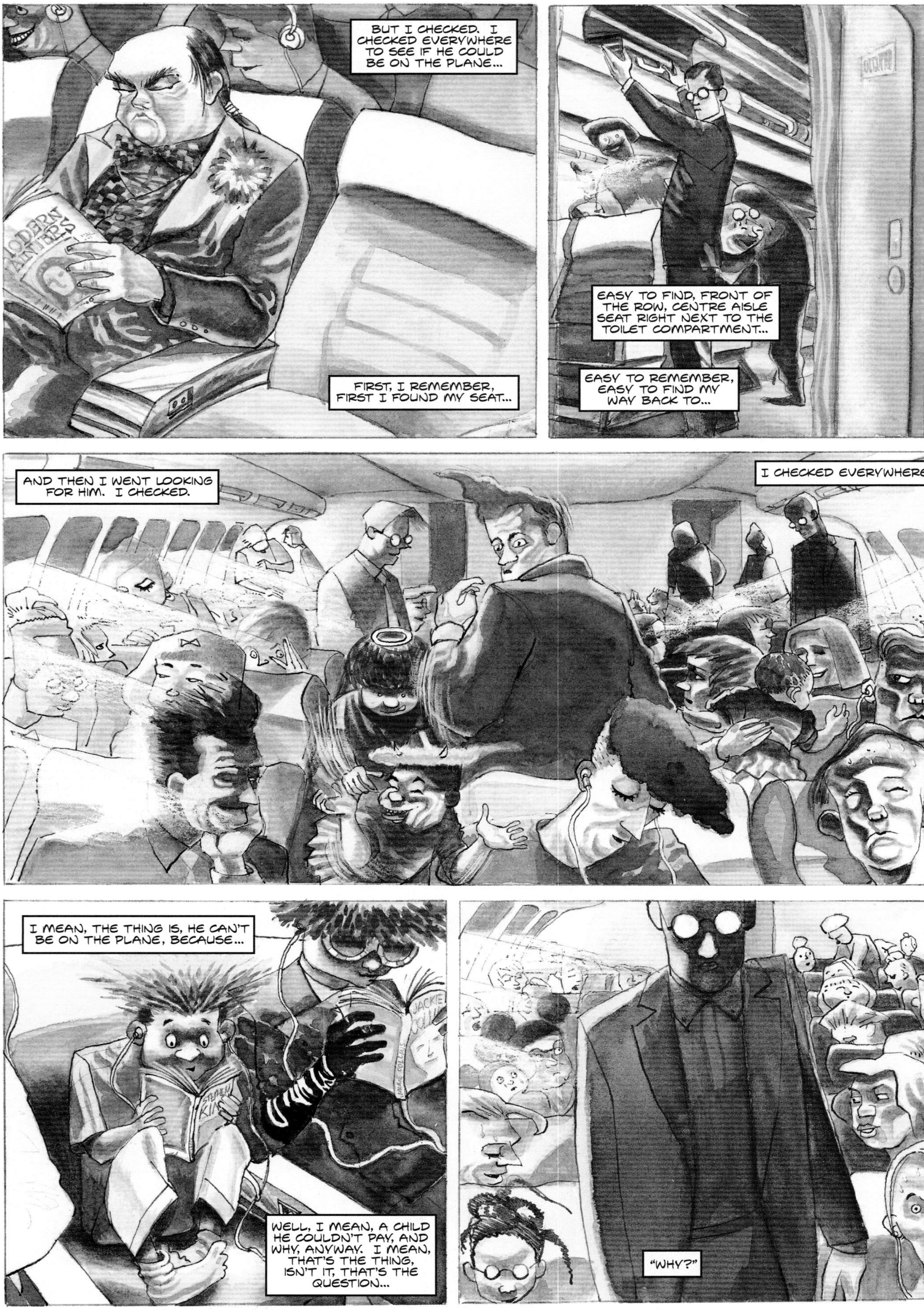
BUT I CHECKED. I CHECKED EVERYWHERE TO SEE IF HE COULD BE ON THE PLANE...
FIRST, I REMEMBER, FIRST I FOUND MY SEAT...
EASY TO FIND, FRONT OF THE ROW, CENTRE AISLE SEAT RIGHT NEXT TO THE TOILET COMPARTMENT...
EASY TO REMEMBER, EASY TO FIND MY WAY BACK TO...
AND THEN I WENT LOOKING FOR HIM. I CHECKED.
I CHECKED EVERYWHERE.
I MEAN, THE THING IS, HE CAN'T BE ON THE PLANE, BECAUSE...
WELL, I MEAN, A CHILD HE COULDN'T PAY, AND WHY, ANYWAY. I MEAN, THAT'S THE THING, ISN'T IT, THAT'S THE QUESTION...
"WHY?"

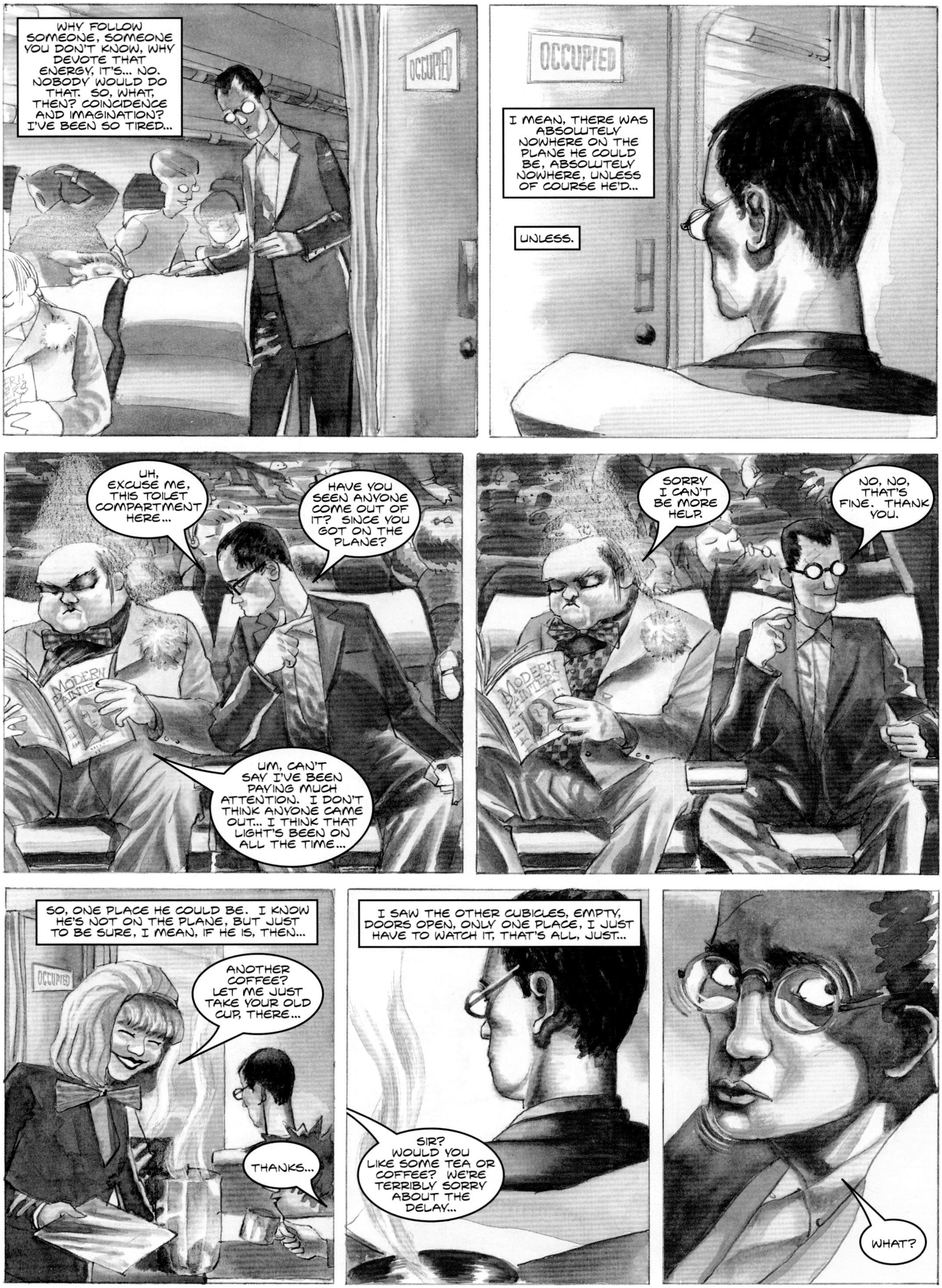
WHY FOLLOW SOMEONE, SOMEONE YOU DON'T KNOW, WHY DEVOTE THAT ENERGY, IT'S... NO. NOBODY WOULD DO THAT. SO, WHAT, THEN? COINCIDENCE AND IMAGINATION? I'VE BEEN SO TIRED...
OCCUPIED
OCCUPIED
I MEAN, THERE WAS ABSOLUTELY NOWHERE ON THE PLANE HE COULD BE, ABSOLUTELY NOWHERE, UNLESS OF COURSE HE'D...
UNLESS.
UH, EXCUSE ME, THIS TOILET COMPARTMENT HERE...
HAVE YOU SEEN ANYONE COME OUT OF IT? SINCE YOU GOT ON THE PLANE?
UM, CAN'T SAY I'VE BEEN PAYING MUCH ATTENTION. I DON'T THINK ANYONE CAME OUT... I THINK THAT LIGHT'S BEEN ON ALL THE TIME...
SORRY I CAN'T BE MORE HELP.
NO, NO, THAT'S FINE. THANK YOU.
SO, ONE PLACE HE COULD BE. I KNOW HE'S NOT ON THE PLANE, BUT JUST TO BE SURE, I MEAN, IF HE IS, THEN...
OCCUPIED
ANOTHER COFFEE? LET ME JUST TAKE YOUR OLD CUP, THERE...
THANKS...
I SAW THE OTHER CUBICLES, EMPTY, DOORS OPEN, ONLY ONE PLACE, I JUST HAVE TO WATCH IT, THAT'S ALL, JUST...
SIR? WOULD YOU LIKE SOME TEA OR COFFEE? WE'RE TERRIBLY SORRY ABOUT THE DELAY...
WHAT?

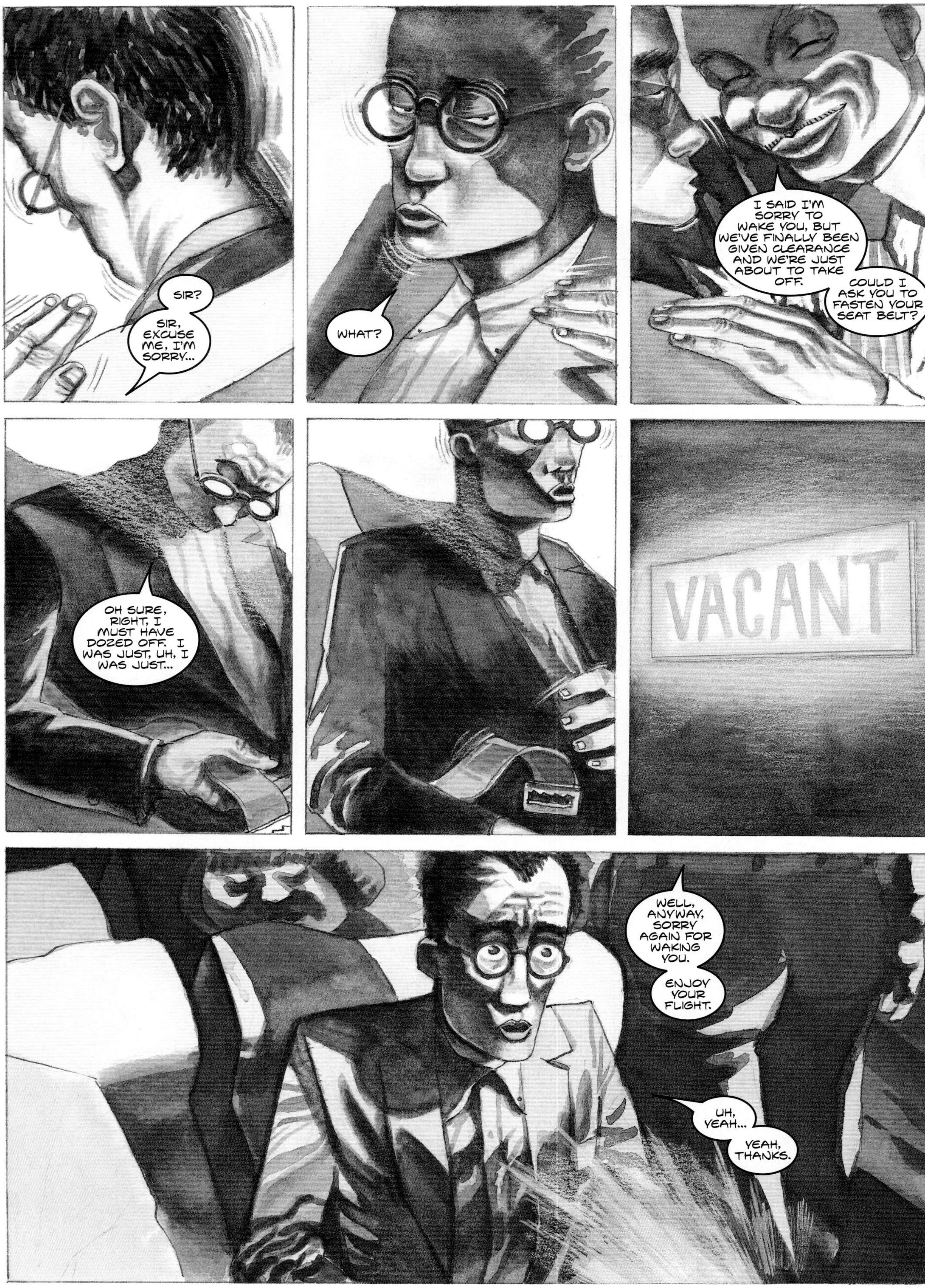
SIR?
SIR, EXCUSE ME, I'M SORRY...
WHAT?
I SAID I'M SORRY TO WAKE YOU, BUT WE'VE FINALLY BEEN GIVEN CLEARANCE AND WE'RE JUST ABOUT TO TAKE OFF.
COULD I ASK YOU TO FASTEN YOUR SEAT BELT?
OH SURE, RIGHT, I MUST HAVE DOZED OFF. I WAS JUST, UH, I WAS JUST...
VACANT
WELL, ANYWAY, SORRY AGAIN FOR WAKING YOU.
ENJOY YOUR FLIGHT.
UH, YEAH...
YEAH, THANKS.

THAT SKY, THE SKY IN MY DREAM...

IT WAS SO CLEAR.

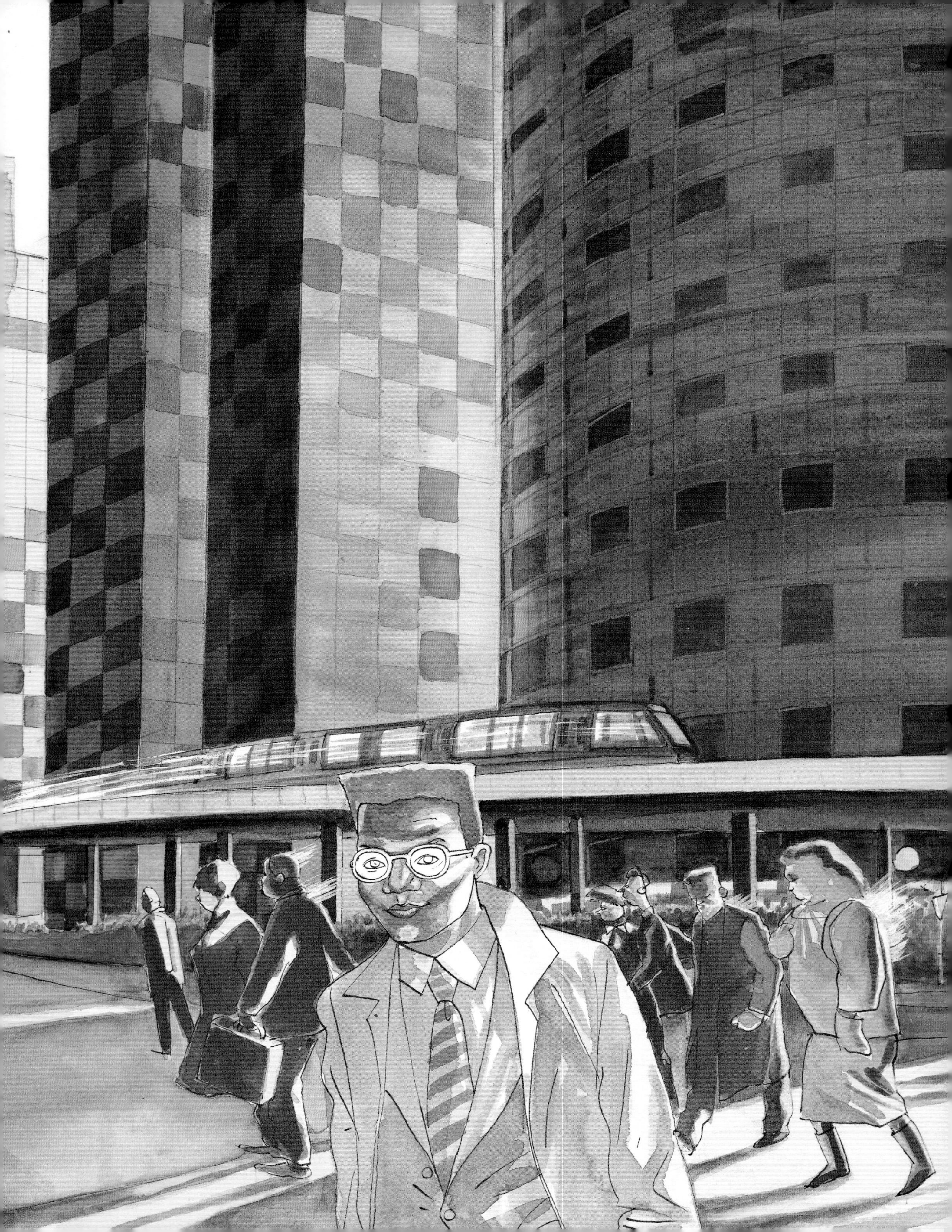

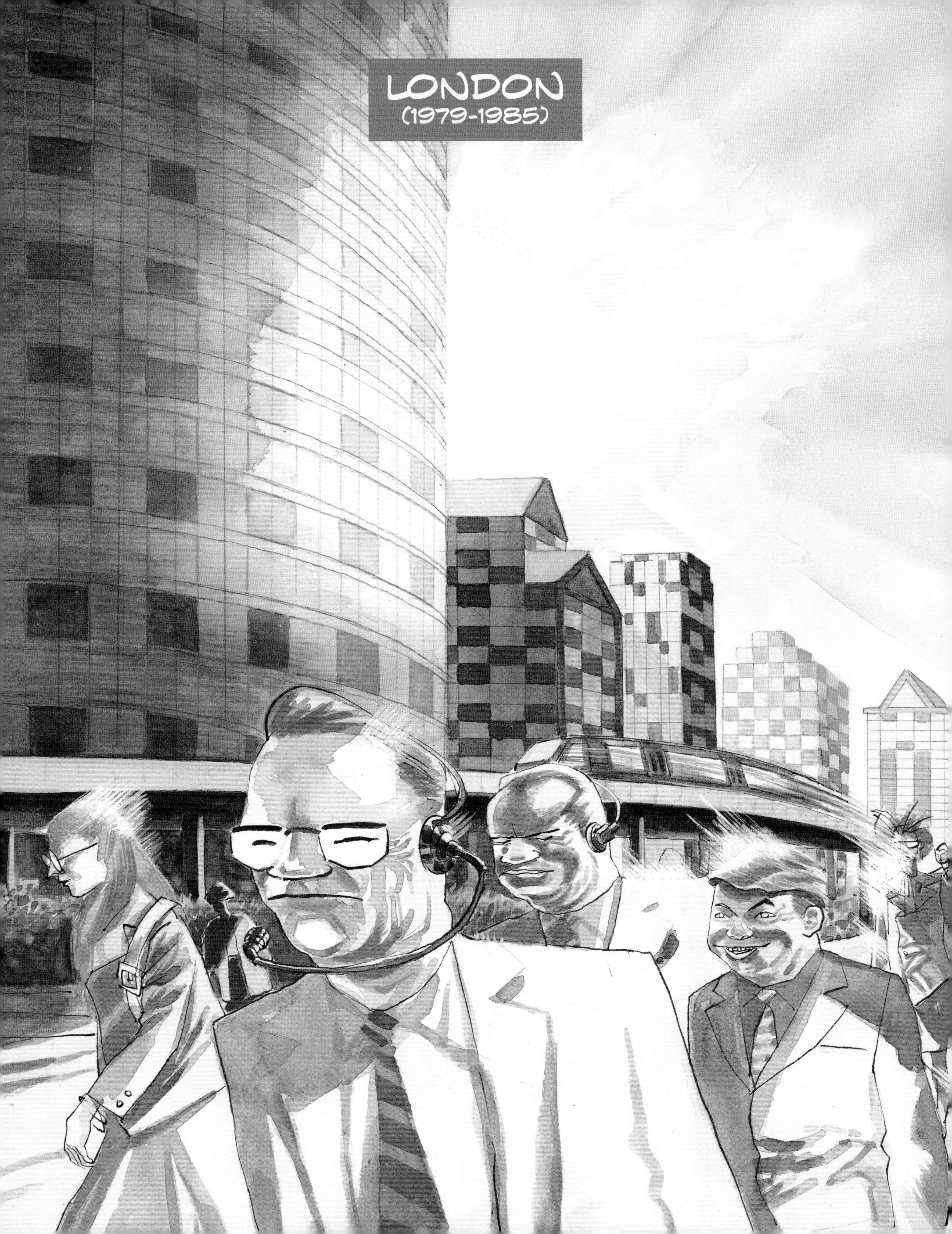
LONDON
(1979-1985)

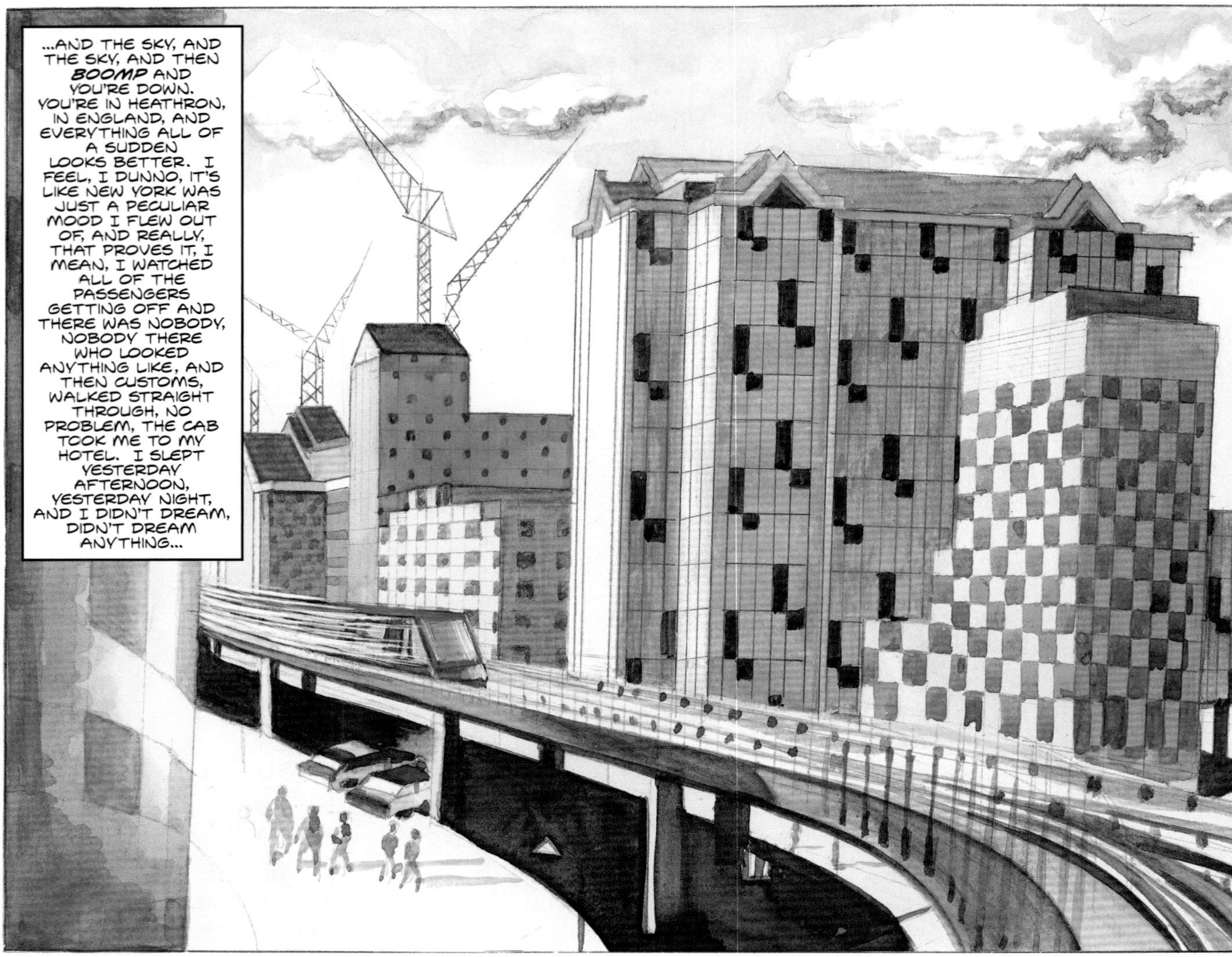
...AND THE SKY, AND THE SKY, AND THEN *BOOMP* AND YOU'RE DOWN. YOU'RE IN HEATHRON, IN ENGLAND, AND EVERYTHING ALL OF A SUDDEN LOOKS BETTER. I FEEL, I DUNNO, IT'S LIKE NEW YORK WAS JUST A PECULIAR MOOD I FLEW OUT OF, AND REALLY, THAT PROVES IT, I MEAN, I WATCHED ALL OF THE PASSENGERS GETTING OFF AND THERE WAS NOBODY, NOBODY THERE WHO LOOKED ANYTHING LIKE, AND THEN CUSTOMS, WALKED STRAIGHT THROUGH, NO PROBLEM, THE CAB TOOK ME TO MY HOTEL. I SLEPT YESTERDAY AFTERNOON, YESTERDAY NIGHT, AND I DIDN'T DREAM, DIDN'T DREAM ANYTHING...

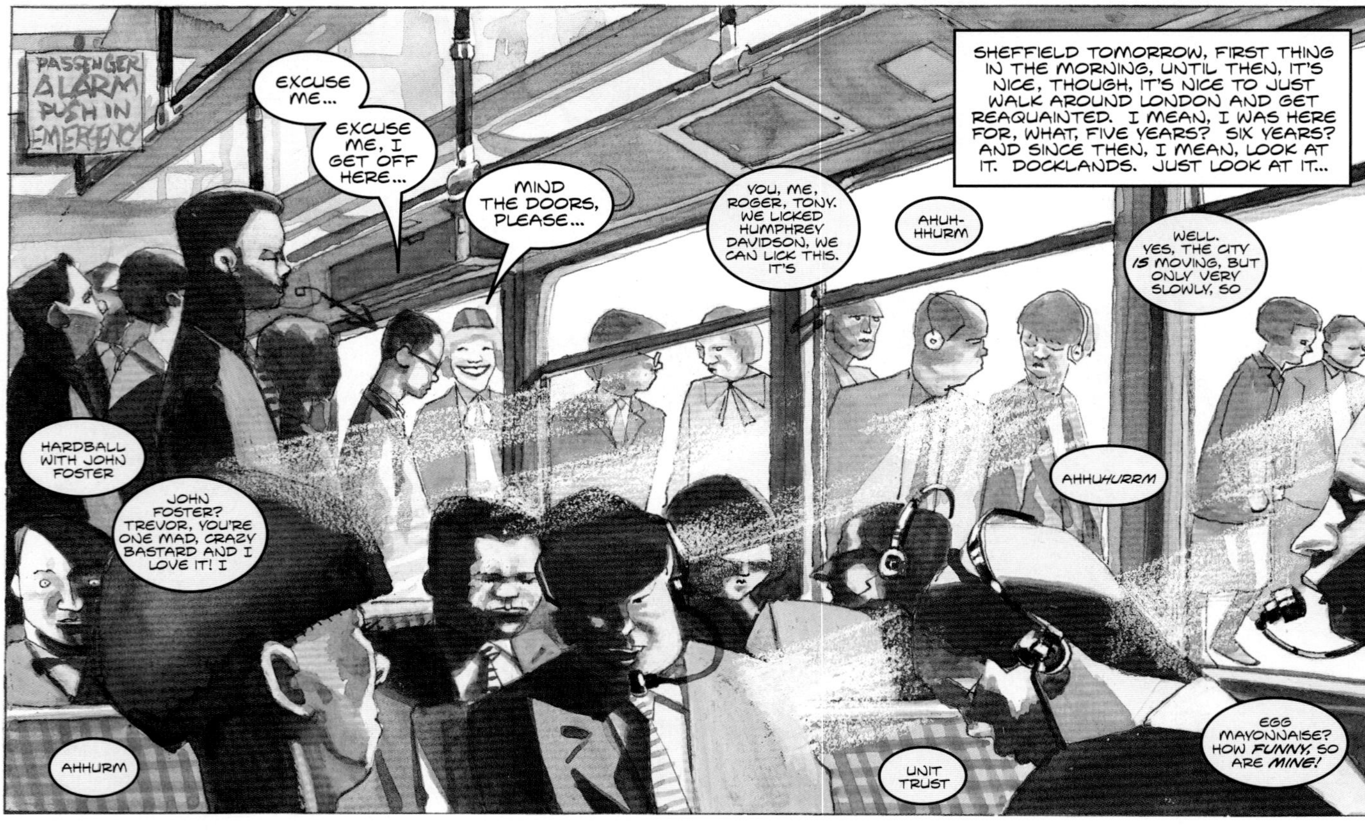
SHEFFIELD TOMORROW, FIRST THING IN THE MORNING, UNTIL THEN, IT'S NICE, THOUGH, IT'S NICE TO JUST WALK AROUND LONDON AND GET REAQUAINTED. I MEAN, I WAS HERE FOR, WHAT, FIVE YEARS? SIX YEARS? AND SINCE THEN, I MEAN, LOOK AT IT. DOCKLANDS. JUST LOOK AT IT...
PASSENGER ALARM PUSH IN EMERGENCY
EXCUSE ME...
EXCUSE ME, I GET OFF HERE...
MIND THE DOORS, PLEASE...
YOU, ME, ROGER, TONY. WE LICKED HUMPHREY DAVIDSON, WE CAN LICK THIS. IT'S
AHUH-HHURM
WELL. YES, THE CITY *IS* MOVING, BUT ONLY VERY SLOWLY, SO
HARDBALL WITH JOHN FOSTER
JOHN FOSTER? TREVOR, YOU'RE ONE MAD, CRAZY BASTARD AND I LOVE IT! I
AHHUHURRM
AHHURM
UNIT TRUST
EGG MAYONNAISE? HOW *FUNNY*, SO ARE *MINE!*

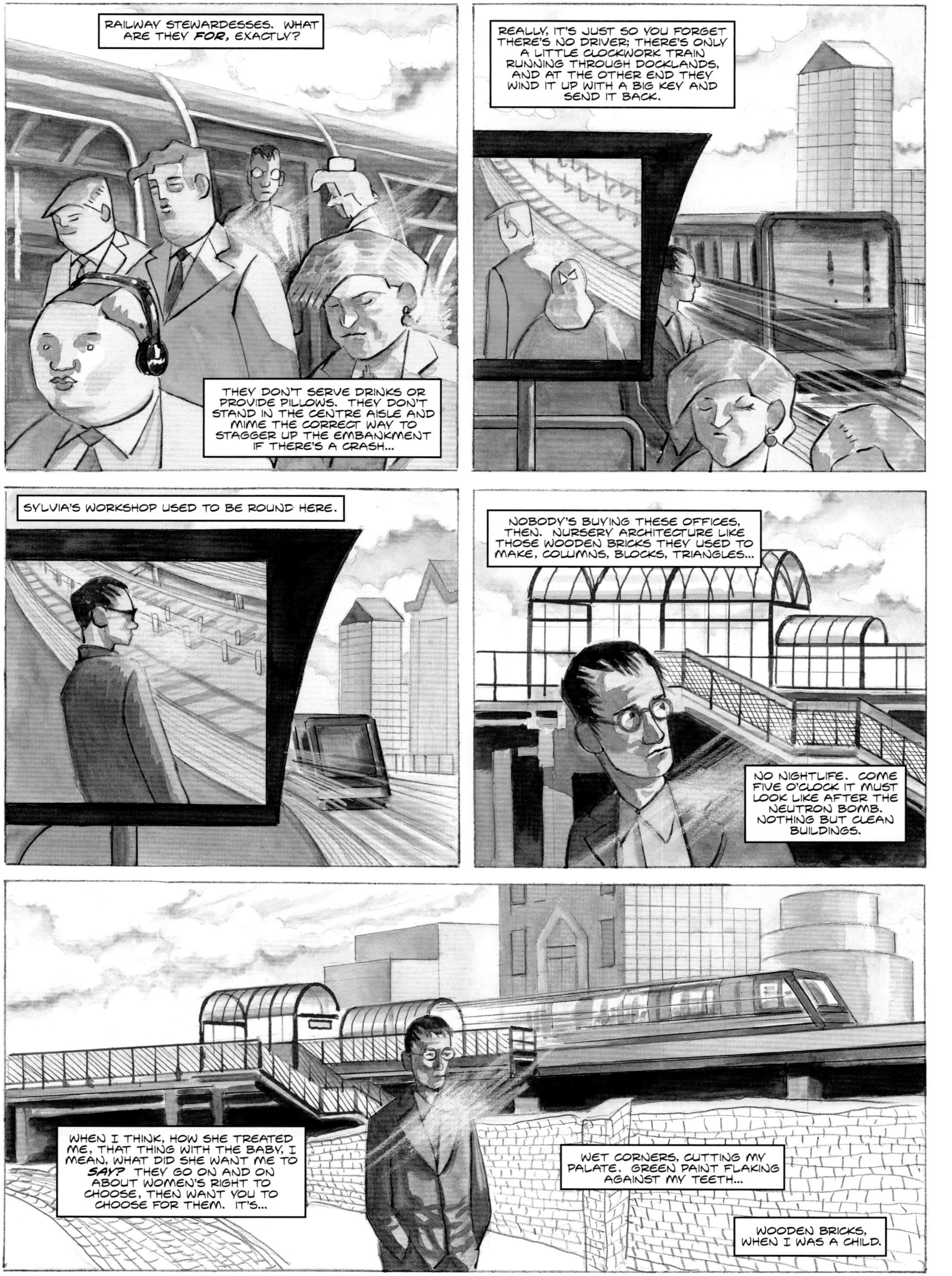
RAILWAY STEWARDESSES. WHAT ARE THEY *FOR,* EXACTLY?
THEY DON'T SERVE DRINKS OR PROVIDE PILLOWS. THEY DON'T STAND IN THE CENTRE AISLE AND MIME THE CORRECT WAY TO STAGGER UP THE EMBANKMENT IF THERE'S A CRASH...
REALLY, IT'S JUST SO YOU FORGET THERE'S NO DRIVER; THERE'S ONLY A LITTLE CLOCKWORK TRAIN RUNNING THROUGH DOCKLANDS, AND AT THE OTHER END THEY WIND IT UP WITH A BIG KEY AND SEND IT BACK.
SYLVIA'S WORKSHOP USED TO BE ROUND HERE.
NOBODY'S BUYING THESE OFFICES, THEN. NURSERY ARCHITECTURE LIKE THOSE WOODEN BRICKS THEY USED TO MAKE, COLUMNS, BLOCKS, TRIANGLES...
NO NIGHTLIFE. COME FIVE O'CLOCK IT MUST LOOK LIKE AFTER THE NEUTRON BOMB. NOTHING BUT CLEAN BUILDINGS.
WHEN I THINK, HOW SHE TREATED ME, THAT THING WITH THE BABY, I MEAN, WHAT DID SHE WANT ME TO *SAY?* THEY GO ON AND ON ABOUT WOMEN'S RIGHT TO CHOOSE, THEN WANT YOU TO CHOOSE FOR THEM. IT'S...
WET CORNERS, CUTTING MY PALATE. GREEN PAINT FLAKING AGAINST MY TEETH...
WOODEN BRICKS, WHEN I WAS A CHILD.

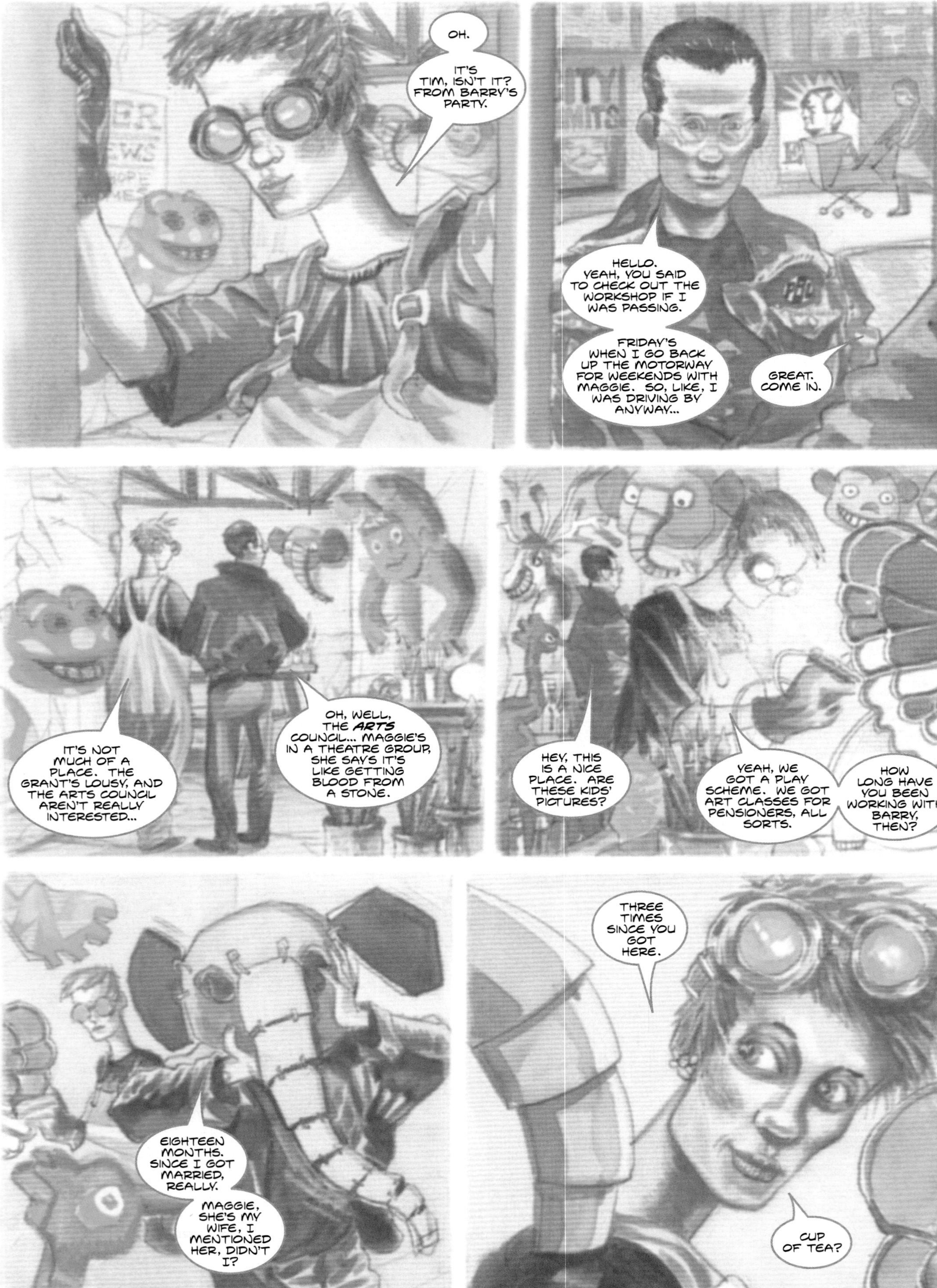
OH.
IT'S TIM, ISN'T IT? FROM BARRY'S PARTY.
HELLO. YEAH, YOU SAID TO CHECK OUT THE WORKSHOP IF I WAS PASSING.
FRIDAY'S WHEN I GO BACK UP THE MOTORWAY FOR WEEKENDS WITH MAGGIE. SO, LIKE, I WAS DRIVING BY ANYWAY...
GREAT. COME IN.
IT'S NOT MUCH OF A PLACE. THE GRANT'S LOUSY, AND THE ARTS COUNCIL AREN'T REALLY INTERESTED...
OH, WELL, THE ***ARTS*** COUNCIL... MAGGIE'S IN A THEATRE GROUP, SHE SAYS IT'S LIKE GETTING BLOOD FROM A STONE.
HEY, THIS IS A NICE PLACE. ARE THESE KIDS' PICTURES?
YEAH, WE GOT A PLAY SCHEME. WE GOT ART CLASSES FOR PENSIONERS, ALL SORTS.
HOW LONG HAVE YOU BEEN WORKING WITH BARRY, THEN?
EIGHTEEN MONTHS. SINCE I GOT MARRIED, REALLY.
MAGGIE, SHE'S MY WIFE, I MENTIONED HER, DIDN'T I?
THREE TIMES SINCE YOU GOT HERE.
CUP OF TEA?

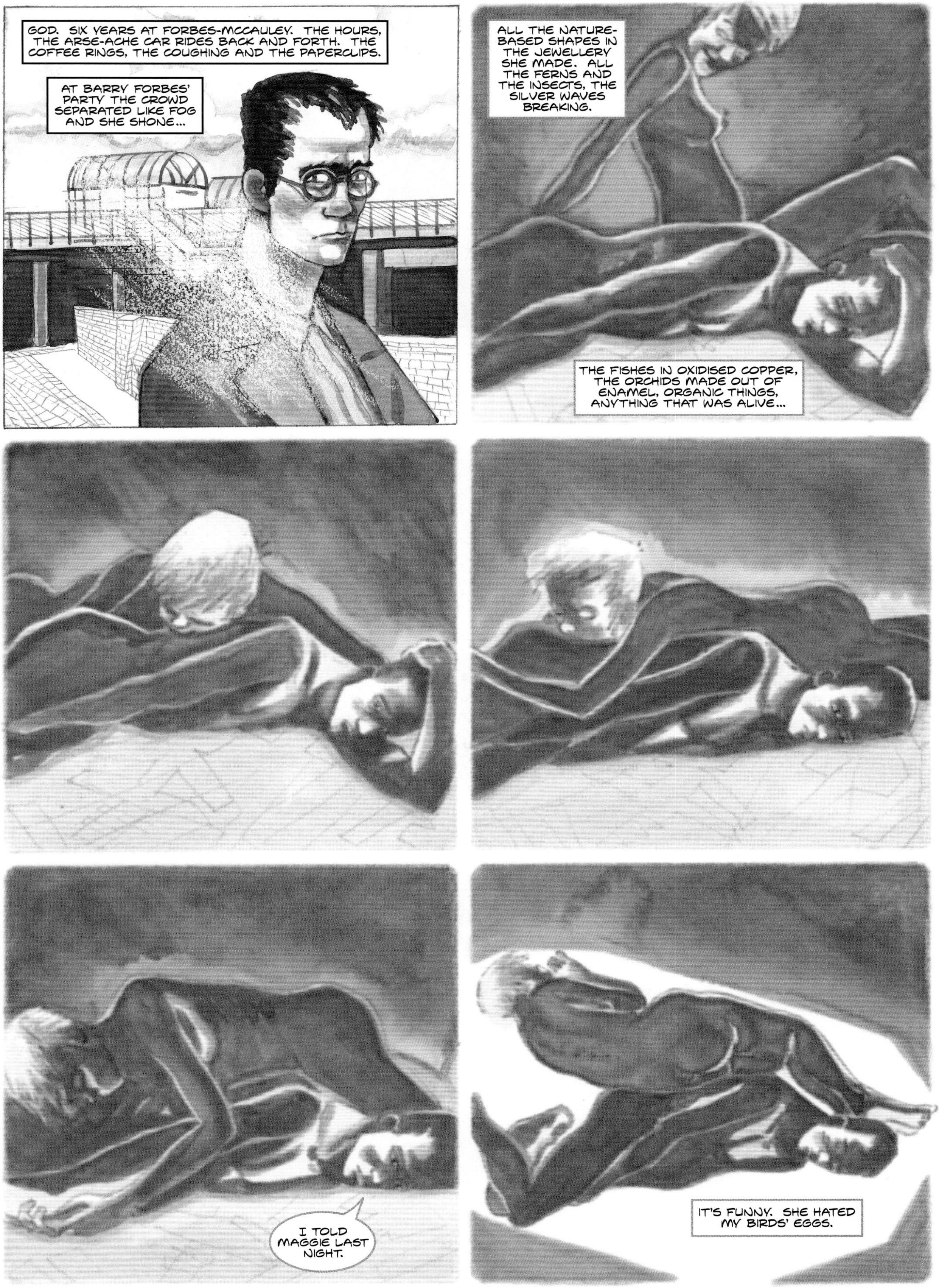
GOD. SIX YEARS AT FORBES-MCCAULEY. THE HOURS, THE ARSE-ACHE CAR RIDES BACK AND FORTH. THE COFFEE RINGS, THE COUGHING AND THE PAPERCLIPS.
AT BARRY FORBES' PARTY THE CROWD SEPARATED LIKE FOG AND SHE SHONE...
ALL THE NATURE-BASED SHAPES IN THE JEWELLERY SHE MADE. ALL THE FERNS AND THE INSECTS, THE SILVER WAVES BREAKING.
THE FISHES IN OXIDISED COPPER, THE ORCHIDS MADE OUT OF ENAMEL, ORGANIC THINGS, ANYTHING THAT WAS ALIVE...
I TOLD MAGGIE LAST NIGHT.
IT'S FUNNY. SHE HATED MY BIRDS' EGGS.

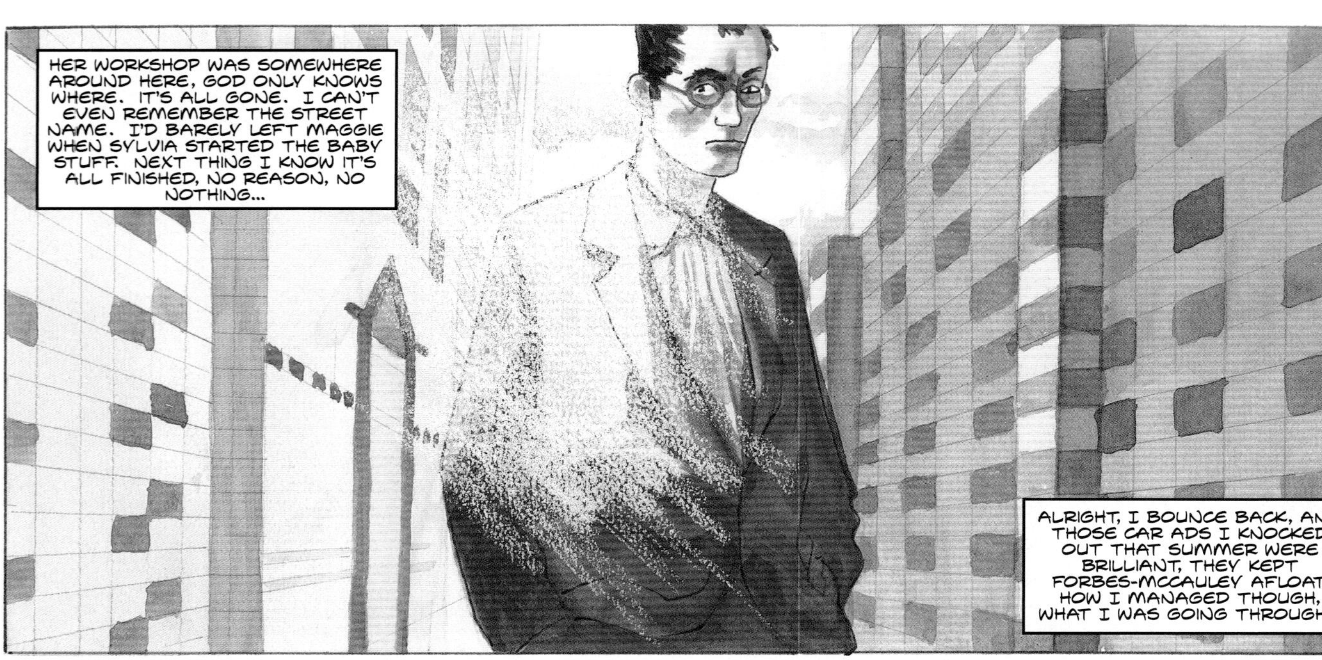
HER WORKSHOP WAS SOMEWHERE AROUND HERE, GOD ONLY KNOWS WHERE. IT'S ALL GONE. I CAN'T EVEN REMEMBER THE STREET NAME. I'D BARELY LEFT MAGGIE WHEN SYLVIA STARTED THE BABY STUFF. NEXT THING I KNOW IT'S ALL FINISHED, NO REASON, NO NOTHING...
ALRIGHT, I BOUNCE BACK, AND THOSE CAR ADS I KNOCKED OUT THAT SUMMER WERE BRILLIANT, THEY KEPT FORBES-MCCAULEY AFLOAT. HOW I MANAGED THOUGH, WHAT I WAS GOING THROUGH...
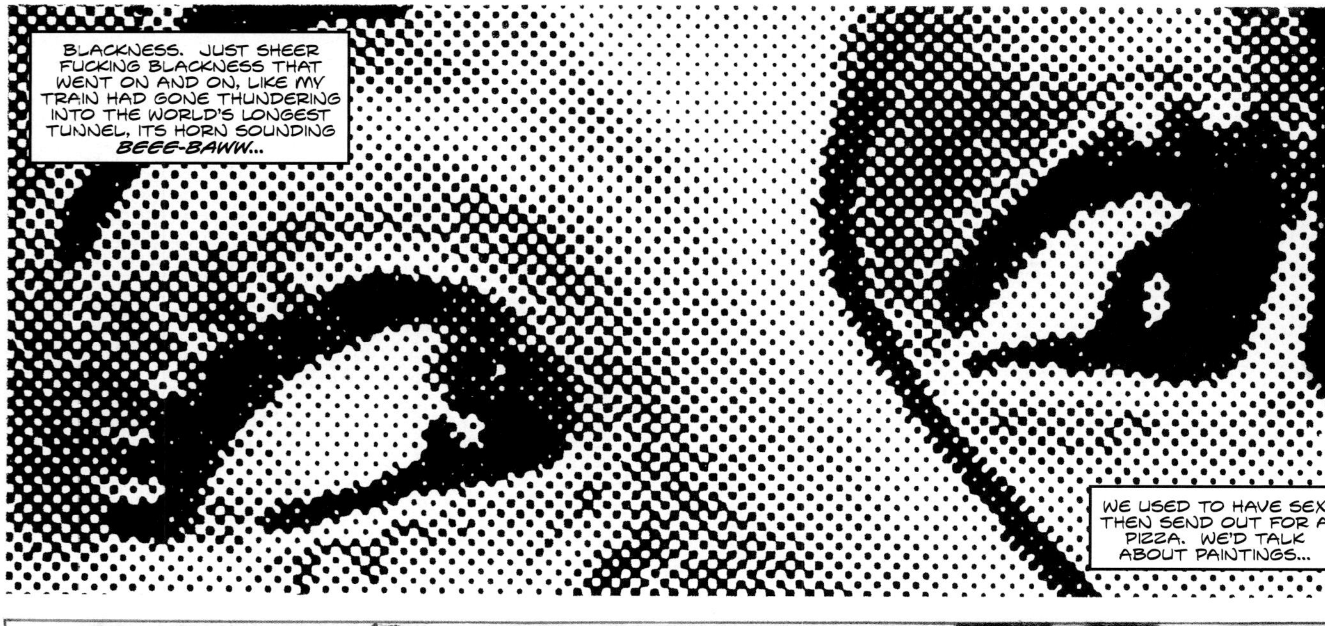
BLACKNESS. JUST SHEER FUCKING BLACKNESS THAT WENT ON AND ON, LIKE MY TRAIN HAD GONE THUNDERING INTO THE WORLD'S LONGEST TUNNEL, ITS HORN SOUNDING ***BEEE-BAWW***...
WE USED TO HAVE SEX THEN SEND OUT FOR A PIZZA. WE'D TALK ABOUT PAINTINGS...
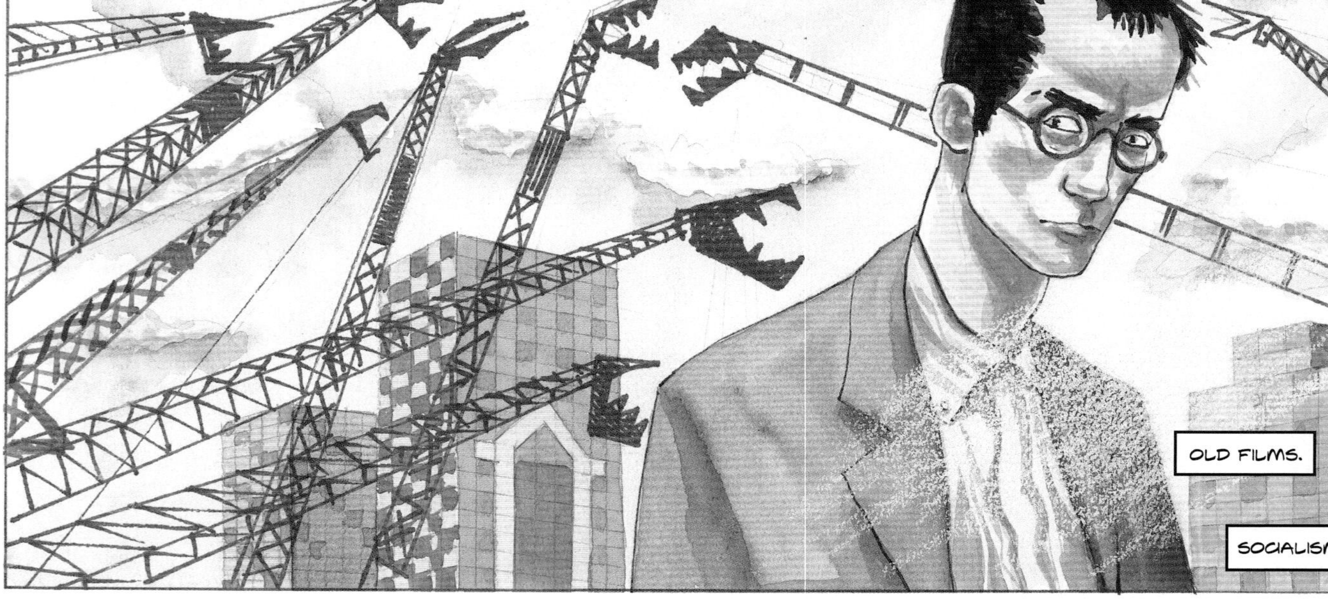
OLD FILMS.
SOCIALISM.

...AND THATCHER, THAT SECOND ELECTION, WE COULDN'T BELIEVE IT. I'M GLAD I WASN'T AROUND FOR THE *THIRD*, ALTHOUGH, REALLY, NEW YORK, IT'S A BIT OF A FRYING PAN/FIRE SITUATION...

WHETHER IT'S HER WITH HER BELGRANOS AND MISSING LOGBOOKS OR BUSH WITH HIS CONTRAS AND COKE DEALS, THEY BRAZEN IT OUT, REWRITE HISTORY, MAKE BELIEVE NOTHING HAS HAPPENED AND EVERYONE JUST GOES ALONG WITH IT...

EVERYBODY VOTES FOR THEM. EVERYBODY PRETENDS THAT IT'S...

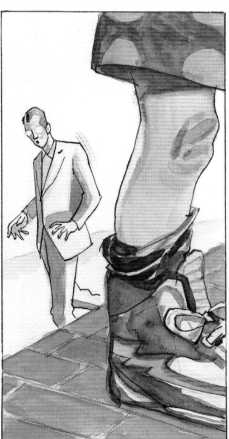

HEY!

YOU LITTLE BASTARD! YOU COME BACK HERE!

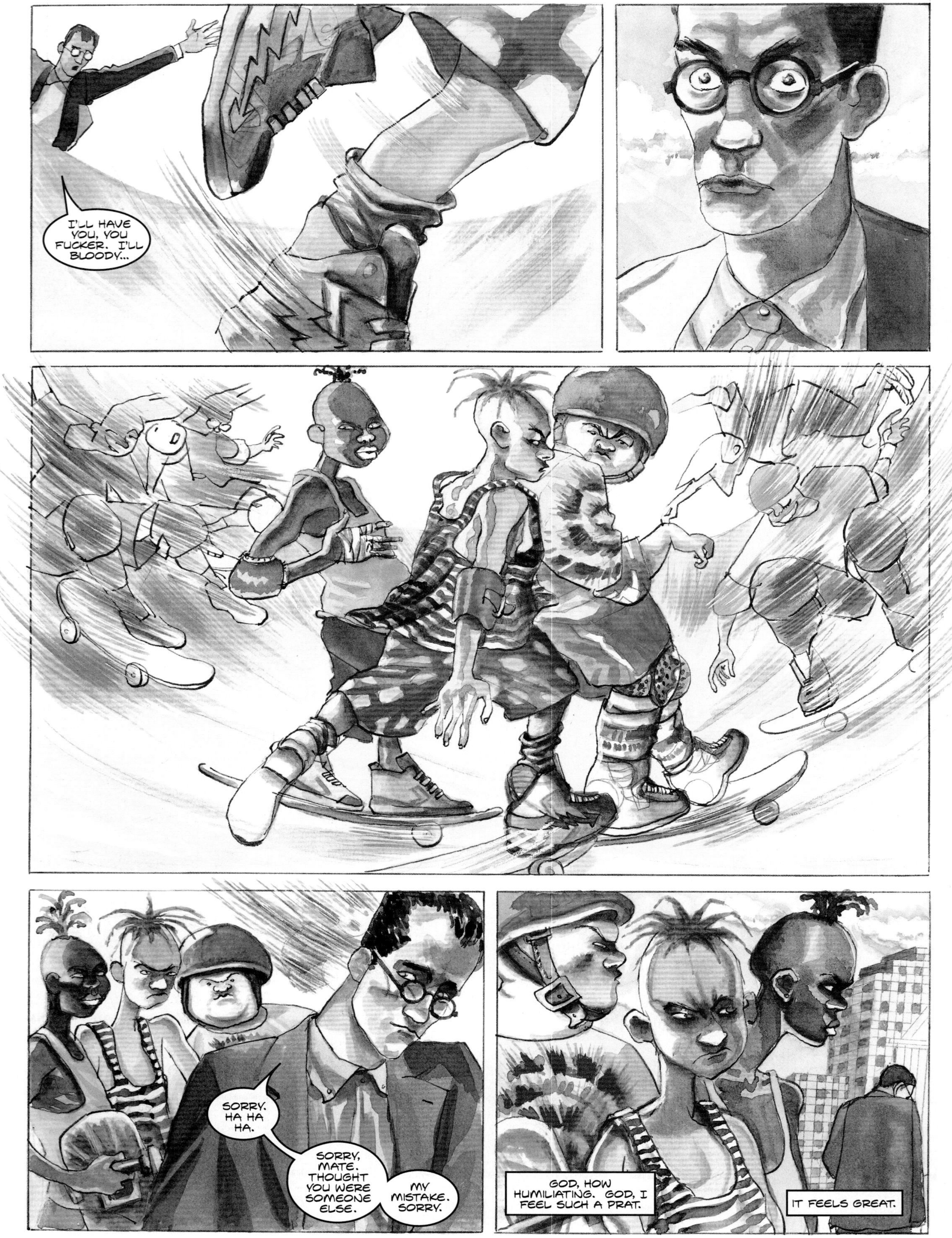
I'LL HAVE YOU, YOU FUCKER. I'LL BLOODY...
SORRY. HA HA HA.
SORRY, MATE. THOUGHT YOU WERE SOMEONE ELSE.
MY MISTAKE. SORRY.
GOD, HOW HUMILIATING. GOD, I FEEL SUCH A PRAT.
IT FEELS GREAT.

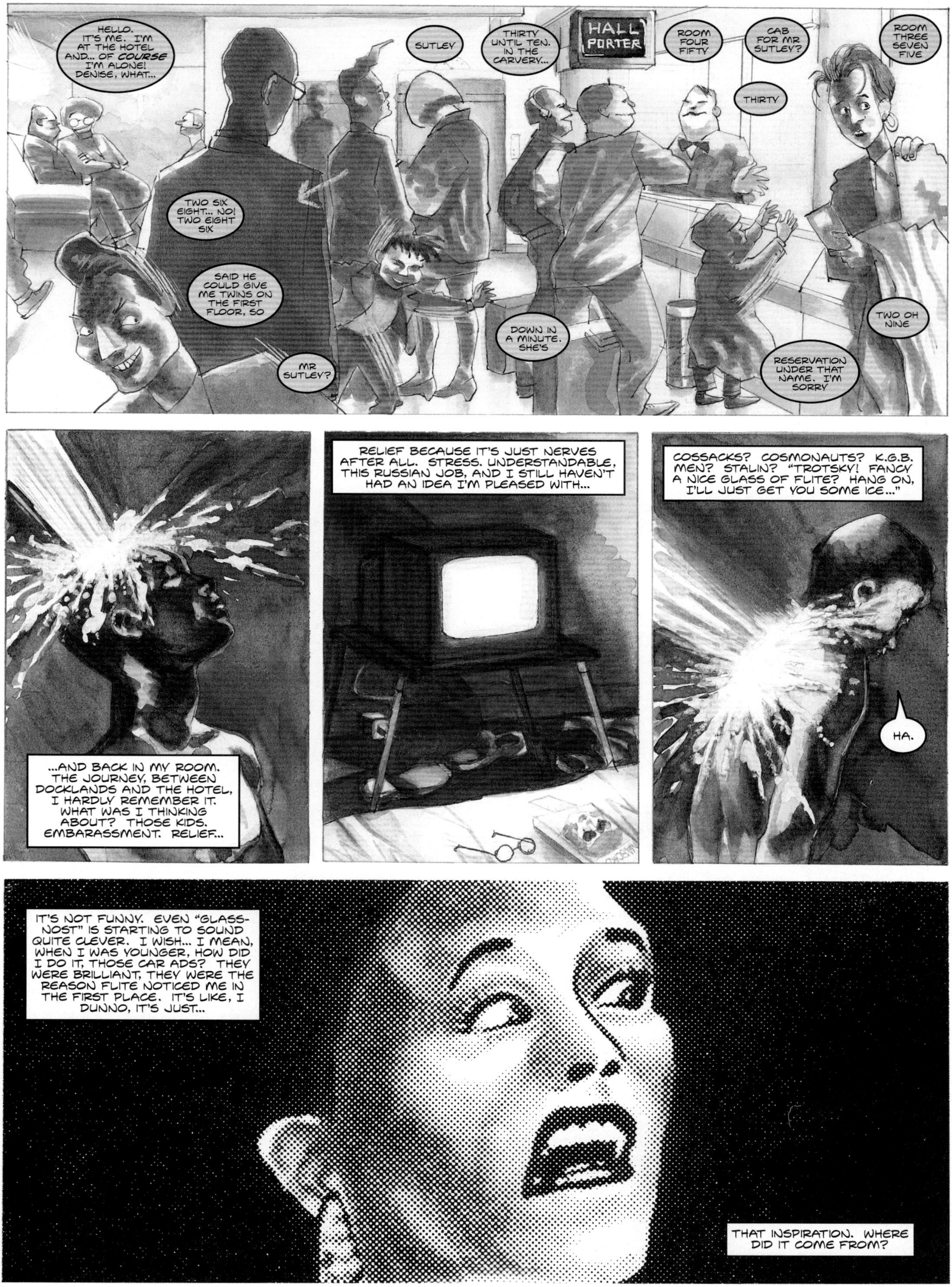
HELLO. IT'S ME. I'M AT THE HOTEL AND... OF *COURSE* I'M ALONE! DENISE, WHAT...
SUTLEY
THIRTY UNTIL TEN. IN THE CARVERY...
HALL PORTER
ROOM FOUR FIFTY
CAB FOR MR SUTLEY?
ROOM THREE SEVEN FIVE
THIRTY
TWO SIX EIGHT... NO! TWO EIGHT SIX
SAID HE COULD GIVE ME TWINS ON THE FIRST FLOOR, SO
MR SUTLEY?
DOWN IN A MINUTE. SHE'S
TWO OH NINE
RESERVATION UNDER THAT NAME. I'M SORRY
...AND BACK IN MY ROOM. THE JOURNEY, BETWEEN DOCKLANDS AND THE HOTEL, I HARDLY REMEMBER IT. WHAT WAS I THINKING ABOUT? THOSE KIDS. EMBARASSMENT. RELIEF...
RELIEF BECAUSE IT'S JUST NERVES AFTER ALL. STRESS. UNDERSTANDABLE, THIS RUSSIAN JOB, AND I STILL HAVEN'T HAD AN IDEA I'M PLEASED WITH...
COSSACKS? COSMONAUTS? K.G.B. MEN? STALIN? "TROTSKY! FANCY A NICE GLASS OF FLITE? HANG ON, I'LL JUST GET YOU SOME ICE..."
HA.
IT'S NOT FUNNY. EVEN "GLASS-NOST" IS STARTING TO SOUND QUITE CLEVER. I WISH... I MEAN, WHEN I WAS YOUNGER, HOW DID I DO IT, THOSE CAR ADS? THEY WERE BRILLIANT, THEY WERE THE REASON FLITE NOTICED ME IN THE FIRST PLACE. IT'S LIKE, I DUNNO, IT'S JUST...
THAT INSPIRATION. WHERE DID IT COME FROM?

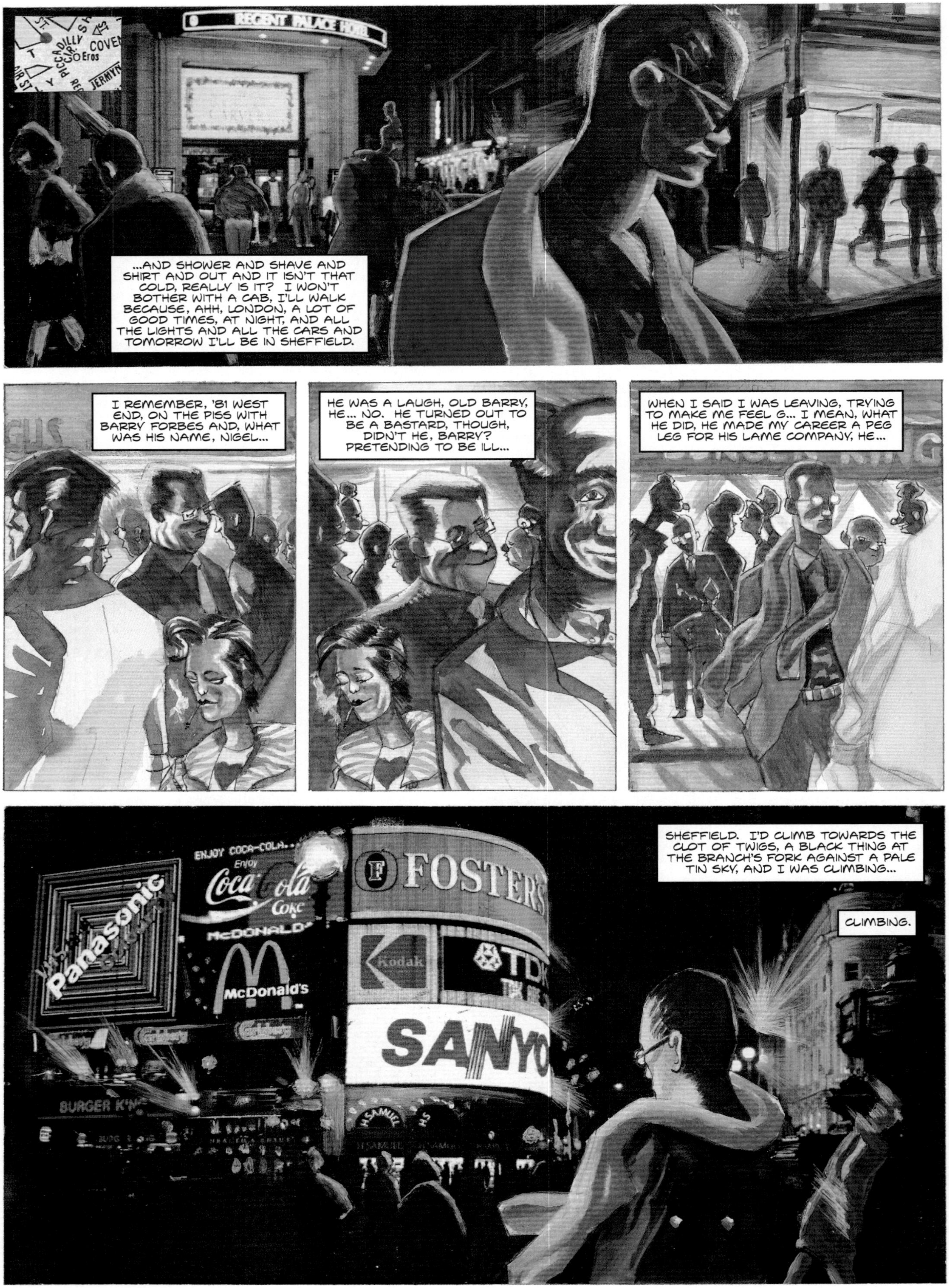
REGENT PALACE HOTEL
...AND SHOWER AND SHAVE AND SHIRT AND OUT AND IT ISN'T THAT COLD, REALLY IS IT? I WON'T BOTHER WITH A CAB, I'LL WALK BECAUSE, AHH, LONDON, A LOT OF GOOD TIMES, AT NIGHT, AND ALL THE LIGHTS AND ALL THE CARS AND TOMORROW I'LL BE IN SHEFFIELD.
I REMEMBER, '81 WEST END, ON THE PISS WITH BARRY FORBES AND, WHAT WAS HIS NAME, NIGEL...
HE WAS A LAUGH, OLD BARRY, HE... NO. HE TURNED OUT TO BE A BASTARD, THOUGH, DIDN'T HE, BARRY? PRETENDING TO BE ILL...
WHEN I SAID I WAS LEAVING, TRYING TO MAKE ME FEEL G... I MEAN, WHAT HE DID, HE MADE MY CAREER A PEG LEG FOR HIS LAME COMPANY, HE...
ENJOY COCA-COLA
Coca-Cola
McDONALD'S
McDonald's
Panasonic
FOSTER'S
Kodak
SANYO
BURGER KING
SHEFFIELD. I'D CLIMB TOWARDS THE CLOT OF TWIGS, A BLACK THING AT THE BRANCH'S FORK AGAINST A PALE TIN SKY, AND I WAS CLIMBING...
CLIMBING.

I'M WELL IMPRESSED, TIM.

WELL IMPRESSED.

WAR.

PEACE.

TUM·FEZ

REALLY, MR FORBES, THAT'S GREAT. YOU DON'T KNOW WHAT LANDING WORK WITH *FORBES-MCCAULEY* MEANS TO ME AND MAGGIE.

I MEAN, I KNOW YOU'RE CARRYING A LOT OF PEOPLE ANYWAY...

WELL, YEAH, WE'RE A BIT OVERSTAFFED, BUT I KNOW TALENT WHEN I SEE IT. YOU'RE A LONG TERM INVESTMENT, TIM, BUT I RECKON YOU'LL PAY OFF, AY?

MONDAY START SUIT YOU?

Stop the Bomb

End all nuclear colla with South Africa

OH YEAH, THAT'S BRILLIANT. THANKS A LOT, MR FORBES...

BARRY.

"BARRY."

AND THE COMMUTING, SHEFFIELD TO LONDON, IT WAS LIKE COMING FROM THE PAST INTO THE PRESENT, AND EVENTUALLY, INTO AMERICA, INTO THE FUTURE, AND MAGGIE LEFT AT HOME BACK IN THE DARK AGES WITH...

CHARING CROSS ROAD... HANG ON A MINUTE, WHICH WAY AM I GOING?

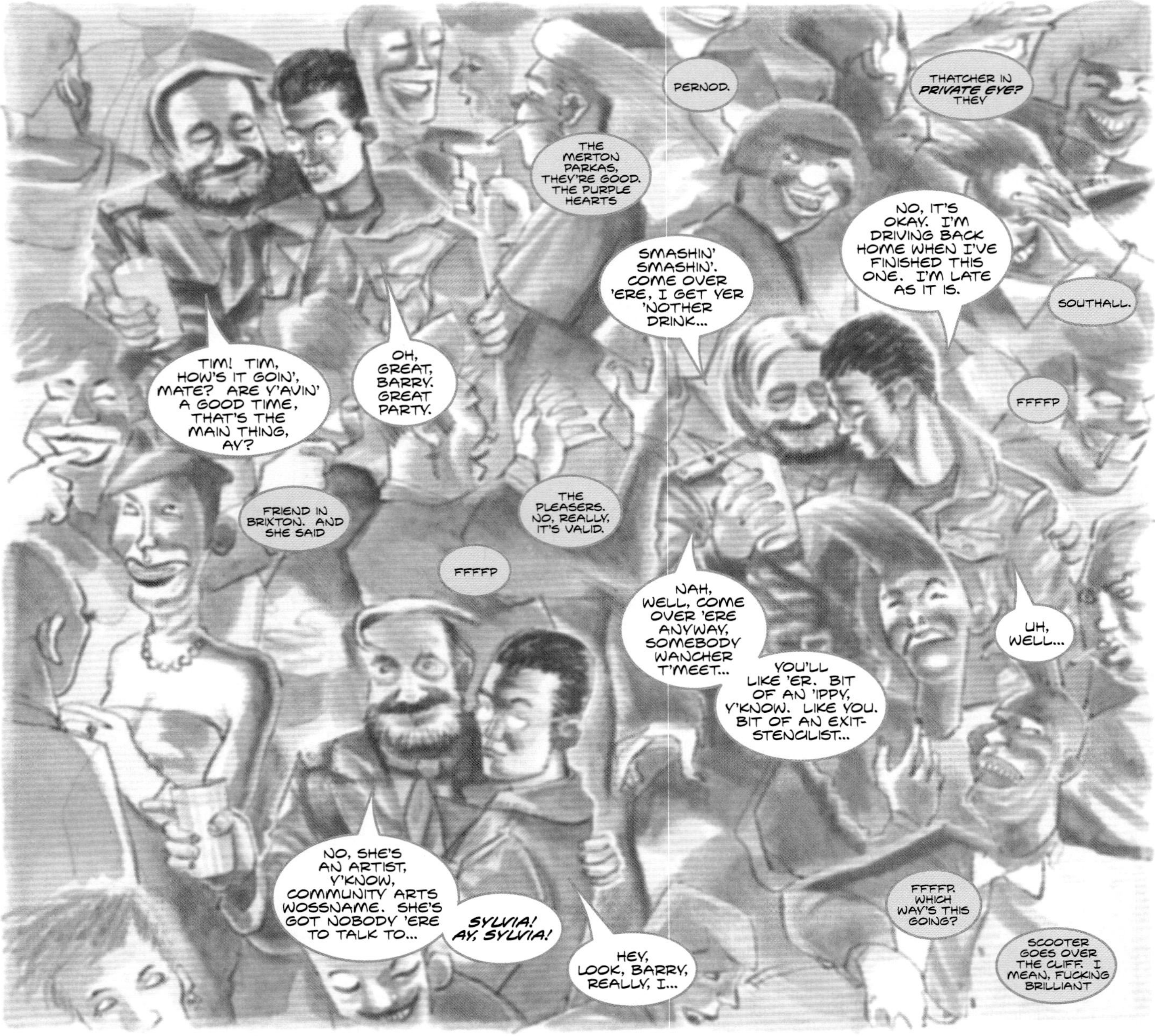

PERNOD.
THATCHER IN *PRIVATE EYE?* THEY
THE MERTON PARKAS, THEY'RE GOOD. THE PURPLE HEARTS
SMASHIN' SMASHIN'. COME OVER 'ERE, I GET YER 'NOTHER DRINK...
NO, IT'S OKAY. I'M DRIVING BACK HOME WHEN I'VE FINISHED THIS ONE. I'M LATE AS IT IS.
SOUTHALL.
TIM! TIM, HOW'S IT GOIN', MATE? ARE Y'AVIN' A GOOD TIME, THAT'S THE MAIN THING, AY?
OH, GREAT, BARRY. GREAT PARTY.
FFFFP
FRIEND IN BRIXTON. AND SHE SAID
THE PLEASERS. NO, REALLY, IT'S VALID.
FFFFP
NAH, WELL, COME OVER 'ERE ANYWAY, SOMEBODY WANCHER T'MEET...
YOU'LL LIKE 'ER. BIT OF AN 'IPPY, Y'KNOW. LIKE YOU. BIT OF AN EXIT-STENCILIST...
UH, WELL...
NO, SHE'S AN ARTIST, Y'KNOW, COMMUNITY ARTS WOSSNAME. SHE'S GOT NOBODY 'ERE TO TALK TO...
SYLVIA! AY, SYLVIA!
HEY, LOOK, BARRY, REALLY, I...
FFFFP. WHICH WAY'S THIS GOING?
SCOOTER GOES OVER THE CLIFF. I MEAN, FUCKING BRILLIANT

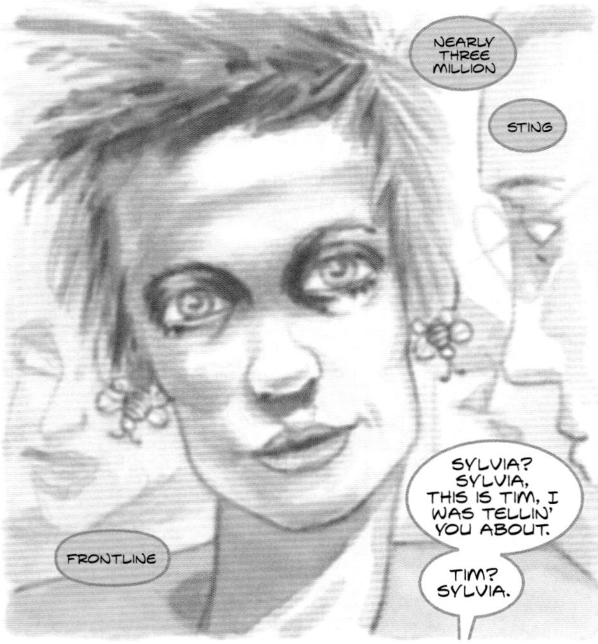

NEARLY THREE MILLION
STING
SYLVIA? SYLVIA, THIS IS TIM, I WAS TELLIN' YOU ABOUT.
TIM? SYLVIA.
FRONTLINE

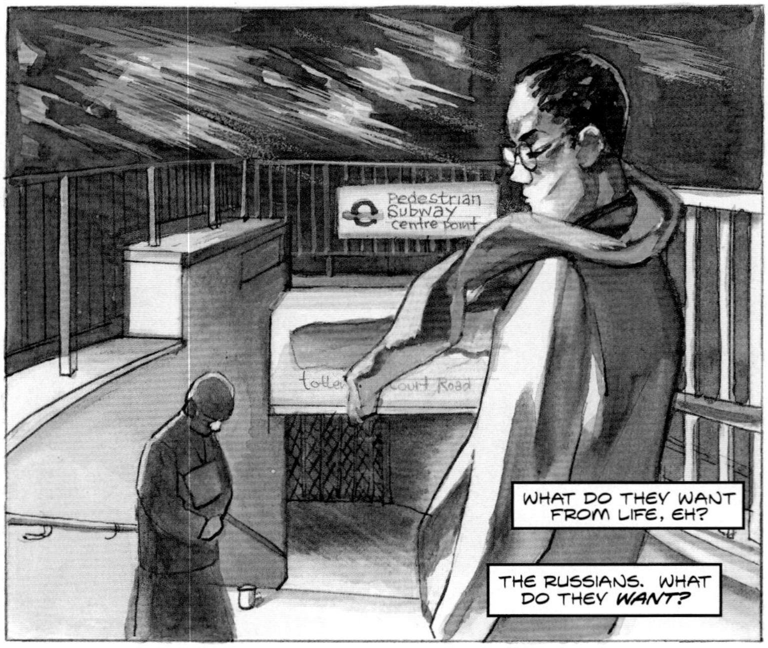

Pedestrian Subway centre point
WHAT DO THEY WANT FROM LIFE, EH?
THE RUSSIANS. WHAT DO THEY *WANT?*

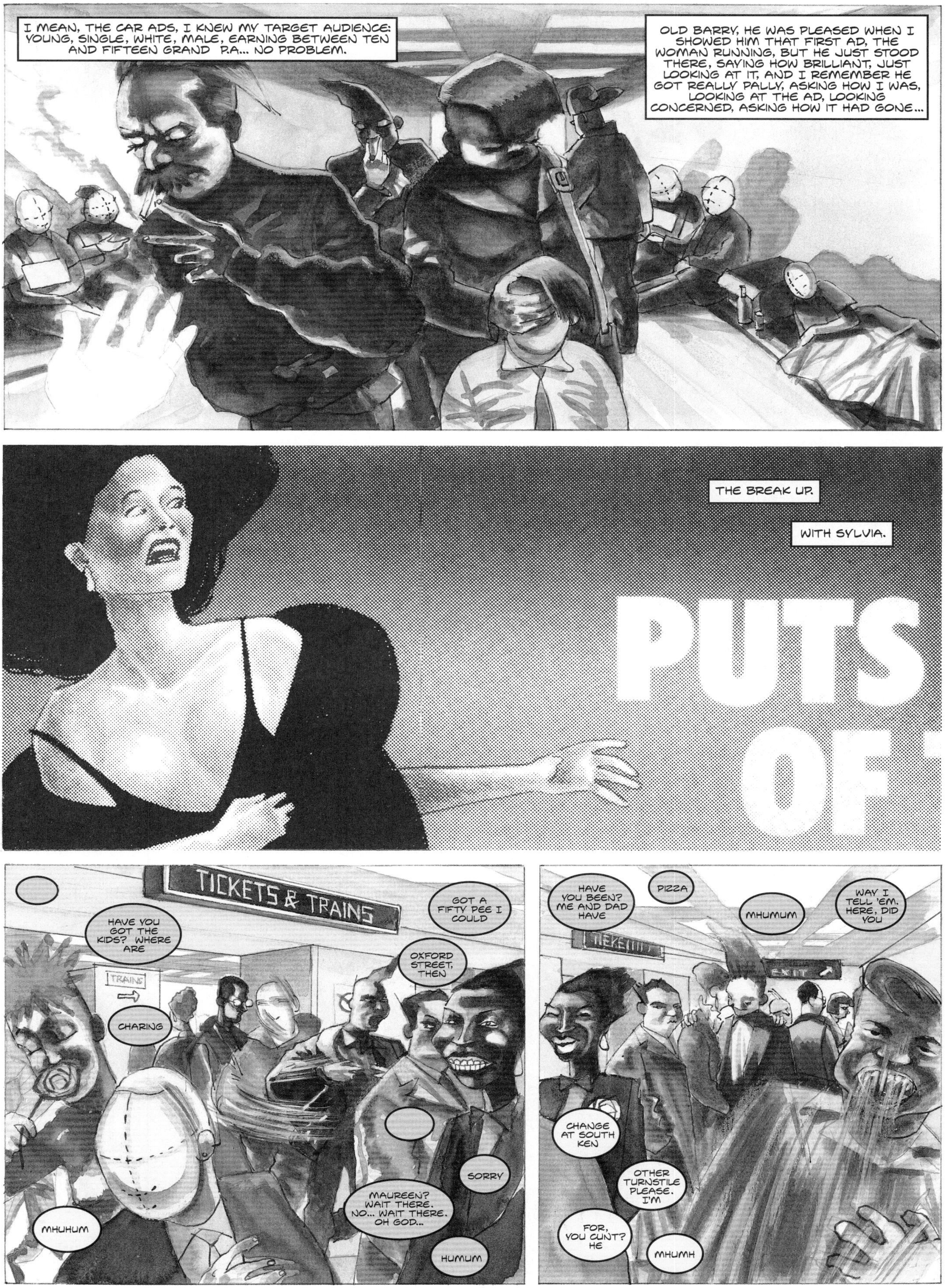
I MEAN, THE CAR ADS, I KNEW MY TARGET AUDIENCE: YOUNG, SINGLE, WHITE, MALE, EARNING BETWEEN TEN AND FIFTEEN GRAND P.A... NO PROBLEM.
OLD BARRY, HE WAS PLEASED WHEN I SHOWED HIM THAT FIRST AD, THE WOMAN RUNNING, BUT HE JUST STOOD THERE, SAYING HOW BRILLIANT, JUST LOOKING AT IT, AND I REMEMBER HE GOT REALLY PALLY, ASKING HOW I WAS, LOOKING AT THE AD, LOOKING CONCERNED, ASKING HOW IT HAD GONE...
THE BREAK UP.
WITH SYLVIA.
PUTS
OF
TICKETS & TRAINS
HAVE YOU GOT THE KIDS? WHERE ARE
GOT A FIFTY PEE I COULD
OXFORD STREET, THEN
TRAINS
CHARING
SORRY
MAUREEN? WAIT THERE. NO... WAIT THERE. OH GOD...
MHUHUM
HUMUM
HAVE YOU BEEN? ME AND DAD HAVE
PIZZA
MHUMUM
WAY I TELL 'EM. HERE, DID YOU
EXIT
CHANGE AT SOUTH KEN
OTHER TURNSTILE PLEASE. I'M
FOR, YOU CUNT? HE
MHUMH

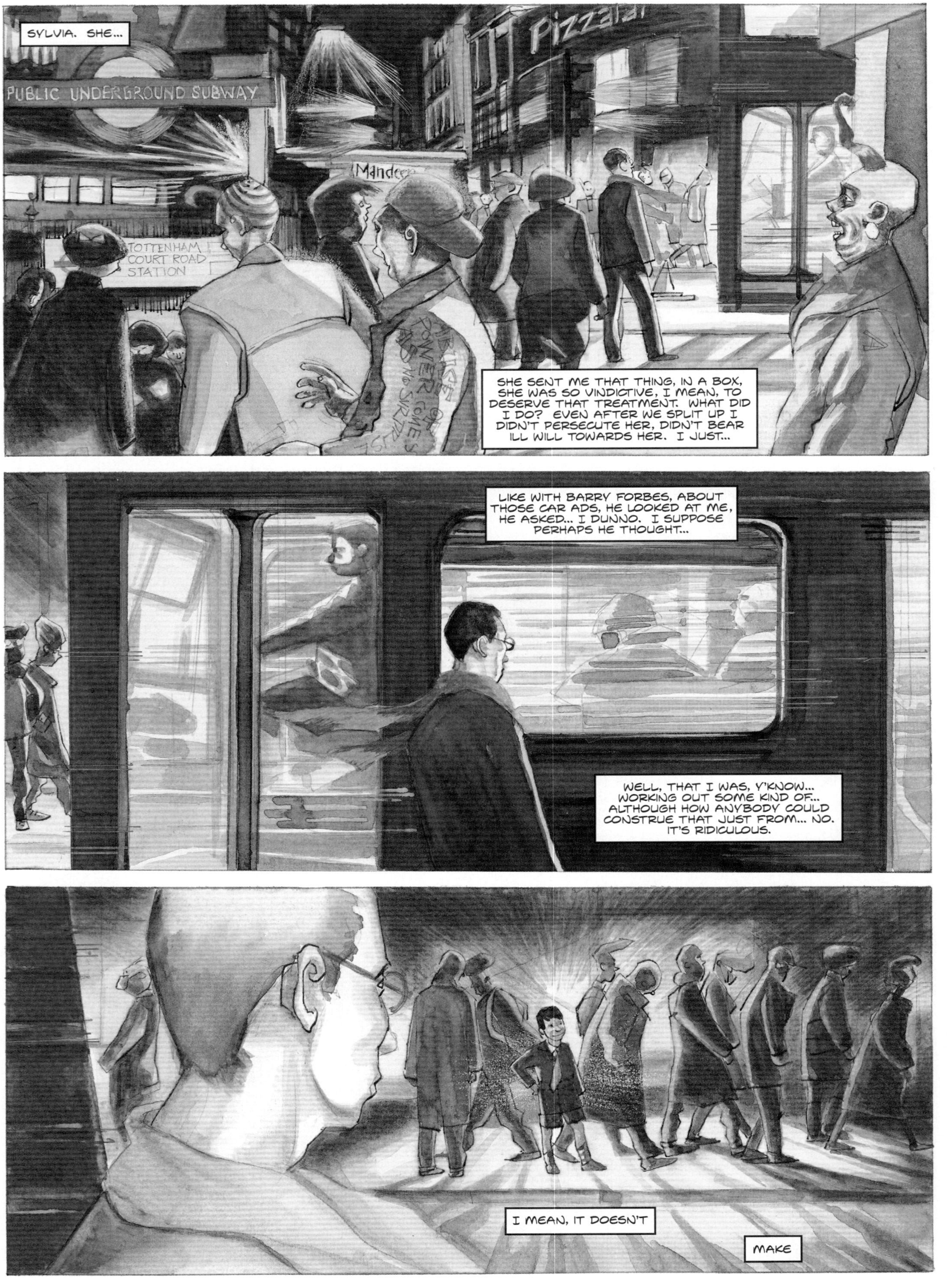
SYLVIA. SHE...
PUBLIC UNDERGROUND SUBWAY
TOTTENHAM COURT ROAD STATION
SHE SENT ME THAT THING, IN A BOX, SHE WAS SO VINDICTIVE, I MEAN, TO DESERVE THAT TREATMENT. WHAT DID I DO? EVEN AFTER WE SPLIT UP I DIDN'T PERSECUTE HER, DIDN'T BEAR ILL WILL TOWARDS HER. I JUST...
LIKE WITH BARRY FORBES, ABOUT THOSE CAR ADS, HE LOOKED AT ME, HE ASKED... I DUNNO. I SUPPOSE PERHAPS HE THOUGHT...
WELL, THAT I WAS, Y'KNOW... WORKING OUT SOME KIND OF... ALTHOUGH HOW ANYBODY COULD CONSTRUE THAT JUST FROM... NO. IT'S RIDICULOUS.
I MEAN, IT DOESN'T
MAKE

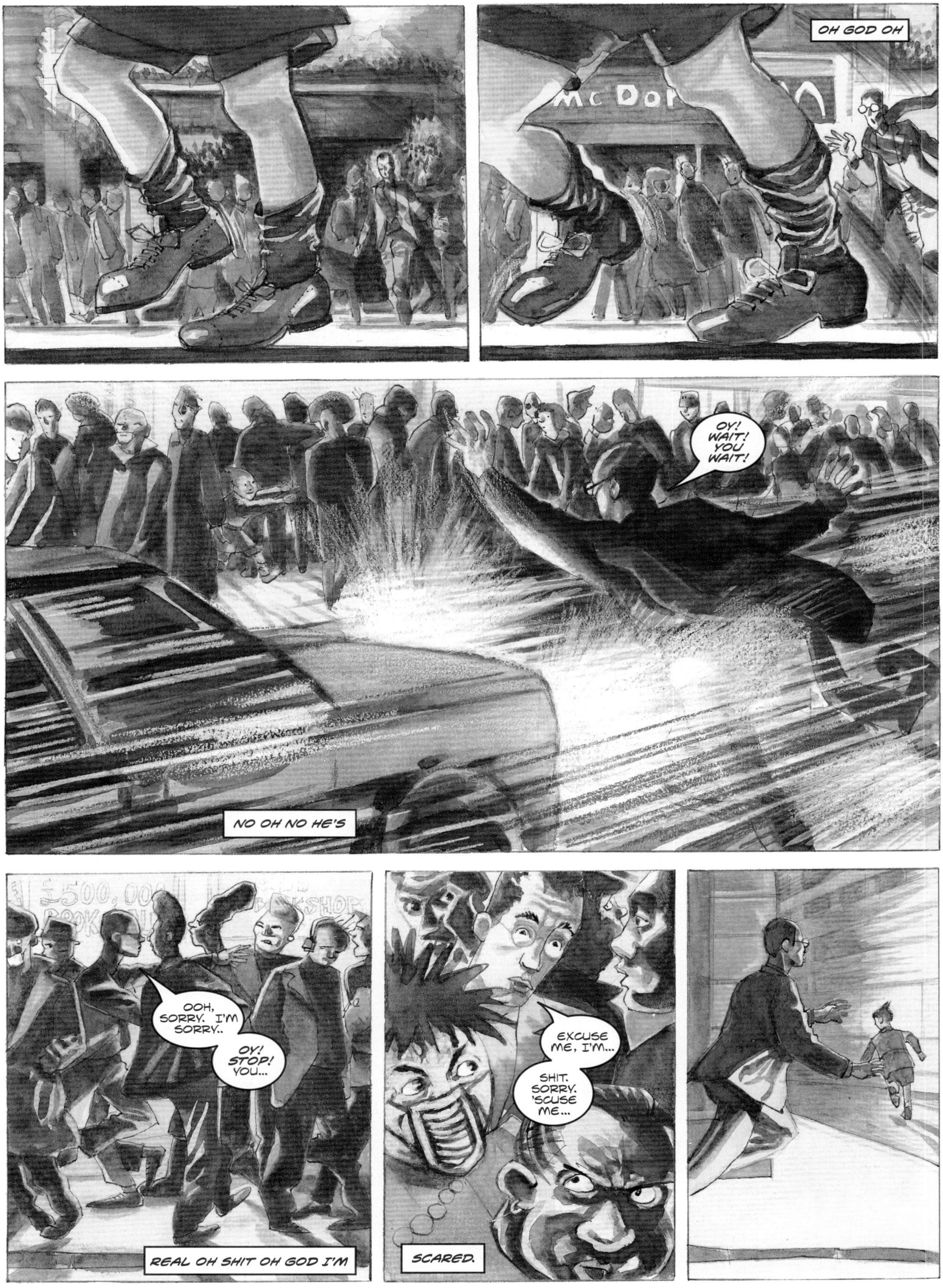
OH GOD OH
OY! WAIT! YOU WAIT!
NO OH NO HE'S
OOH, SORRY. I'M SORRY..
OY! STOP! YOU...
REAL OH SHIT OH GOD I'M
EXCUSE ME, I'M...
SHIT. SORRY. 'SCUSE ME...
SCARED.

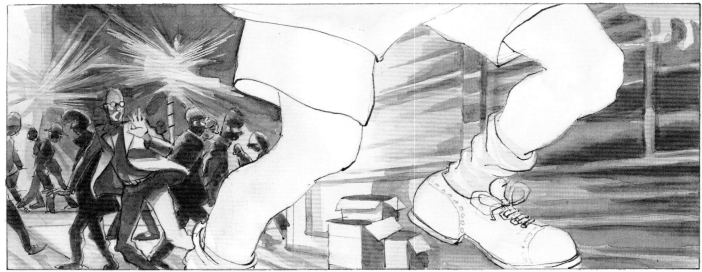

WAY I SEE IT, IT'S YOUR BODY, I CAN'T MAKE DECISIONS FOR..

TIM, *PLEASE.* I DON'T WANT YOU TO MAKE MY DECISIONS. I JUST WANT TO KNOW HOW YOU *FEEL* ABOUT IT.

I DON'T THINK I COULD HANDLE A BABY RIGHT NOW.

I DON'T THINK *YOU* COULD EITHER, BUT IT'S OUR BABY AND I WANT TO KNOW WHAT *YOU* THINK AND WHAT *YOU* WANT..

I... LOOK, I JUST WANT WHAT'S BEST FOR *YOU,* THAT'S ALL.

I JUST WANT WHAT *YOU* WANT.

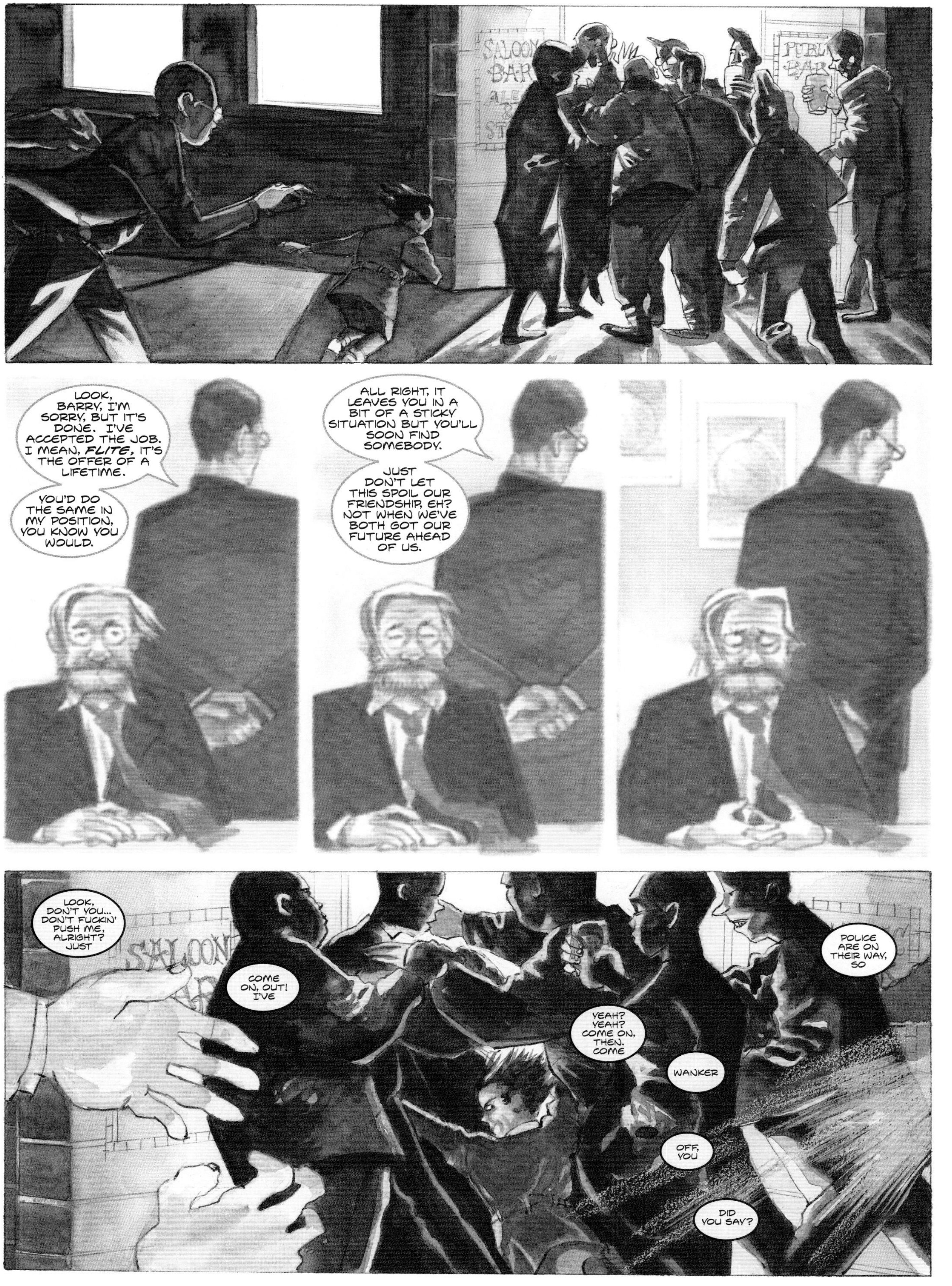
SALOON BAR
LOOK, BARRY, I'M SORRY, BUT IT'S DONE. I'VE ACCEPTED THE JOB. I MEAN, *FLITE,* IT'S THE OFFER OF A LIFETIME.
YOU'D DO THE SAME IN MY POSITION, YOU KNOW YOU WOULD.
ALL RIGHT, IT LEAVES YOU IN A BIT OF A STICKY SITUATION BUT YOU'LL SOON FIND SOMEBODY.
JUST DON'T LET THIS SPOIL OUR FRIENDSHIP, EH? NOT WHEN WE'VE BOTH GOT OUR FUTURE AHEAD OF US.
LOOK, DON'T YOU... DON'T FUCKIN' PUSH ME, ALRIGHT? JUST
COME ON, OUT! I'VE
YEAH? YEAH? COME ON, THEN. COME
WANKER
OFF, YOU
DID YOU SAY?
POLICE ARE ON THEIR WAY, SO

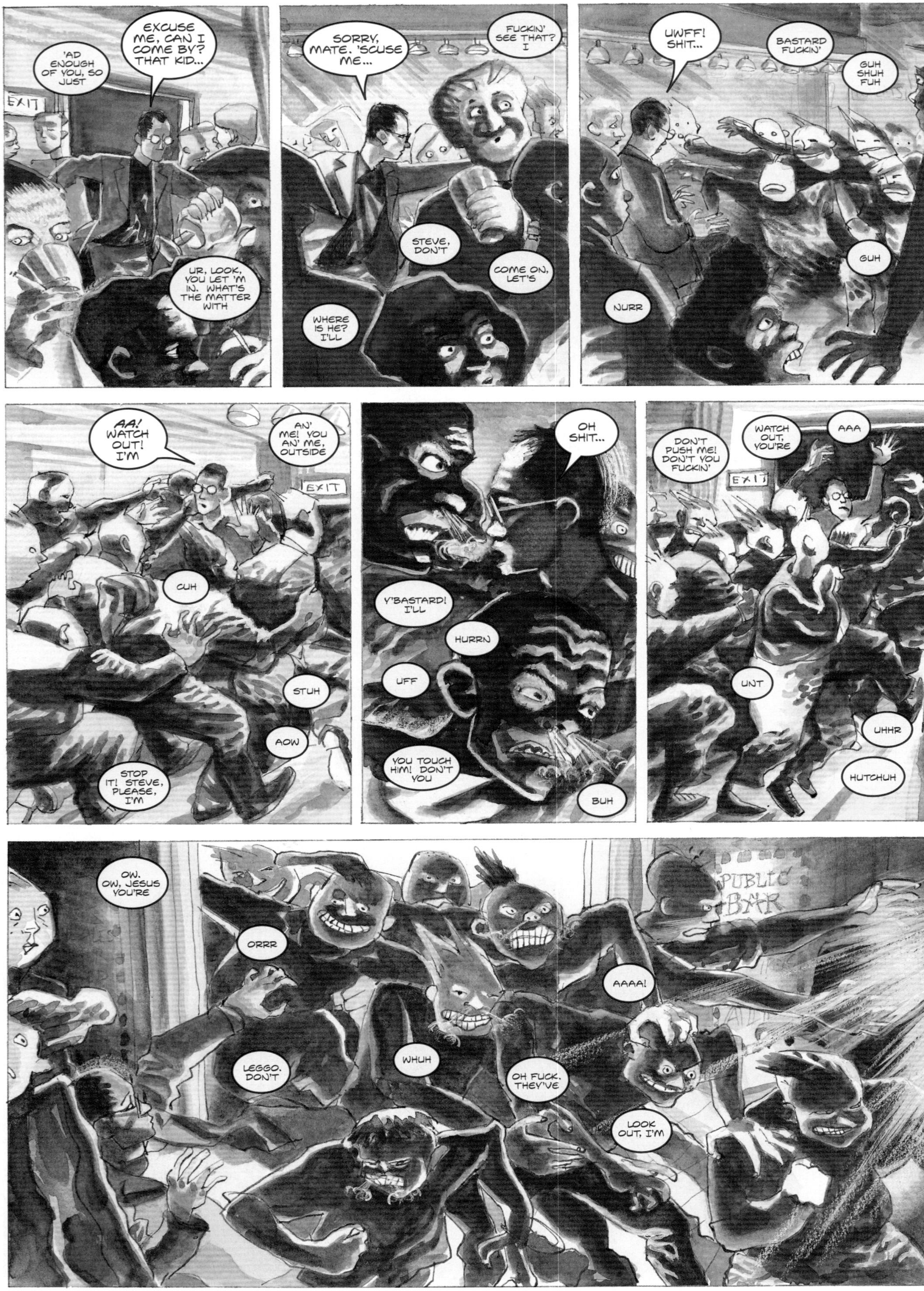
'AD ENOUGH OF YOU, SO JUST
EXCUSE ME, CAN I COME BY? THAT KID...
UR, LOOK, YOU LET 'M IN. WHAT'S THE MATTER WITH
SORRY, MATE. 'SCUSE ME...
FUCKIN' SEE THAT? I
STEVE, DON'T
COME ON, LET'S
WHERE IS HE? I'LL
UWFF! SHIT...
BASTARD FUCKIN'
GUH SHUH FUH
GUH
NURR
AA! WATCH OUT! I'M
AN' ME! YOU AN' ME, OUTSIDE
CUH
STUH
AOW
STOP IT! STEVE, PLEASE, I'M
OH SHIT...
Y'BASTARD! I'LL
HURRN
UFF
YOU TOUCH HIM! DON'T YOU
BUH
DON'T PUSH ME! DON'T YOU FUCKIN'
WATCH OUT, YOU'RE
AAA
UNT
UHHR
HUTCHUH
OW. OW, JESUS YOU'RE
ORRR
AAAA!
LEGGO. DON'T
WHUH
OH FUCK. THEY'VE
LOOK OUT, I'M
PUBLIC BAR

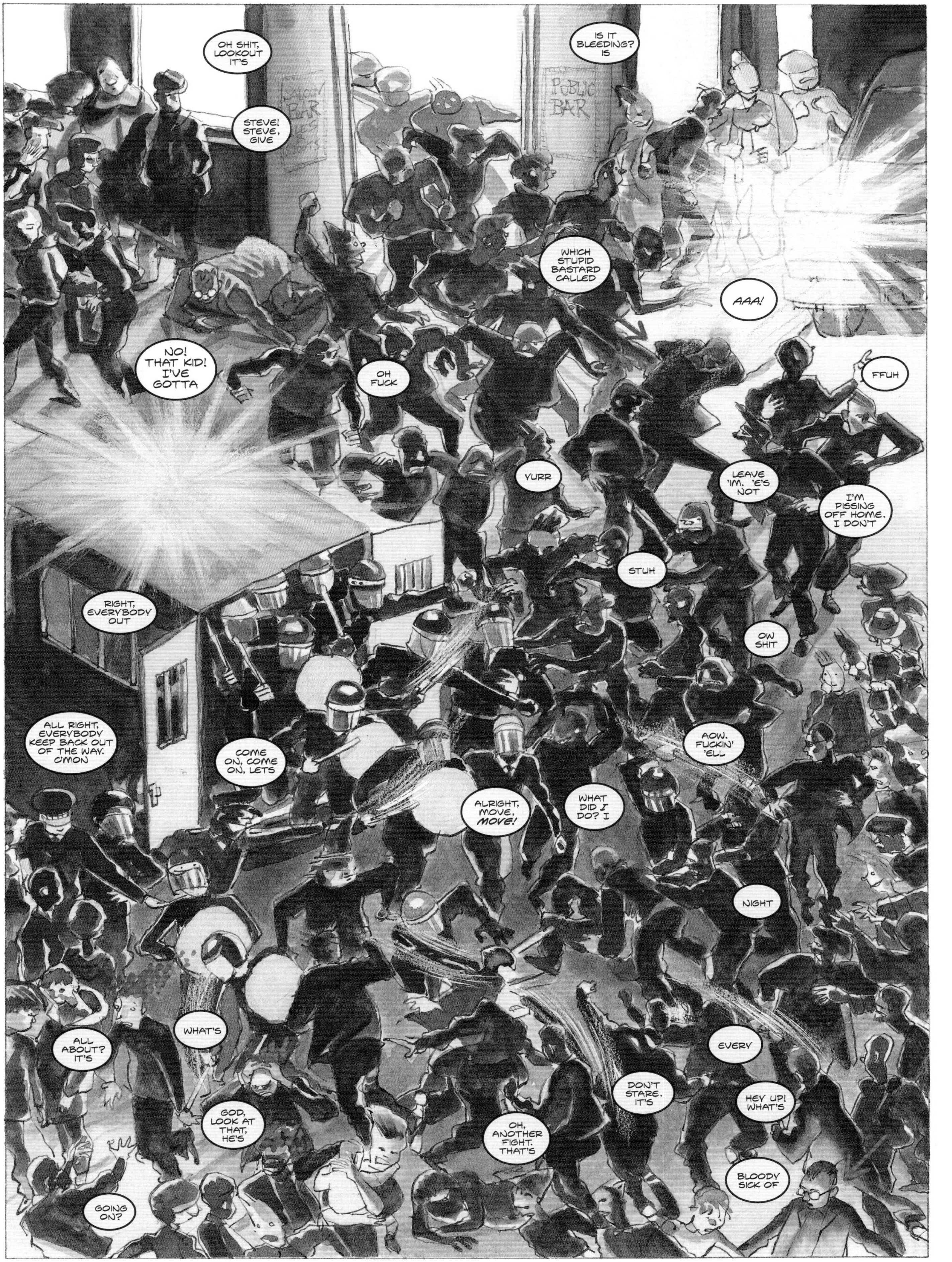

OH SHIT, LOOKOUT IT'S
STEVE! STEVE, GIVE
SALOON BAR
PUBLIC BAR
IS IT BLEEDING? IS
WHICH STUPID BASTARD CALLED
AAA!
NO! THAT KID! I'VE GOTTA
OH FUCK
FFUH
YURR
LEAVE 'IM. 'E'S NOT
I'M PISSING OFF HOME. I DON'T
STUH
RIGHT, EVERYBODY OUT
OW SHIT
ALL RIGHT, EVERYBODY KEEP BACK OUT OF THE WAY. C'MON
COME ON, COME ON, LETS
AOW. FUCKIN' 'ELL
ALRIGHT, MOVE, MOVE!
WHAT DID I DO? I
NIGHT
WHAT'S
ALL ABOUT? IT'S
EVERY
DON'T STARE. IT'S
HEY UP! WHAT'S
GOD, LOOK AT THAT, HE'S
OH, ANOTHER FIGHT. THAT'S
BLOODY SICK OF
GOING ON?

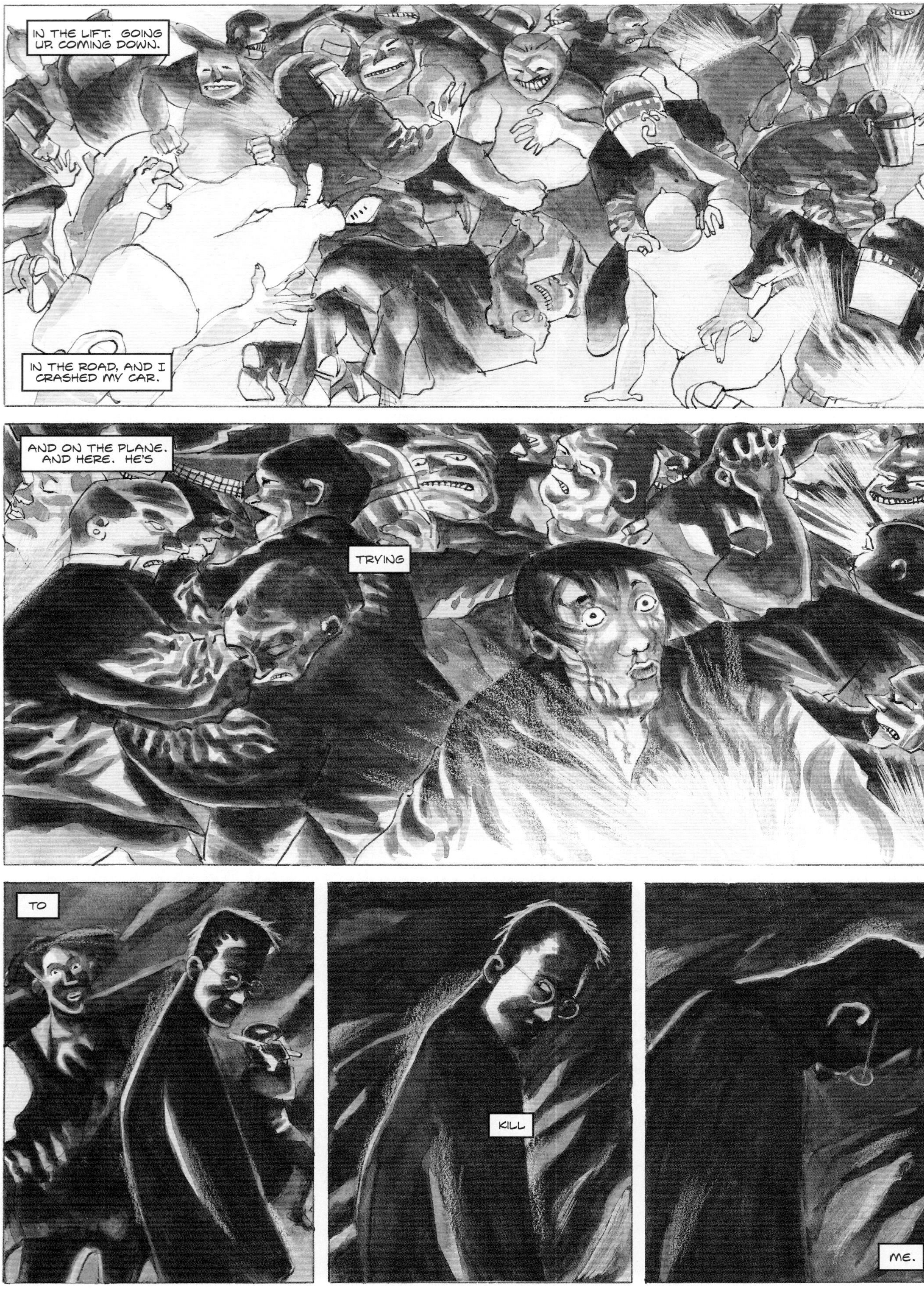
IN THE LIFT. GOING UP. COMING DOWN.
IN THE ROAD, AND I CRASHED MY CAR.
AND ON THE PLANE. AND HERE. HE'S
TRYING
TO
KILL
ME.

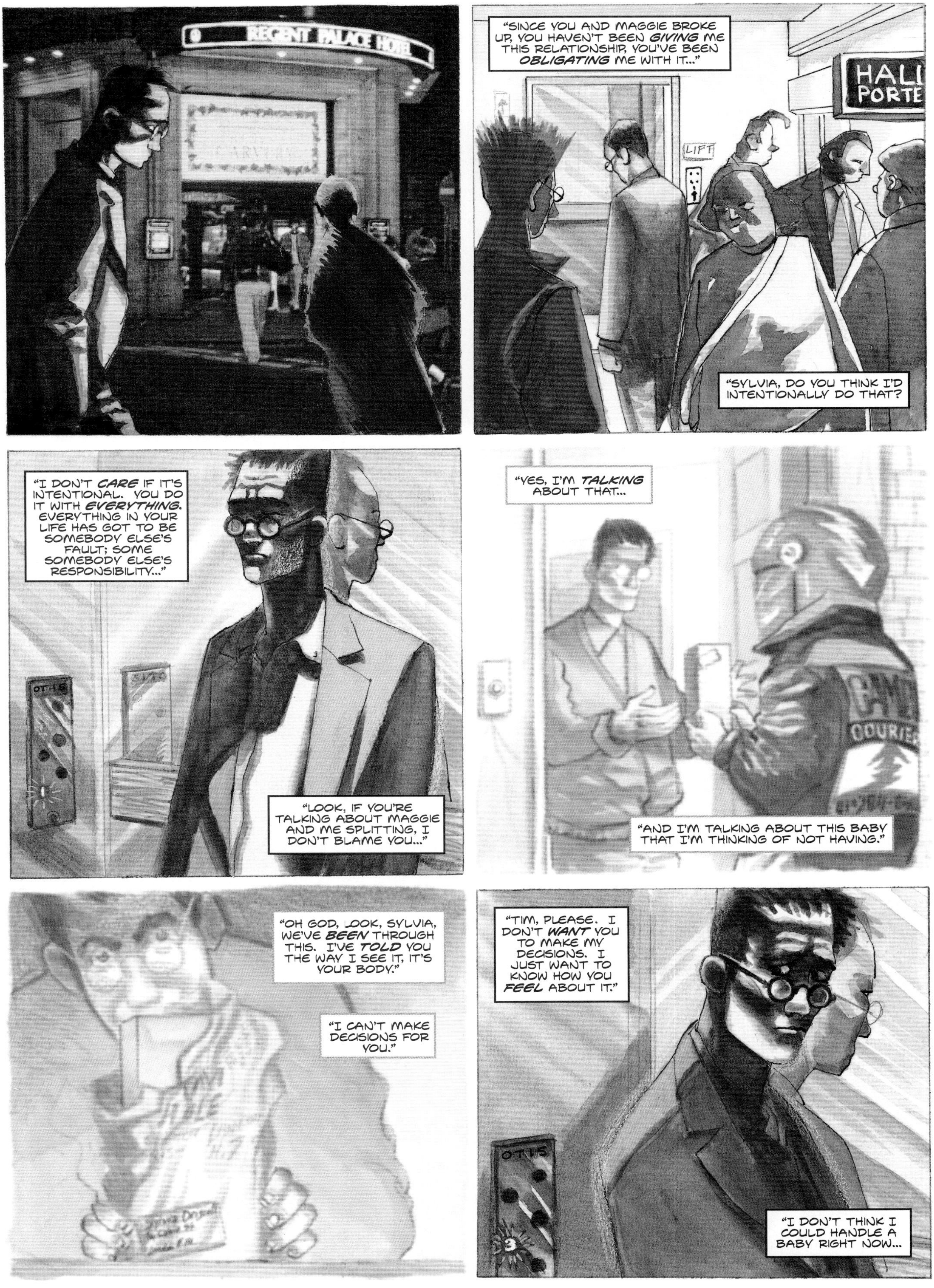
REGENT PALACE HOTEL
"SINCE YOU AND MAGGIE BROKE UP, YOU HAVEN'T BEEN *GIVING* ME THIS RELATIONSHIP, YOU'VE BEEN *OBLIGATING* ME WITH IT..."
LIFT
"SYLVIA, DO YOU THINK I'D INTENTIONALLY DO THAT?
"I DON'T *CARE* IF IT'S INTENTIONAL. YOU DO IT WITH *EVERYTHING*. EVERYTHING IN YOUR LIFE HAS GOT TO BE SOMEBODY ELSE'S FAULT; SOME SOMEBODY ELSE'S RESPONSIBILITY..."
OTIS
"LOOK, IF YOU'RE TALKING ABOUT MAGGIE AND ME SPLITTING, I DON'T BLAME YOU..."
"YES, I'M *TALKING* ABOUT THAT...
"AND I'M TALKING ABOUT THIS BABY THAT I'M THINKING OF NOT HAVING."
"OH GOD, LOOK, SYLVIA, WE'VE *BEEN* THROUGH THIS. I'VE *TOLD* YOU THE WAY I SEE IT, IT'S YOUR BODY."
"I CAN'T MAKE DECISIONS FOR YOU."
"TIM, PLEASE. I DON'T *WANT* YOU TO MAKE MY DECISIONS. I JUST WANT TO KNOW HOW YOU *FEEL* ABOUT IT."
OTIS
"I DON'T THINK I COULD HANDLE A BABY RIGHT NOW...

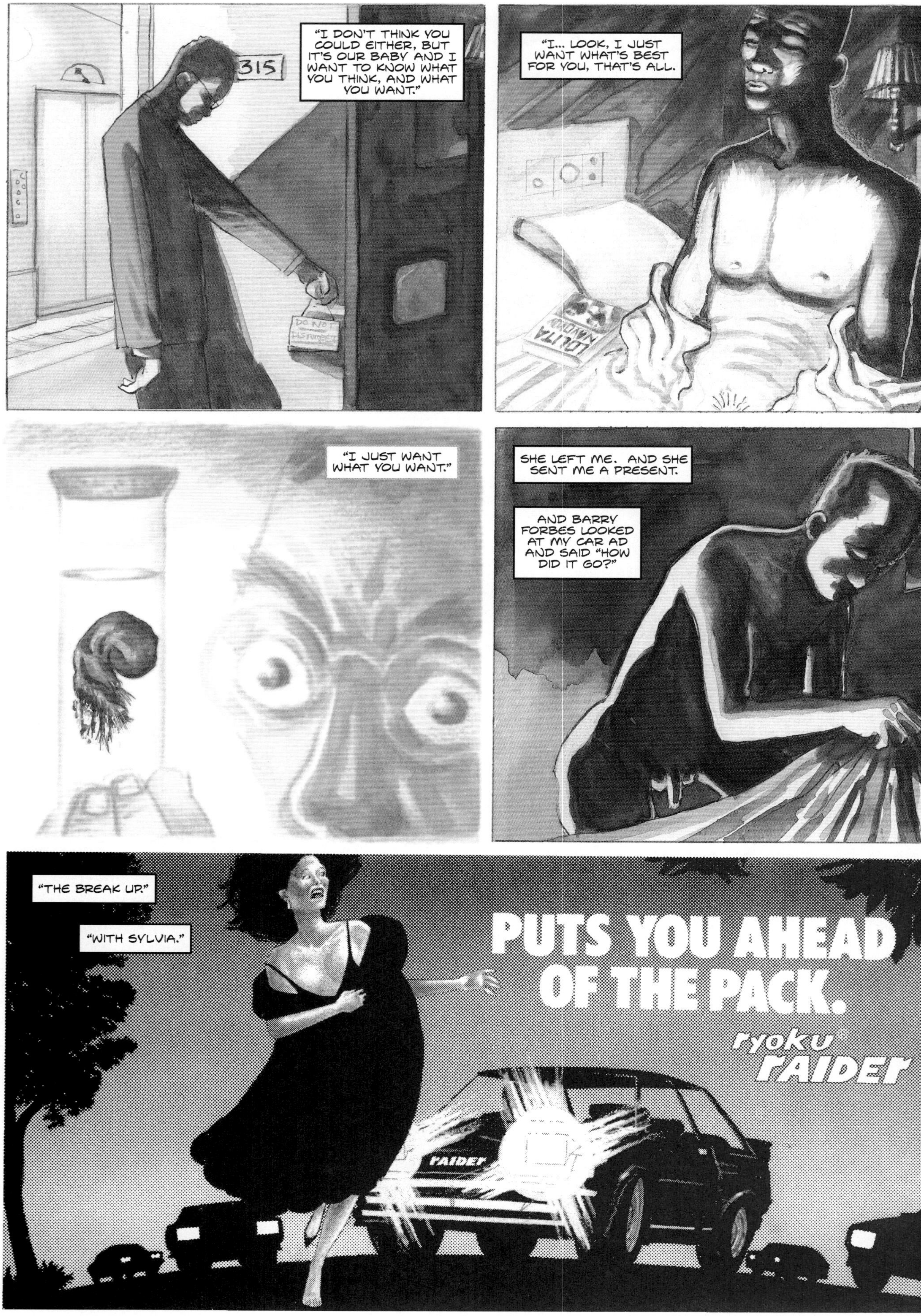

"I DON'T THINK YOU COULD EITHER, BUT IT'S OUR BABY AND I WANT TO KNOW WHAT YOU THINK, AND WHAT YOU WANT."
315
"I... LOOK, I JUST WANT WHAT'S BEST FOR YOU, THAT'S ALL.
"I JUST WANT WHAT YOU WANT."
SHE LEFT ME. AND SHE SENT ME A PRESENT.
AND BARRY FORBES LOOKED AT MY CAR AD AND SAID "HOW DID IT GO?"
"THE BREAK UP."
"WITH SYLVIA."
PUTS YOU AHEAD OF THE PACK.
ryoku RAIDER
RAIDER

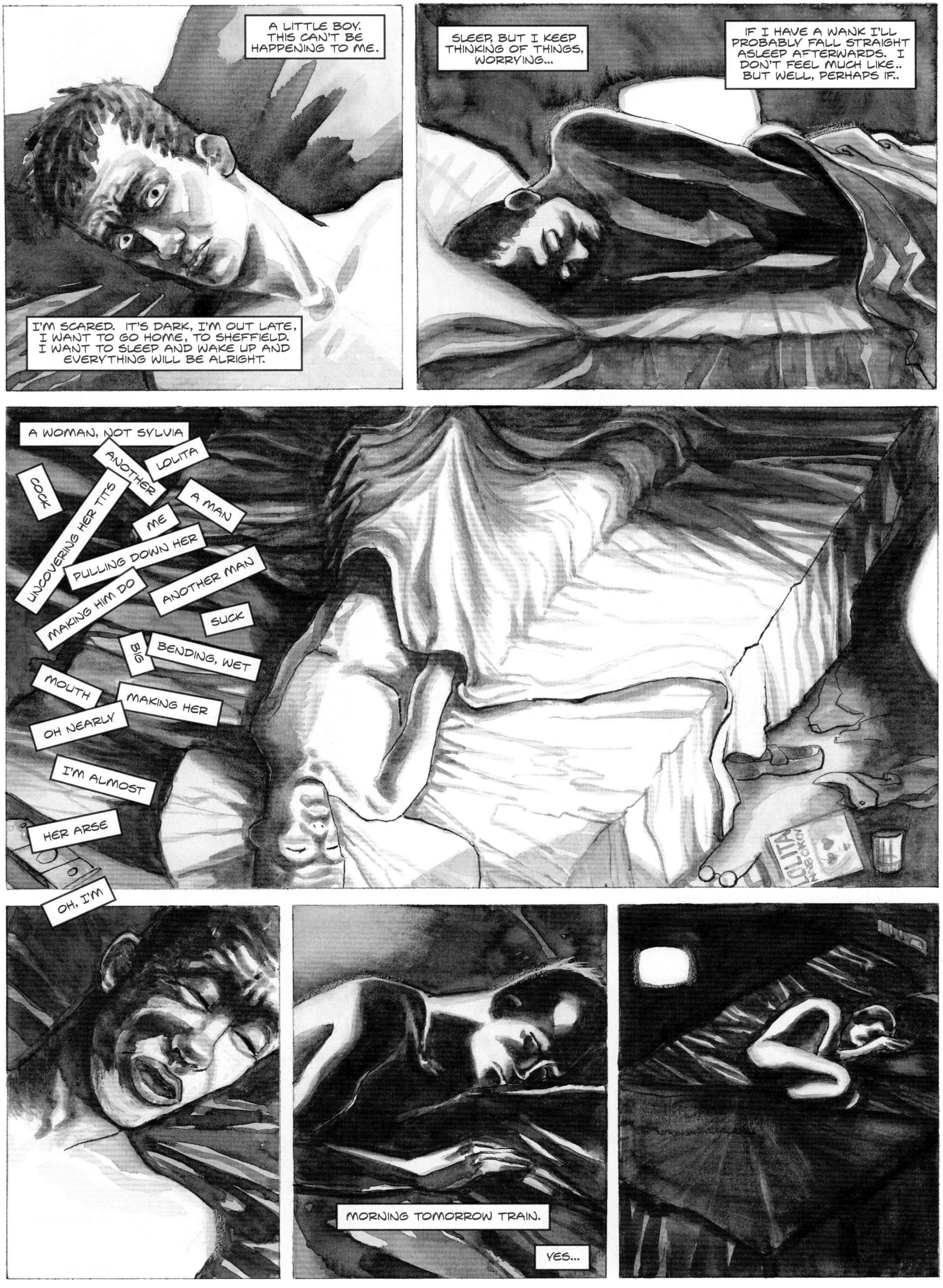
A LITTLE BOY. THIS CAN'T BE HAPPENING TO ME.
I'M SCARED. IT'S DARK, I'M OUT LATE, I WANT TO GO HOME, TO SHEFFIELD. I WANT TO SLEEP AND WAKE UP AND EVERYTHING WILL BE ALRIGHT.
SLEEP, BUT I KEEP THINKING OF THINGS, WORRYING...
IF I HAVE A WANK I'LL PROBABLY FALL STRAIGHT ASLEEP AFTERWARDS. I DON'T FEEL MUCH LIKE.. BUT WELL, PERHAPS IF..
A WOMAN, NOT SYLVIA
ANOTHER
LOLITA
COCK
UNCOVERING HER TITS
A MAN
ME
PULLING DOWN HER
MAKING HIM DO
ANOTHER MAN
SUCK
BIG
BENDING, WET
MOUTH
MAKING HER
OH NEARLY
I'M ALMOST
HER ARSE
LOLITA
NABOKOV
OH, I'M
MORNING TOMORROW TRAIN.
YES...

...WORK, THINK ABOUT WORK AND NOT ABOUT... GORKY PARK. BLACK MARKET. BLUE JEANS... BUT... BLUE JEANS. THAT'S IT, ISN'T IT? BLUE JEANS IS *IT.*

TICKETS PLEASE. THANK YOU...

THANK YOU. HERE YOU ARE...

CAN YOU HAVE YOUR TICKETS READY, PLEASE?

WHATEVER THE WEST MEANS TO THEM, THAT'S WHAT WE ASSOCIATE FLITE WITH...

TICKETS PLEASE... THANK YOU.

THEY WANT TO BE AMERICAN.

IT'S OBVIOUS. NO POINT SECOND-GUESSING *THEIR* NEEDS. WE JUST SELL THEM *OURS.* OUR CULTURE, OUR APPETITES, OUR...

TICKETS, PLEASE.

SORRY?

I SAID CAN I SEE YOUR TICKET, PLEASE, SIR.

OH, SORRY... MILES AWAY...

HERE.

WHATEVER THE WEST MEANS TO THEM, THAT'S WHAT WE ASSOCIATE FLITE WITH...

FREEDOM. CHOICE. CONSUMER GOODS. SEX, OF COURSE, IN MODERATION... OH YES, THIS IS BETTER, STARTING TO COME TOGETHER, MAYBE THINGS AREN'T SO BLACK. IF I GET A GOOD WORKING IDEA FROM THIS HOLIDAY...

HMM.

I'M SORRY, SIR...

I'M AFRAID YOU'LL HAVE TO PAY THE FULL FARE FROM LONDON TO SHEFFIELD. I'LL HAVE TO LOOK IT UP...

WHAT?

BUT I'VE *PAID* MY FARE. I'VE *PAID* FOR A TICKET TO SHEFFIELD.

AH, THAT'S ALL VERY WELL, BUT SEE FOR YOURSELF. YOU'VE ONLY PAID HALF FARE.

THIS IS A CHILD'S TICKET.

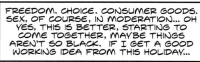

BEEE-BAWW...

SHEFFIELD
(1964-1979)

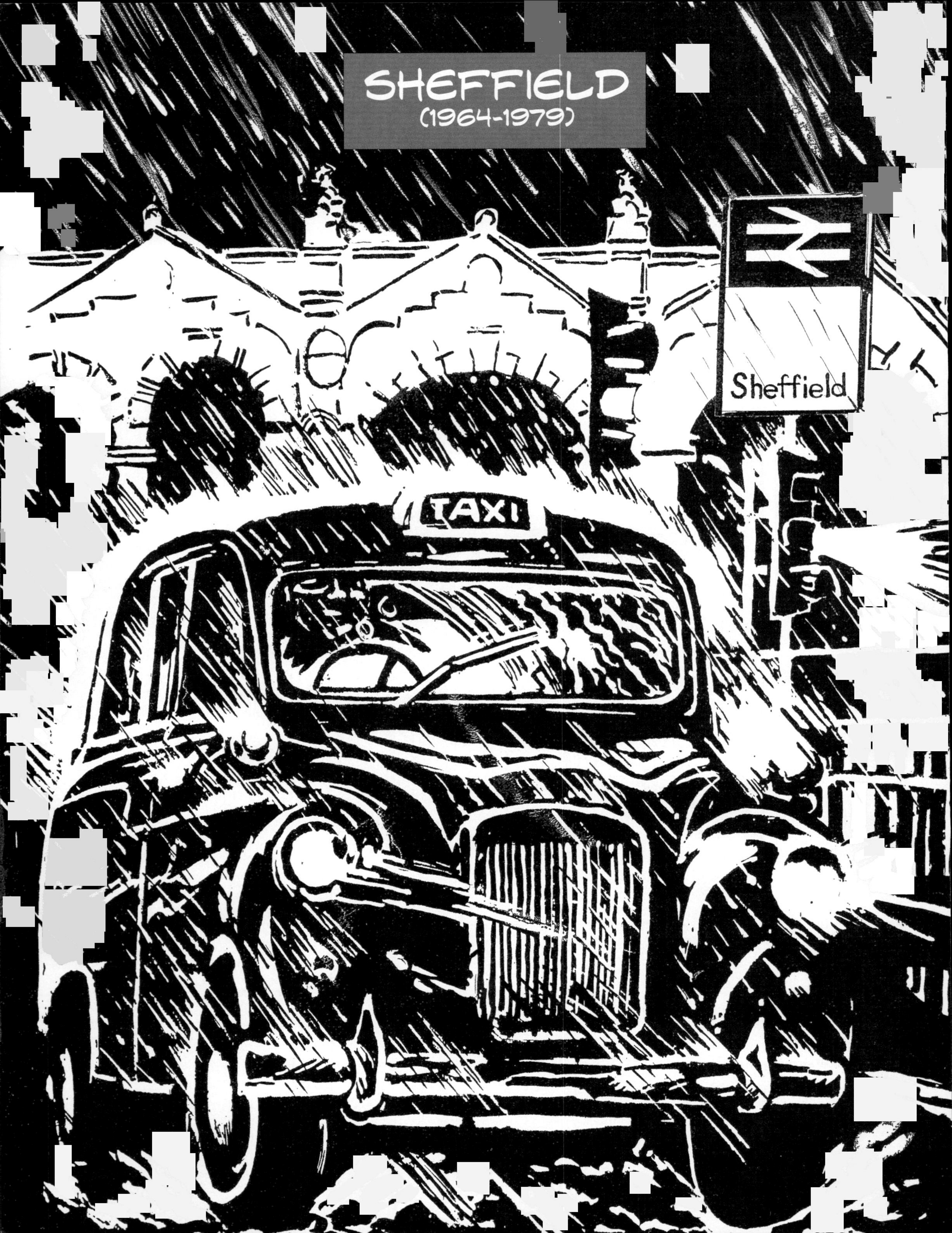
Sheffield
TAXI

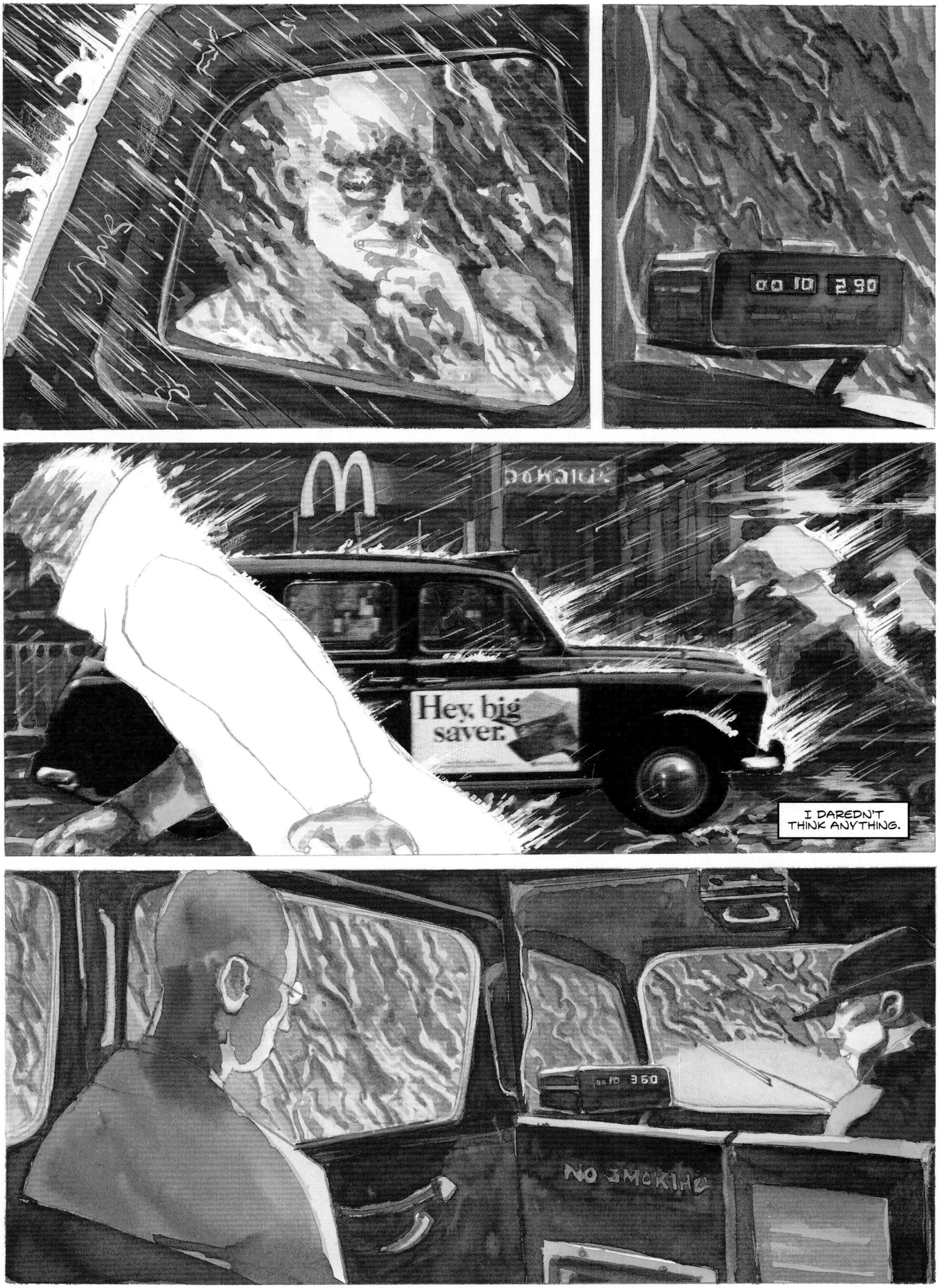
00 10 2.90
Hey, big saver.
I DAREDN'T THINK ANYTHING.
NO SMOKING

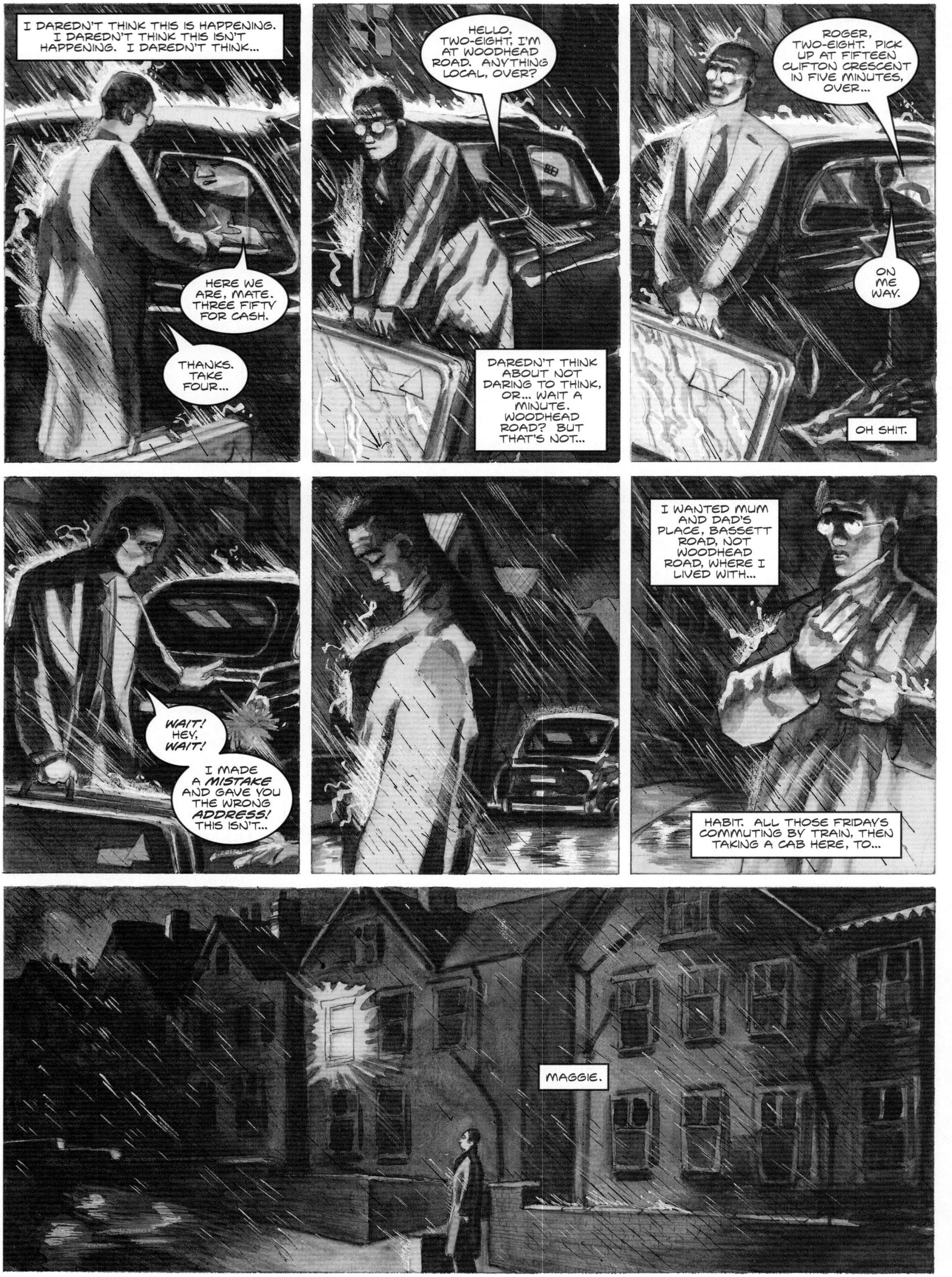
I DAREDN'T THINK THIS IS HAPPENING. I DAREDN'T THINK THIS ISN'T HAPPENING. I DAREDN'T THINK...
HERE WE ARE, MATE. THREE FIFTY FOR CASH.
THANKS. TAKE FOUR...
HELLO, TWO-EIGHT, I'M AT WOODHEAD ROAD. ANYTHING LOCAL, OVER?
DAREDN'T THINK ABOUT NOT DARING TO THINK, OR... WAIT A MINUTE. WOODHEAD ROAD? BUT THAT'S NOT...
ROGER, TWO-EIGHT. PICK UP AT FIFTEEN CLIFTON CRESCENT IN FIVE MINUTES, OVER...
ON ME WAY.
OH SHIT.
WAIT! HEY, WAIT!
I MADE A MISTAKE AND GAVE YOU THE WRONG ADDRESS! THIS ISN'T...
I WANTED MUM AND DAD'S PLACE, BASSETT ROAD, NOT WOODHEAD ROAD, WHERE I LIVED WITH...
HABIT. ALL THOSE FRIDAYS COMMUTING BY TRAIN, THEN TAKING A CAB HERE, TO...
MAGGIE.

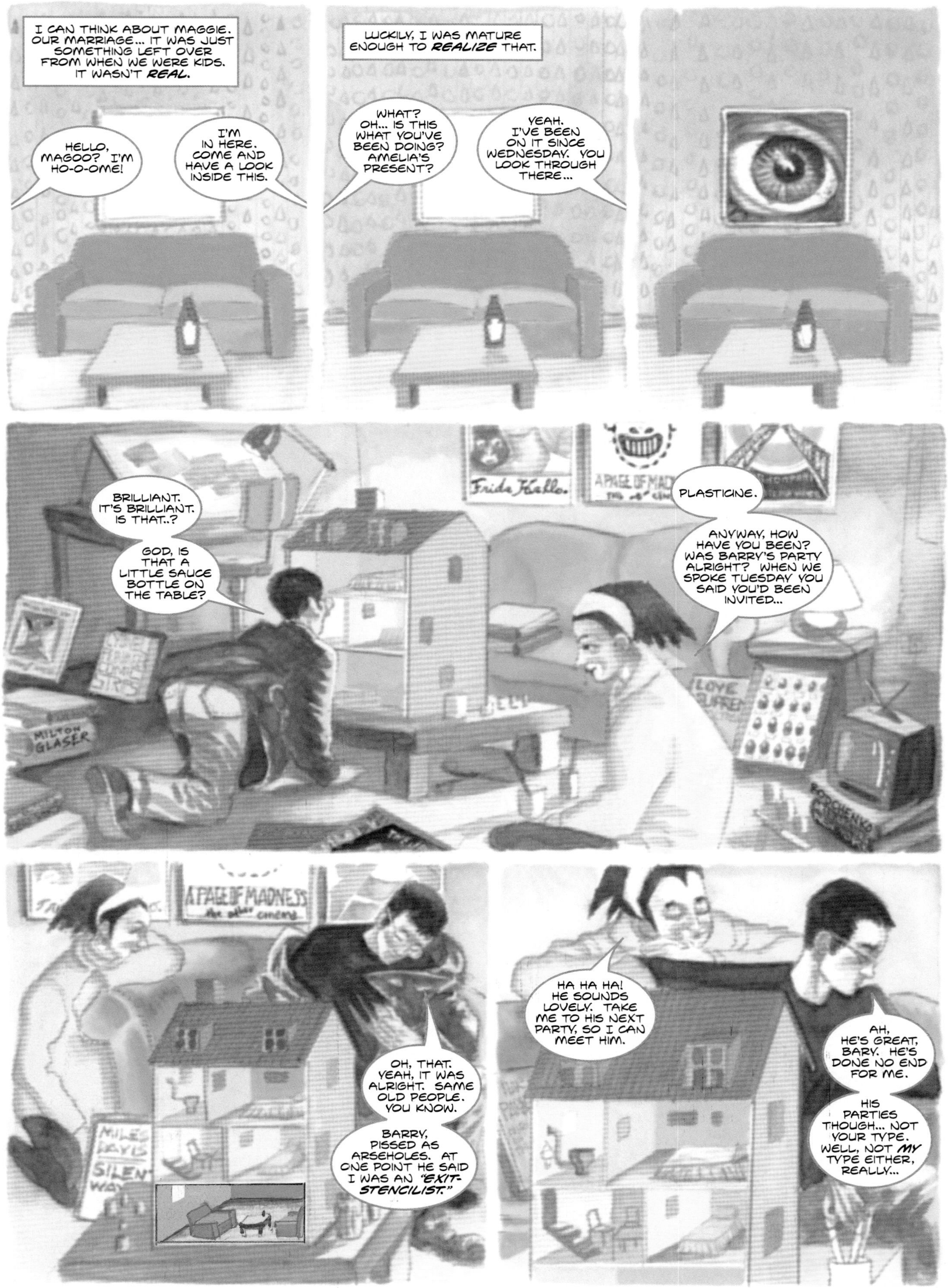
I CAN THINK ABOUT MAGGIE. OUR MARRIAGE... IT WAS JUST SOMETHING LEFT OVER FROM WHEN WE WERE KIDS. IT WASN'T **REAL.**
HELLO, MAGOO? I'M HO-O-OME!
I'M IN HERE. COME AND HAVE A LOOK INSIDE THIS.
LUCKILY, I WAS MATURE ENOUGH TO **REALIZE** THAT.
WHAT? OH... IS THIS WHAT YOU'VE BEEN DOING? AMELIA'S PRESENT?
YEAH. I'VE BEEN ON IT SINCE WEDNESDAY. YOU LOOK THROUGH THERE...
BRILLIANT. IT'S BRILLIANT. IS THAT..?
GOD, IS THAT A LITTLE SAUCE BOTTLE ON THE TABLE?
PLASTICINE.
ANYWAY, HOW HAVE YOU BEEN? WAS BARRY'S PARTY ALRIGHT? WHEN WE SPOKE TUESDAY YOU SAID YOU'D BEEN INVITED...
Frida Kahlo.
A PAGE OF MADNESS
MILTON GLASER
LOVE
A PAGE OF MADNESS the other cinema
OH, THAT. YEAH, IT WAS ALRIGHT. SAME OLD PEOPLE. YOU KNOW.
BARRY, PISSED AS ARSEHOLES. AT ONE POINT HE SAID I WAS AN ***"EXIT-STENCILIST."***
MILES DAVIS SILENT WAY
HA HA HA! HE SOUNDS LOVELY. TAKE ME TO HIS NEXT PARTY, SO I CAN MEET HIM.
AH, HE'S GREAT, BARY. HE'S DONE NO END FOR ME.
HIS PARTIES THOUGH... NOT YOUR TYPE. WELL, NOT ***MY*** TYPE EITHER, REALLY...

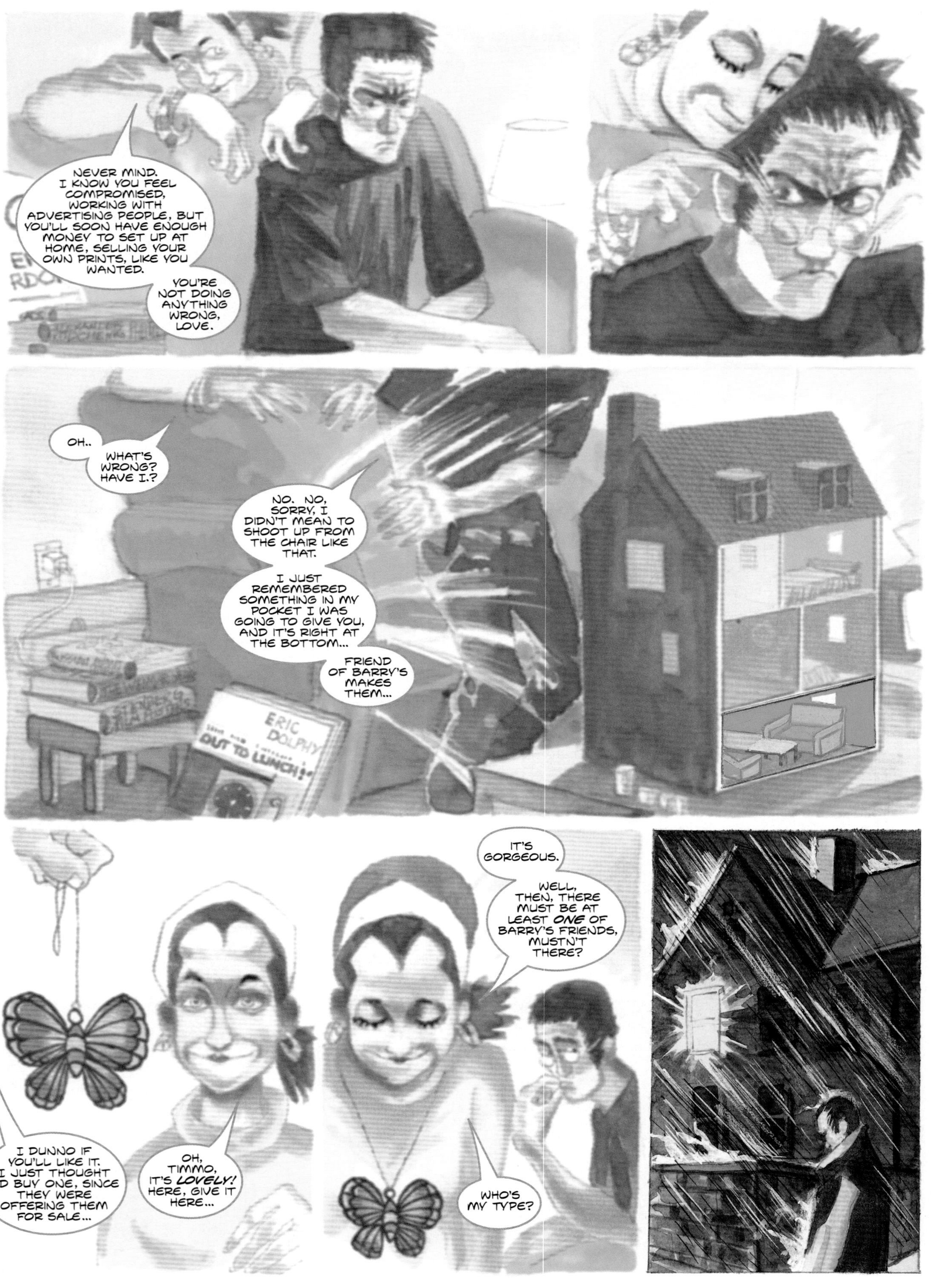
NEVER MIND. I KNOW YOU FEEL COMPROMISED, WORKING WITH ADVERTISING PEOPLE, BUT YOU'LL SOON HAVE ENOUGH MONEY TO SET UP AT HOME, SELLING YOUR OWN PRINTS, LIKE YOU WANTED.
YOU'RE NOT DOING ANYTHING WRONG, LOVE.
OH..
WHAT'S WRONG? HAVE I.?
NO. NO, SORRY, I DIDN'T MEAN TO SHOOT UP FROM THE CHAIR LIKE THAT.
I JUST REMEMBERED SOMETHING IN MY POCKET I WAS GOING TO GIVE YOU, AND IT'S RIGHT AT THE BOTTOM...
FRIEND OF BARRY'S MAKES THEM...
ERIC DOLPHY
OUT TO LUNCH!
I DUNNO IF YOU'LL LIKE IT. I JUST THOUGHT I'D BUY ONE, SINCE THEY WERE OFFERING THEM FOR SALE...
OH, TIMMO, IT'S *LOVELY!* HERE, GIVE IT HERE...
IT'S GORGEOUS.
WELL, THEN, THERE MUST BE AT LEAST *ONE* OF BARRY'S FRIENDS, MUSTN'T THERE?
WHO'S MY TYPE?

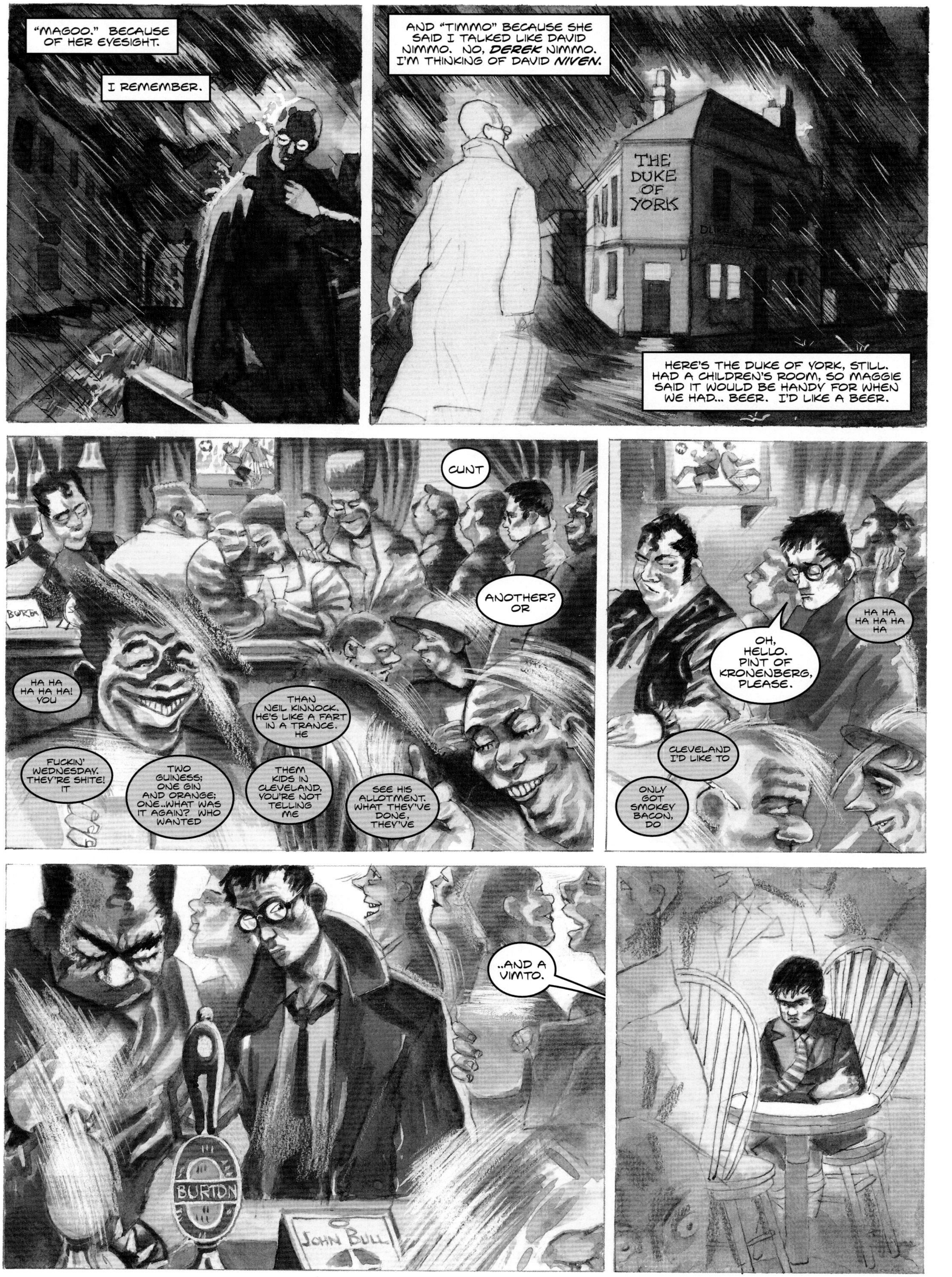
"MAGOO." BECAUSE OF HER EYESIGHT.
I REMEMBER.
AND "TIMMO" BECAUSE SHE SAID I TALKED LIKE DAVID NIMMO. NO, DEREK NIMMO. I'M THINKING OF DAVID NIVEN.
THE DUKE OF YORK
HERE'S THE DUKE OF YORK, STILL. HAD A CHILDREN'S ROOM, SO MAGGIE SAID IT WOULD BE HANDY FOR WHEN WE HAD... BEER. I'D LIKE A BEER.
CUNT
ANOTHER? OR
HA HA HA HA HA! YOU
THAN NEIL KINNOCK. HE'S LIKE A FART IN A TRANCE. HE
FUCKIN' WEDNESDAY. THEY'RE SHITE! IT
TWO GUINESS; ONE GIN AND ORANGE; ONE..WHAT WAS IT AGAIN? WHO WANTED
THEM KIDS IN CLEVELAND, YOU'RE NOT TELLING ME
SEE HIS ALLOTMENT. WHAT THEY'VE DONE, THEY'VE
OH, HELLO. PINT OF KRONENBERG, PLEASE.
HA HA HA HA HA HA
CLEVELAND I'D LIKE TO
ONLY GOT SMOKEY BACON, DO
..AND A VIMTO.
BURTON
JOHN BULL

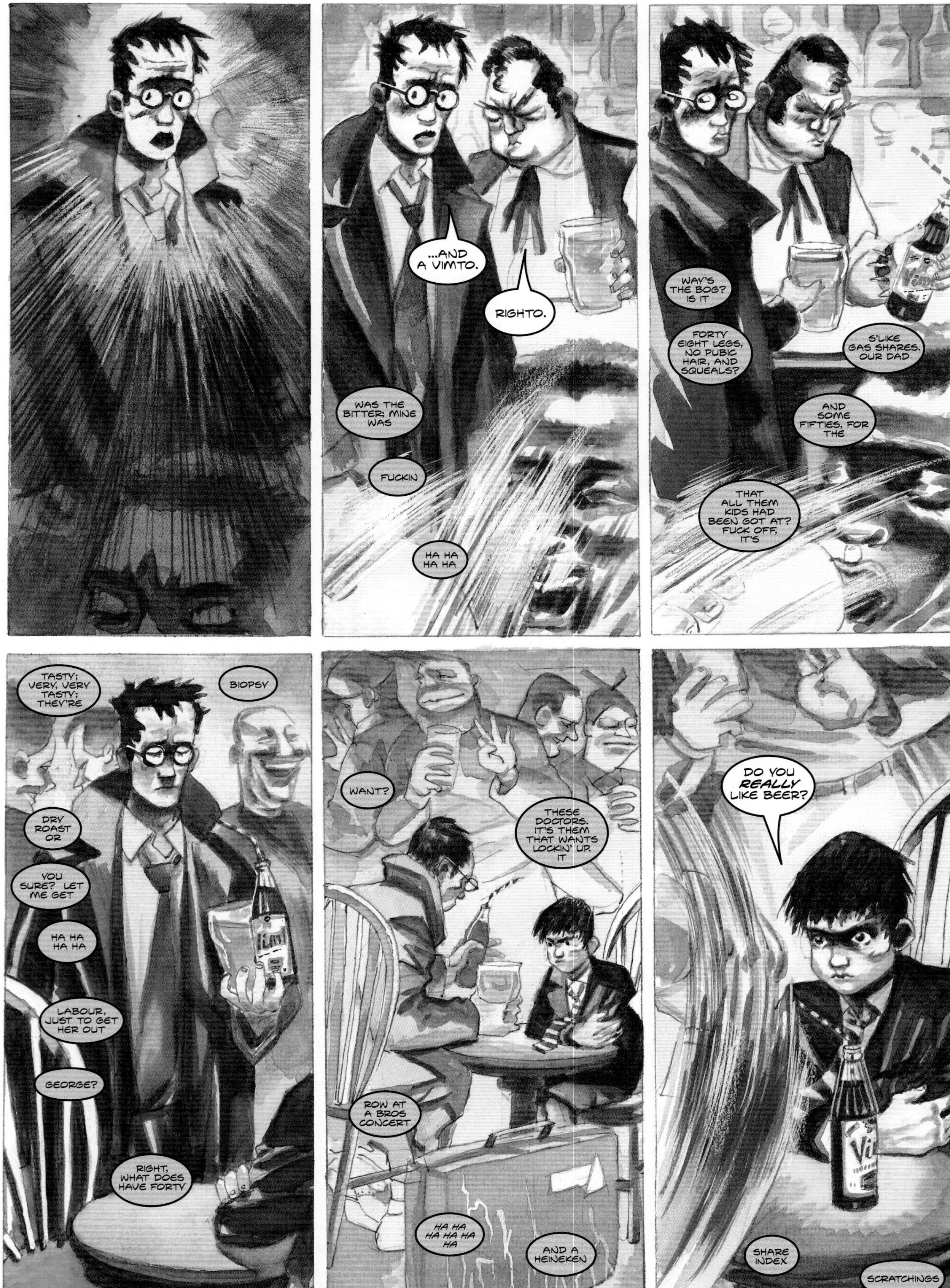
...AND A VIMTO.
RIGHTO.
WAS THE BITTER; MINE WAS
FUCKIN
HA HA HA HA
WAY'S THE BOG? IS IT
FORTY EIGHT LEGS, NO PUBIC HAIR, AND SQUEALS?
S'LIKE GAS SHARES. OUR DAD
AND SOME FIFTIES, FOR THE
THAT ALL THEM KIDS HAD BEEN GOT AT? FUCK OFF, IT'S
TASTY; VERY, VERY TASTY; THEY'RE
BIOPSY
DRY ROAST OR
YOU SURE? LET ME GET
HA HA HA HA
LABOUR, JUST TO GET HER OUT
GEORGE?
RIGHT, WHAT DOES HAVE FORTY
WANT?
THESE DOCTORS. IT'S THEM THAT WANTS LOCKIN' UP. IT
ROW AT A BROS CONCERT
HA HA HA HA HA HA
AND A HEINEKEN
DO YOU REALLY LIKE BEER?
SHARE INDEX
SCRATCHINGS

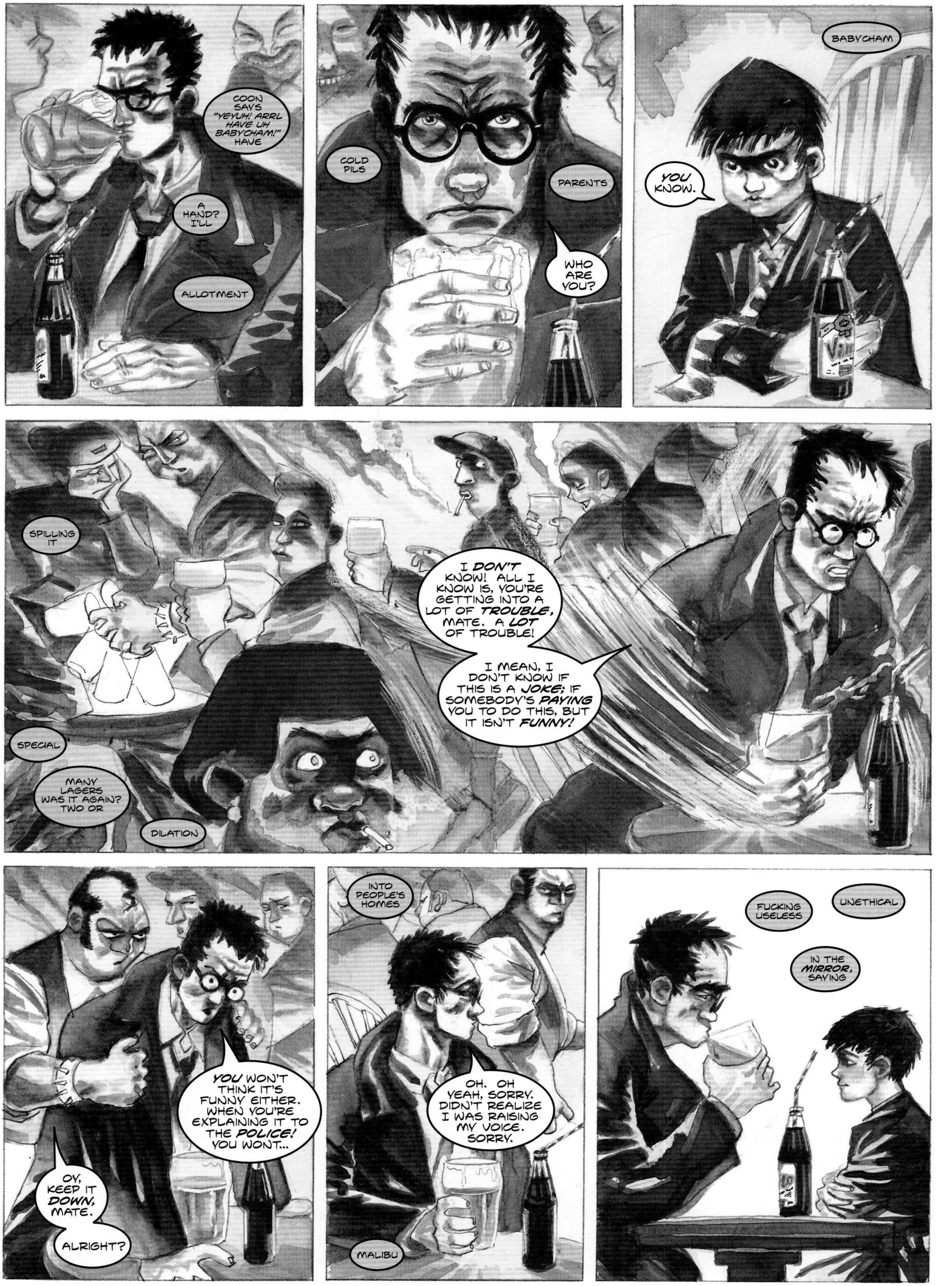
COON SAYS "YEYUH! ARRL HAVE UH BABYCHAM!" HAVE
A HAND? I'LL
ALLOTMENT
COLD PILS
PARENTS
WHO ARE YOU?
BABYCHAM
YOU KNOW.
SPILLING IT
I DON'T KNOW! ALL I KNOW IS, YOU'RE GETTING INTO A LOT OF TROUBLE, MATE. A LOT OF TROUBLE!
I MEAN, I DON'T KNOW IF THIS IS A JOKE; IF SOMEBODY'S PAYING YOU TO DO THIS, BUT IT ISN'T FUNNY!
SPECIAL
MANY LAGERS WAS IT AGAIN? TWO OR
DILATION
YOU WON'T THINK IT'S FUNNY EITHER. WHEN YOU'RE EXPLAINING IT TO THE POLICE! YOU WONT...
OY, KEEP IT DOWN, MATE.
ALRIGHT?
INTO PEOPLE'S HOMES
OH. OH YEAH, SORRY. DIDN'T REALIZE I WAS RAISING MY VOICE. SORRY.
MALIBU
FUCKING USELESS
UNETHICAL
IN THE MIRROR, SAYING

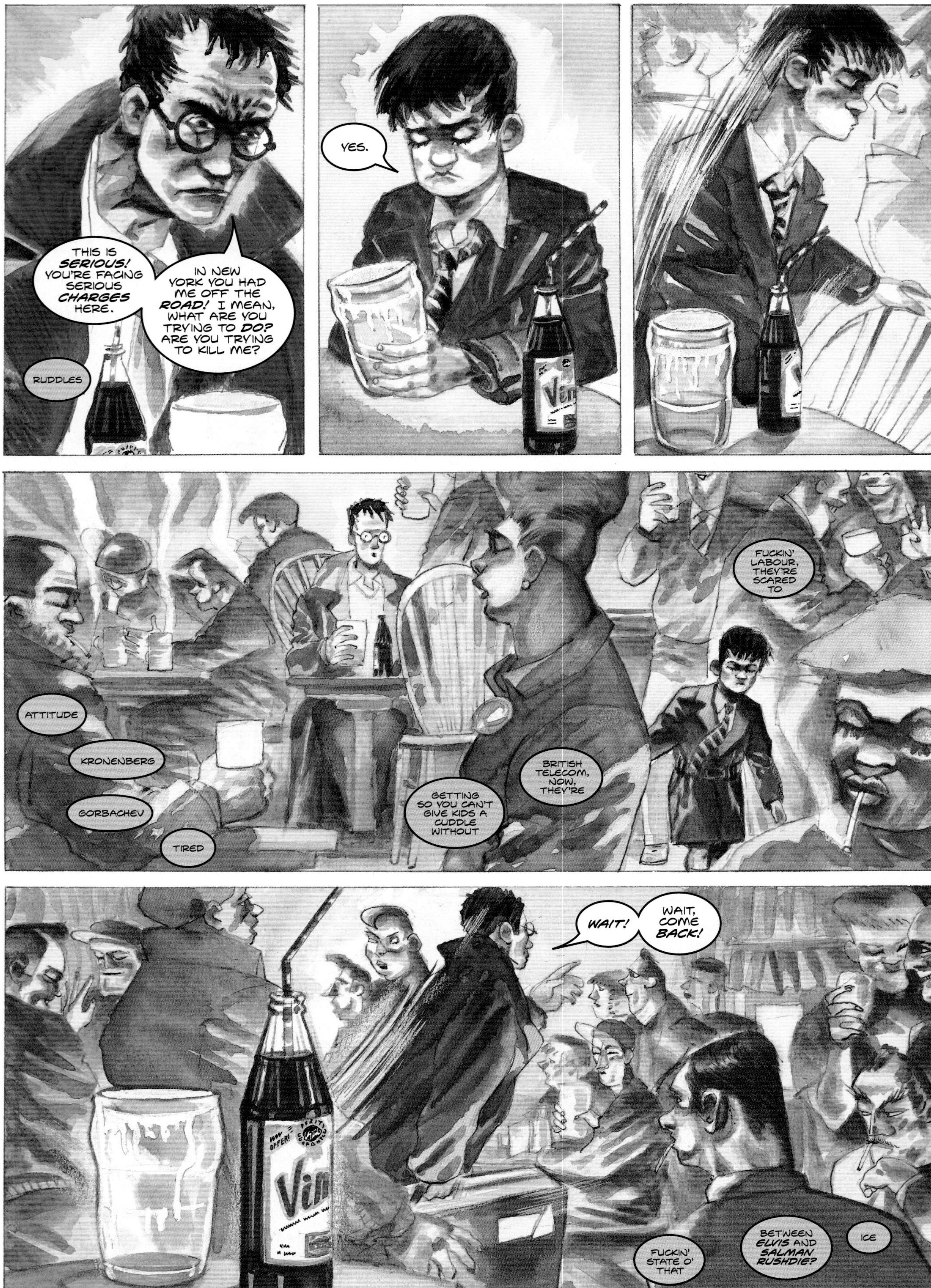
THIS IS **SERIOUS!** YOU'RE FACING SERIOUS **CHARGES** HERE.
IN NEW YORK YOU HAD ME OFF THE **ROAD!** I MEAN, WHAT ARE YOU TRYING TO **DO?** ARE YOU TRYING TO KILL ME?
RUDDLES
YES.
FUCKIN' LABOUR, THEY'RE SCARED TO
ATTITUDE
KRONENBERG
GORBACHEV
TIRED
GETTING SO YOU CAN'T GIVE KIDS A CUDDLE WITHOUT
BRITISH TELECOM, NOW, THEY'RE
WAIT!
WAIT, COME **BACK!**
FUCKIN' STATE O' THAT
BETWEEN **ELVIS** AND **SALMAN RUSHDIE?**
ICE

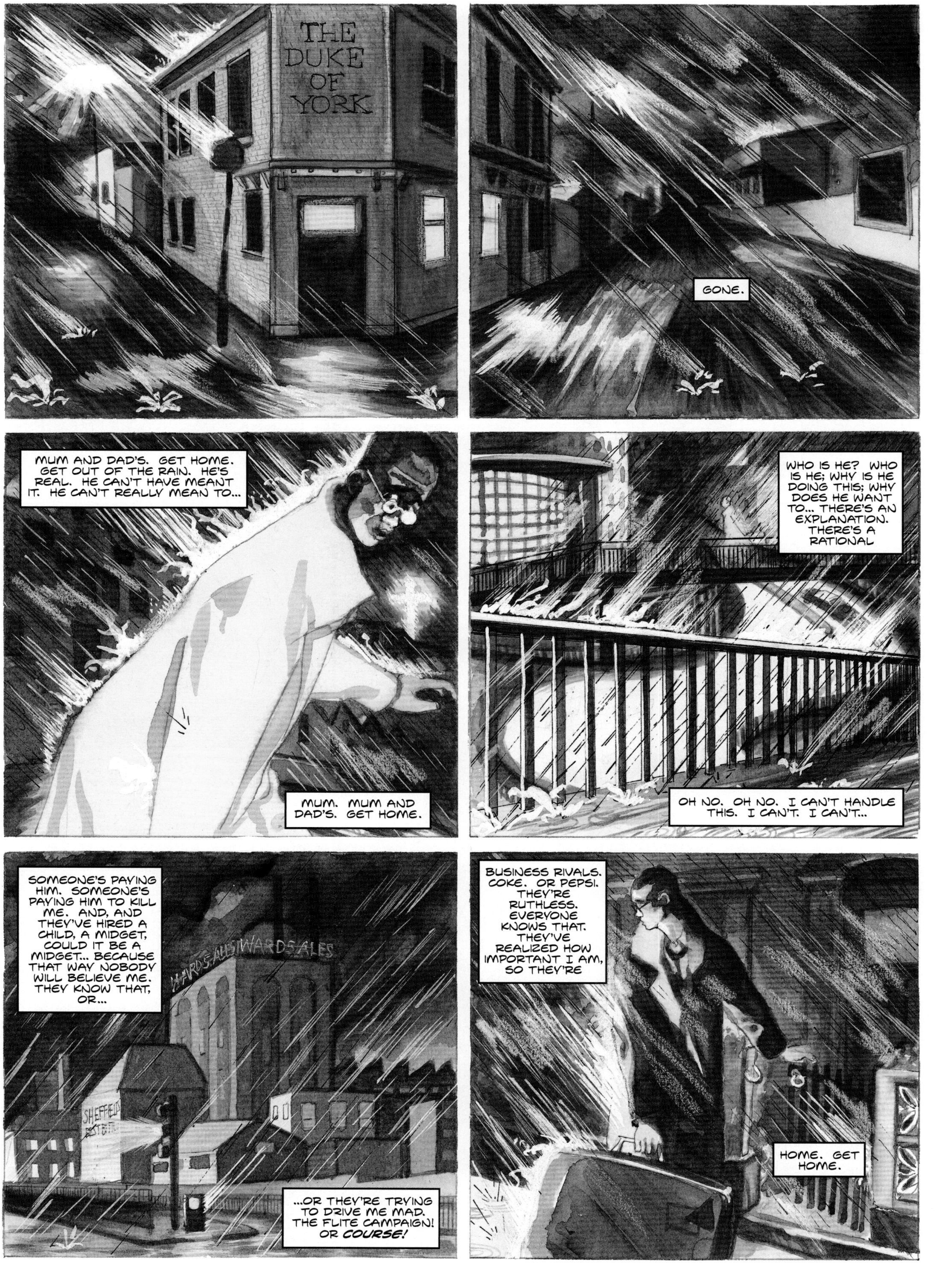
THE DUKE OF YORK
GONE.
MUM AND DAD'S. GET HOME. GET OUT OF THE RAIN. HE'S REAL. HE CAN'T HAVE MEANT IT. HE CAN'T REALLY MEAN TO...
MUM. MUM AND DAD'S. GET HOME.
WHO IS HE? WHO IS HE; WHY IS HE DOING THIS; WHY DOES HE WANT TO... THERE'S AN EXPLANATION. THERE'S A RATIONAL
OH NO. OH NO. I CAN'T HANDLE THIS. I CAN'T. I CAN'T...
SOMEONE'S PAYING HIM. SOMEONE'S PAYING HIM TO KILL ME. AND, AND THEY'VE HIRED A CHILD, A MIDGET, COULD IT BE A MIDGET... BECAUSE THAT WAY NOBODY WILL BELIEVE ME. THEY KNOW THAT, OR...
WARDS ALES WARDS ALES
SHEFFIELD
...OR THEY'RE TRYING TO DRIVE ME MAD. THE FLITE CAMPAIGN! OR ***COURSE!***
BUSINESS RIVALS. COKE. OR PEPSI. THEY'RE RUTHLESS. EVERYONE KNOWS THAT. THEY'VE REALIZED HOW IMPORTANT I AM, SO THEY'RE
HOME. GET HOME.

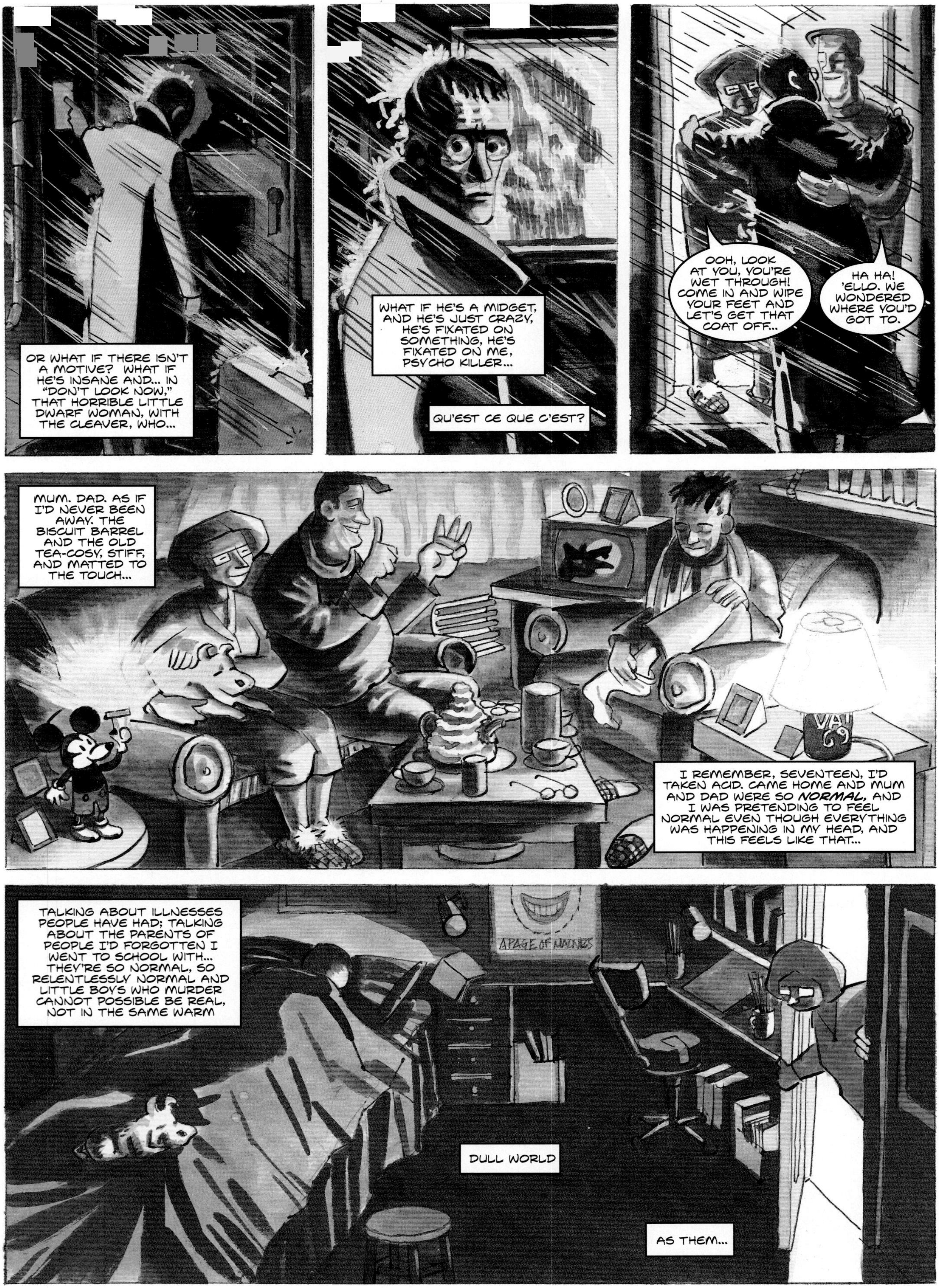
OR WHAT IF THERE ISN'T A MOTIVE? WHAT IF HE'S INSANE AND... IN "DON'T LOOK NOW," THAT HORRIBLE LITTLE DWARF WOMAN, WITH THE CLEAVER, WHO...
WHAT IF HE'S A MIDGET, AND HE'S JUST CRAZY, HE'S FIXATED ON SOMETHING, HE'S FIXATED ON ME, PSYCHO KILLER...
QU'EST CE QUE C'EST?
OOH, LOOK AT YOU, YOU'RE WET THROUGH! COME IN AND WIPE YOUR FEET AND LET'S GET THAT COAT OFF...
HA HA! 'ELLO. WE WONDERED WHERE YOU'D GOT TO.
MUM. DAD. AS IF I'D NEVER BEEN AWAY. THE BISCUIT BARREL AND THE OLD TEA-COSY, STIFF, AND MATTED TO THE TOUCH...
I REMEMBER, SEVENTEEN, I'D TAKEN ACID. CAME HOME AND MUM AND DAD WERE SO *NORMAL,* AND I WAS PRETENDING TO FEEL NORMAL EVEN THOUGH EVERYTHING WAS HAPPENING IN MY HEAD, AND THIS FEELS LIKE THAT...
TALKING ABOUT ILLNESSES PEOPLE HAVE HAD; TALKING ABOUT THE PARENTS OF PEOPLE I'D FORGOTTEN I WENT TO SCHOOL WITH... THEY'RE SO NORMAL, SO RELENTLESSLY NORMAL AND LITTLE BOYS WHO MURDER CANNOT POSSIBLE BE REAL, NOT IN THE SAME WARM
DULL WORLD
AS THEM...

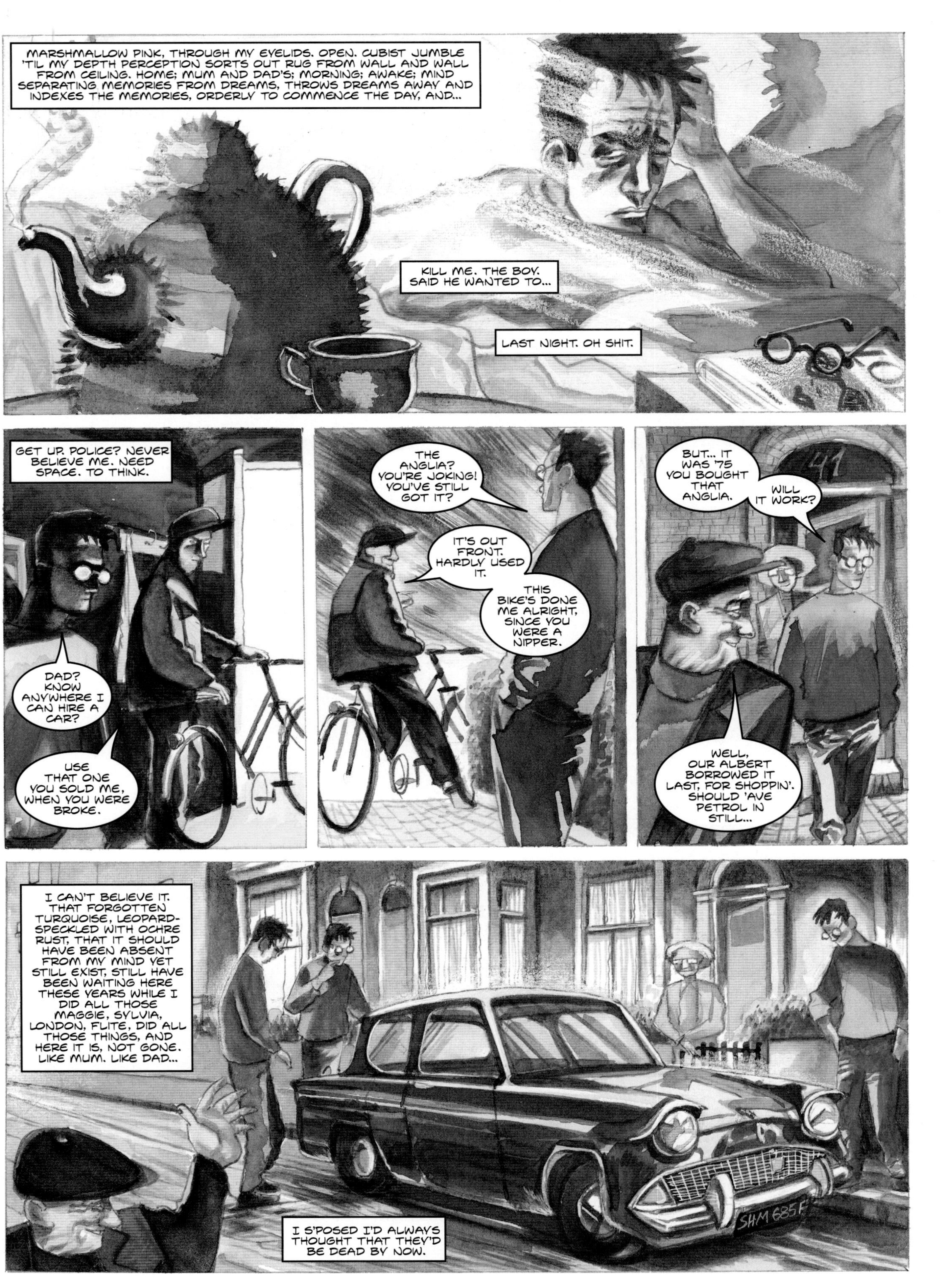
MARSHMALLOW PINK, THROUGH MY EYELIDS. OPEN. CUBIST JUMBLE 'TIL MY DEPTH PERCEPTION SORTS OUT RUG FROM WALL AND WALL FROM CEILING. HOME; MUM AND DAD'S; MORNING; AWAKE; MIND SEPARATING MEMORIES FROM DREAMS, THROWS DREAMS AWAY AND INDEXES THE MEMORIES, ORDERLY TO COMMENCE THE DAY, AND...
KILL ME. THE BOY. SAID HE WANTED TO...
LAST NIGHT. OH SHIT.
GET UP. POLICE? NEVER BELIEVE ME. NEED SPACE. TO THINK.
DAD? KNOW ANYWHERE I CAN HIRE A CAR?
USE THAT ONE YOU SOLD ME, WHEN YOU WERE BROKE.
THE ANGLIA? YOU'RE JOKING! YOU'VE STILL GOT IT?
IT'S OUT FRONT. HARDLY USED IT.
THIS BIKE'S DONE ME ALRIGHT, SINCE YOU WERE A NIPPER.
BUT... IT WAS '75 YOU BOUGHT THAT ANGLIA.
WILL IT WORK?
WELL, OUR ALBERT BORROWED IT LAST, FOR SHOPPIN'. SHOULD 'AVE PETROL IN STILL...
I CAN'T BELIEVE IT. THAT FORGOTTEN TURQUOISE, LEOPARD-SPECKLED WITH OCHRE RUST, THAT IT SHOULD HAVE BEEN ABSENT FROM MY MIND YET STILL EXIST, STILL HAVE BEEN WAITING HERE THESE YEARS WHILE I DID ALL THOSE MAGGIE, SYLVIA, LONDON, FLITE, DID ALL THOSE THINGS, AND HERE IT IS, NOT GONE. LIKE MUM. LIKE DAD...
I S'POSED I'D ALWAYS THOUGHT THAT THEY'D BE DEAD BY NOW.

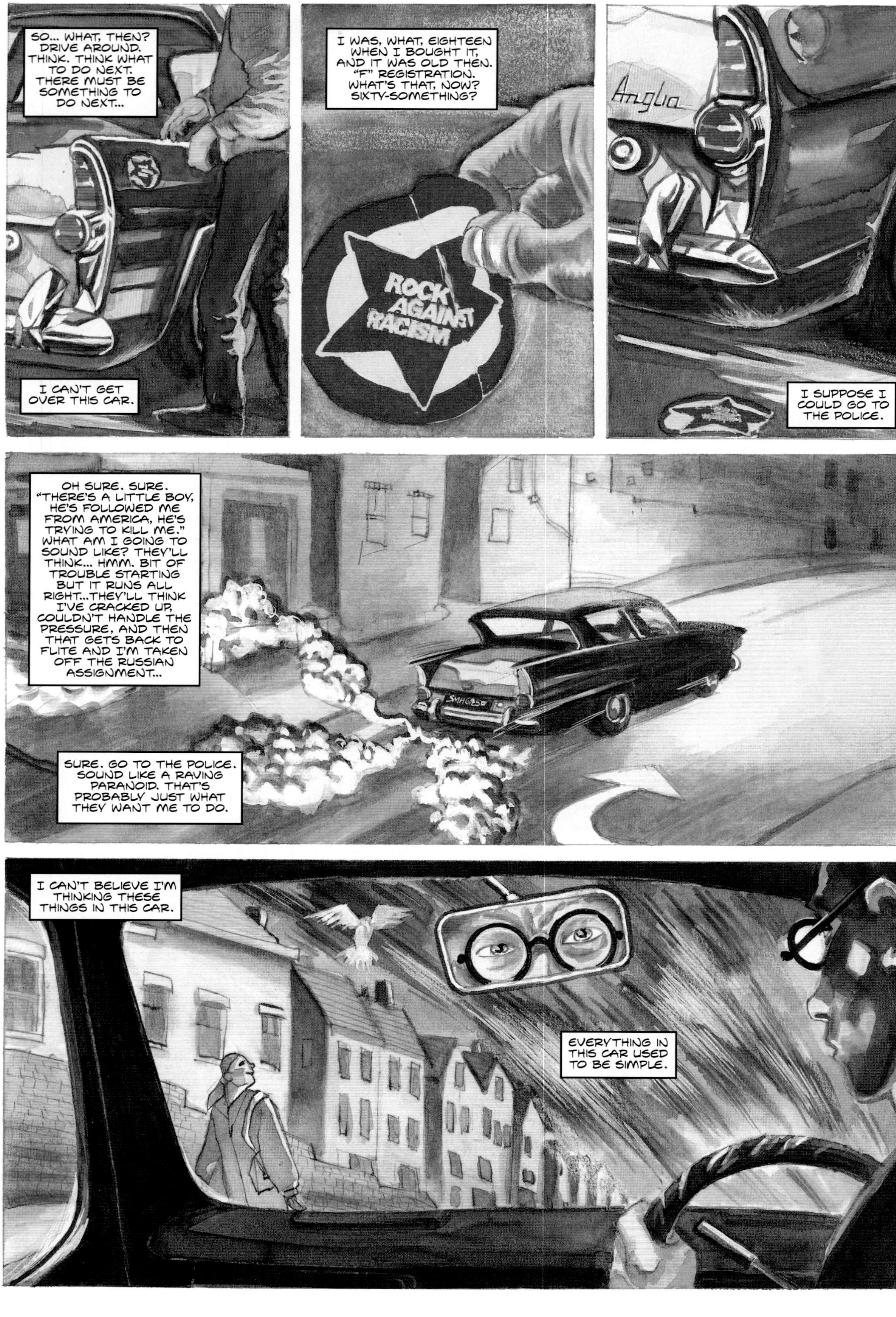

SO... WHAT, THEN? DRIVE AROUND. THINK. THINK WHAT TO DO NEXT. THERE MUST BE SOMETHING TO DO NEXT...
I CAN'T GET OVER THIS CAR.
I WAS, WHAT, EIGHTEEN WHEN I BOUGHT IT, AND IT WAS OLD THEN. "F" REGISTRATION. WHAT'S THAT, NOW? SIXTY-SOMETHING?
ROCK AGAINST RACISM
Anglia
I SUPPOSE I COULD GO TO THE POLICE.
OH SURE. SURE. "THERE'S A LITTLE BOY, HE'S FOLLOWED ME FROM AMERICA, HE'S TRYING TO KILL ME." WHAT AM I GOING TO SOUND LIKE? THEY'LL THINK... HMM. BIT OF TROUBLE STARTING BUT IT RUNS ALL RIGHT...THEY'LL THINK I'VE CRACKED UP, COULDN'T HANDLE THE PRESSURE, AND THEN THAT GETS BACK TO FLITE AND I'M TAKEN OFF THE RUSSIAN ASSIGNMENT...
SURE. GO TO THE POLICE. SOUND LIKE A RAVING PARANOID. THAT'S PROBABLY JUST WHAT THEY WANT ME TO DO.
I CAN'T BELIEVE I'M THINKING THESE THINGS IN THIS CAR.
EVERYTHING IN THIS CAR USED TO BE SIMPLE.

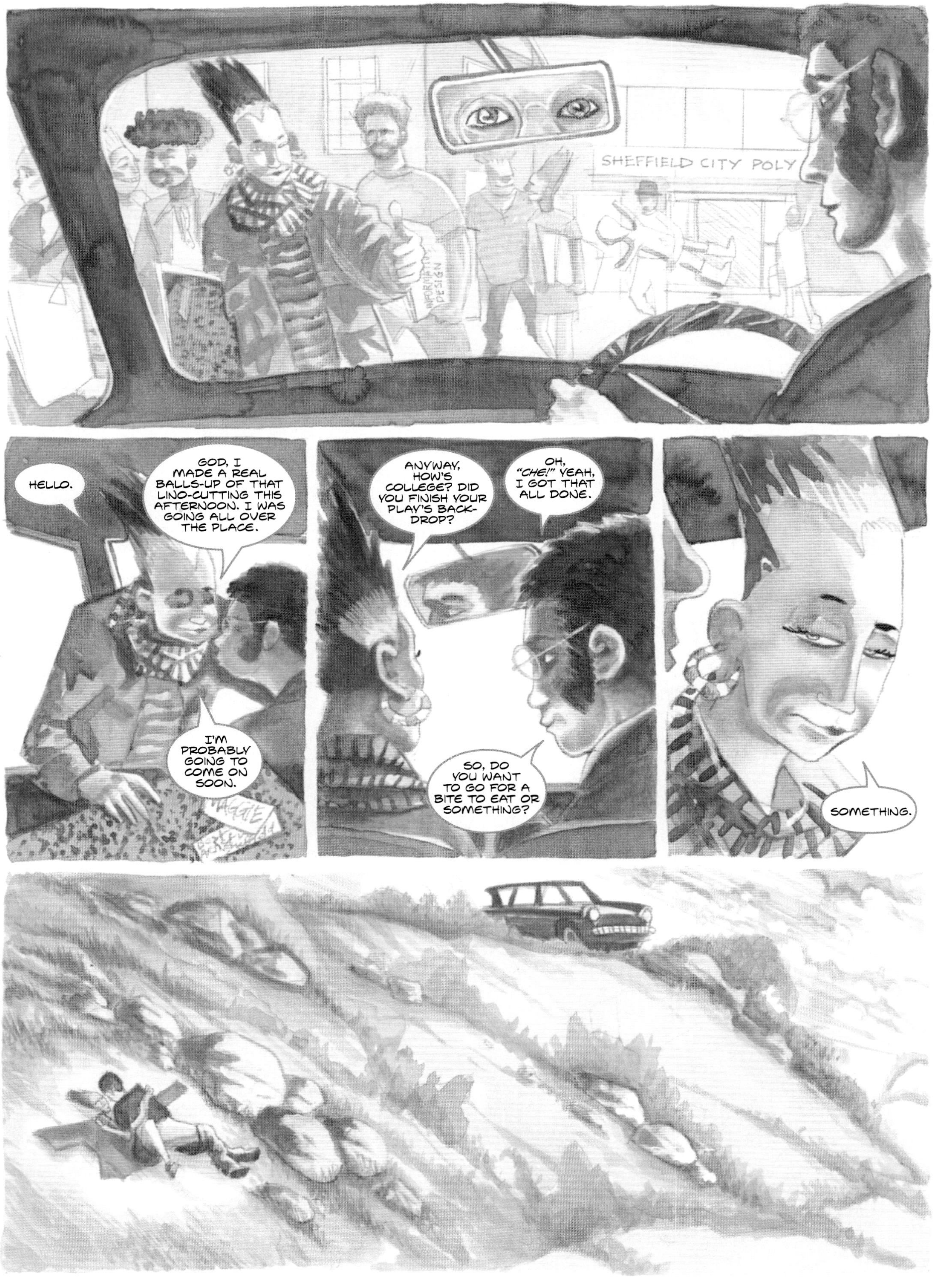
SHEFFIELD CITY POLY
INFORMATION DESIGN
HELLO.
GOD, I MADE A REAL BALLS-UP OF THAT LINO-CUTTING THIS AFTERNOON. I WAS GOING ALL OVER THE PLACE.
I'M PROBABLY GOING TO COME ON SOON.
MAGGIE
ANYWAY, HOW'S COLLEGE? DID YOU FINISH YOUR PLAY'S BACK-DROP?
OH, "CHE!" YEAH, I GOT THAT ALL DONE.
SO, DO YOU WANT TO GO FOR A BITE TO EAT OR SOMETHING?
SOMETHING.

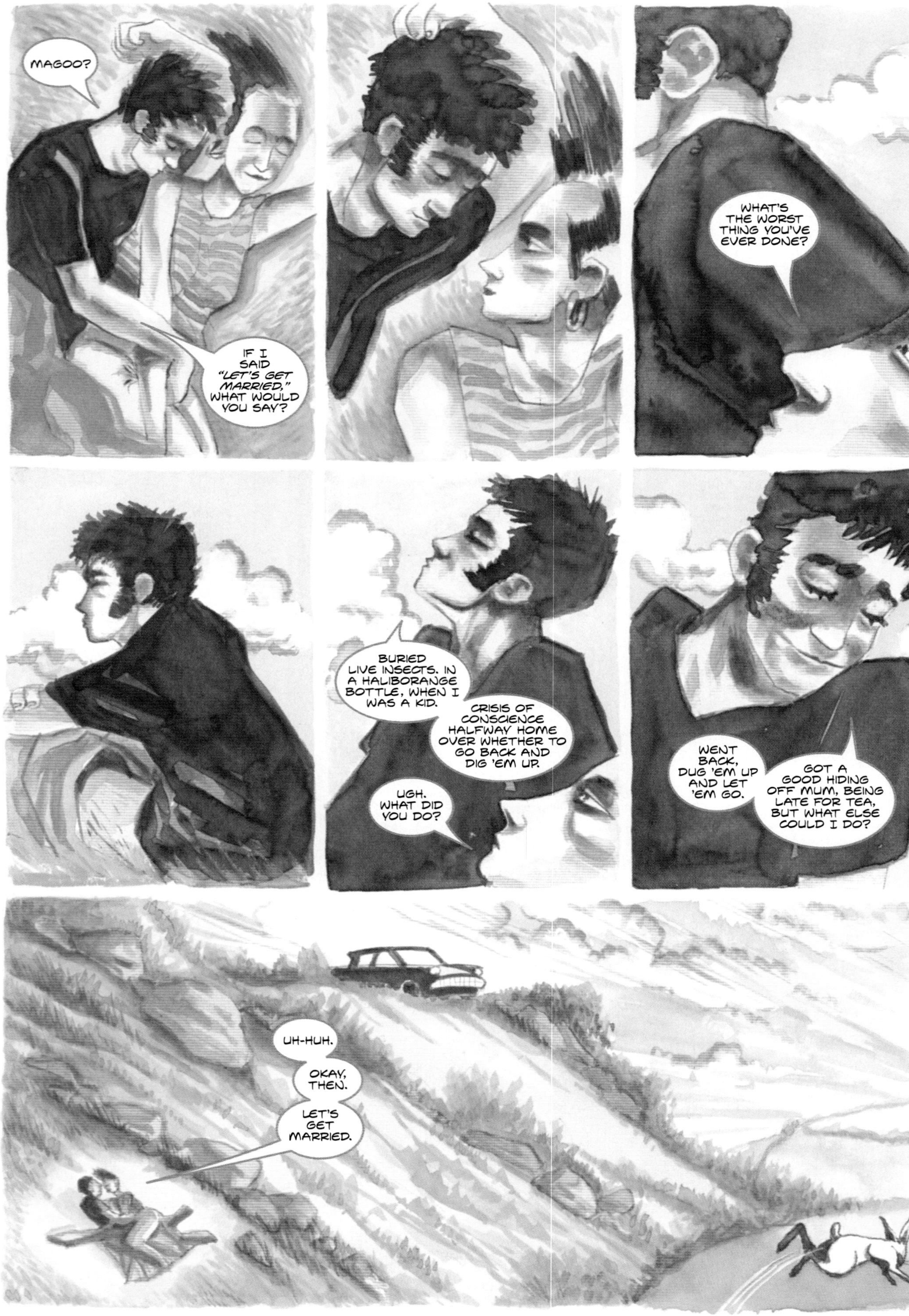
MAGOO?
IF I SAID "LET'S GET MARRIED," WHAT WOULD YOU SAY?
WHAT'S THE WORST THING YOU'VE EVER DONE?
BURIED LIVE INSECTS. IN A HALIBORANGE BOTTLE, WHEN I WAS A KID.
CRISIS OF CONSCIENCE HALFWAY HOME OVER WHETHER TO GO BACK AND DIG 'EM UP.
UGH. WHAT DID YOU DO?
WENT BACK, DUG 'EM UP AND LET 'EM GO.
GOT A GOOD HIDING OFF MUM, BEING LATE FOR TEA, BUT WHAT ELSE COULD I DO?
UH-HUH.
OKAY, THEN.
LET'S GET MARRIED.

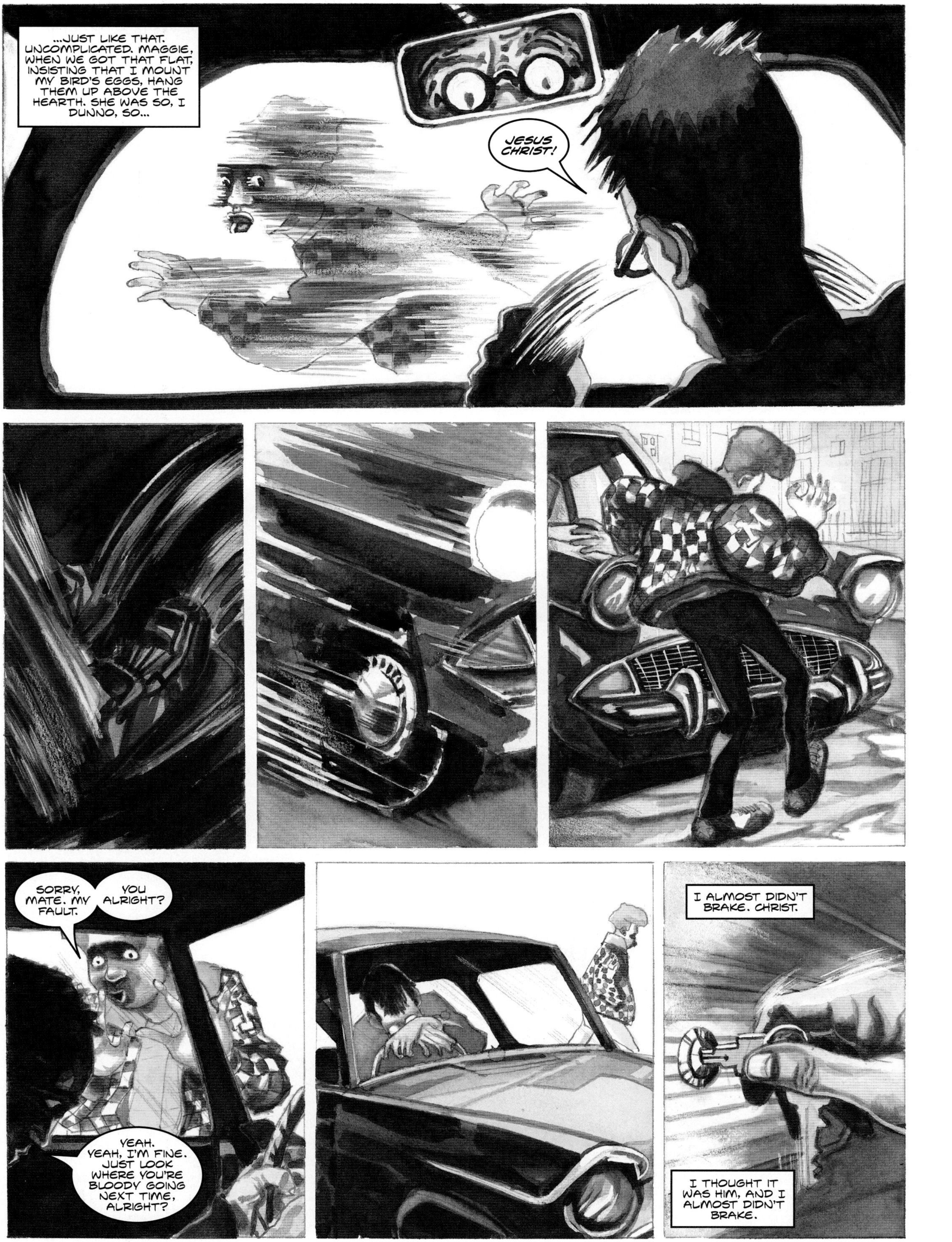
...JUST LIKE THAT. UNCOMPLICATED. MAGGIE, WHEN WE GOT THAT FLAT, INSISTING THAT I MOUNT MY BIRD'S EGGS, HANG THEM UP ABOVE THE HEARTH. SHE WAS SO, I DUNNO, SO...
JESUS CHRIST!
SORRY, MATE. MY FAULT.
YOU ALRIGHT?
YEAH. YEAH, I'M FINE. JUST LOOK WHERE YOU'RE BLOODY GOING NEXT TIME, ALRIGHT?
I ALMOST DIDN'T BRAKE. CHRIST.
I THOUGHT IT WAS HIM, AND I ALMOST DIDN'T BRAKE.

EVERYTHING IS DANGEROUS TO ME, ISN'T IT? WHERE I AM NOW? EVEN ME. *I'M* DANGEROUS TO ME. I...

EH-EH-EH-EH-EH-EH-EH-EH-EH. SHIT.

OH, FOR FUCK'S SAKE. OH, THAT'S GREAT. THAT'S ALL I NEED.

COME ON, YOU WANKER! YOU WORK FOR UNCLE ALBERT; YOU CAN WORK FOR ME. COME ON, JUST...

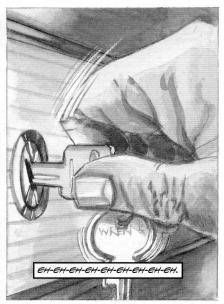

EH-EH-EH-EH-EH-EH-EH-EH-EH.

SHIT.

HANG ON, THIS IS UPPER ALBERT ROAD, NEAR WHERE I WENT TO JUNIOR SCHOOL. OUR OLD HOUSE WAS JUST DOWN THERE. THOSE SORT OF MUSTARDY-YELLOW FLATS, THEY WERE THERE THEN, AND THAT BUILDING WITH THE *"PRESS KNIVES"* SIGN.

I DON'T REMEMBER DRIVING HERE.

SHM 685F

HATED THIS NEIGHBOURHOOD. ALWAYS HATED IT. CHRIST, IT HASN'T CHANGED AT ALL. ALL THE PLACES ROUND HERE THAT *HAVE* CHANGED, AND THAT MAKES ME FEEL WEIRD, BUT IT'S WORSE WHEN THEY *HAVEN'T*.

EYES DOWN. MUM AND DAD'S, MILE AN' HALF AWAY. JUST PUSH. THE YELLOW-GREEN PRIVET WATCHING ME; THE FLAT-FACED MAISONETTES I WALKED PAST ON MY WAY TO SCHOOL...

AHEAD OF THE PACK.

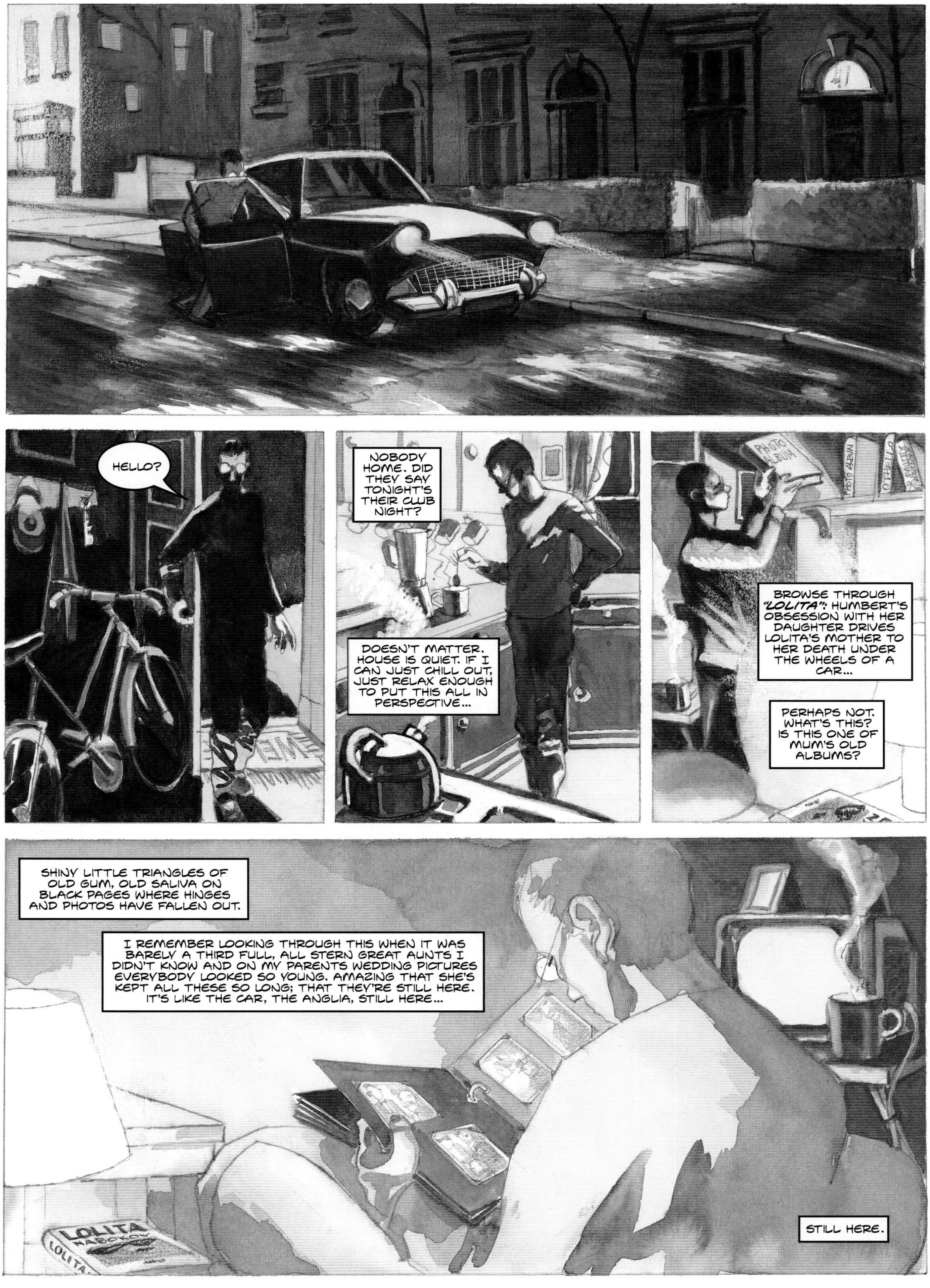
HELLO?
NOBODY HOME. DID THEY SAY TONIGHT'S THEIR CLUB NIGHT?
DOESN'T MATTER. HOUSE IS QUIET. IF I CAN JUST CHILL OUT, JUST RELAX ENOUGH TO PUT THIS ALL IN PERSPECTIVE...
PHOTO ALBUM
BROWSE THROUGH "LOLITA": HUMBERT'S OBSESSION WITH HER DAUGHTER DRIVES LOLITA'S MOTHER TO HER DEATH UNDER THE WHEELS OF A CAR...
PERHAPS NOT. WHAT'S THIS? IS THIS ONE OF MUM'S OLD ALBUMS?
SHINY LITTLE TRIANGLES OF OLD GUM, OLD SALIVA ON BLACK PAGES WHERE HINGES AND PHOTOS HAVE FALLEN OUT.
I REMEMBER LOOKING THROUGH THIS WHEN IT WAS BARELY A THIRD FULL, ALL STERN GREAT AUNTS I DIDN'T KNOW AND ON MY PARENTS WEDDING PICTURES EVERYBODY LOOKED SO YOUNG. AMAZING THAT SHE'S KEPT ALL THESE SO LONG; THAT THEY'RE STILL HERE. IT'S LIKE THE CAR, THE ANGLIA, STILL HERE...
LOLITA
NABOKOV
STILL HERE.

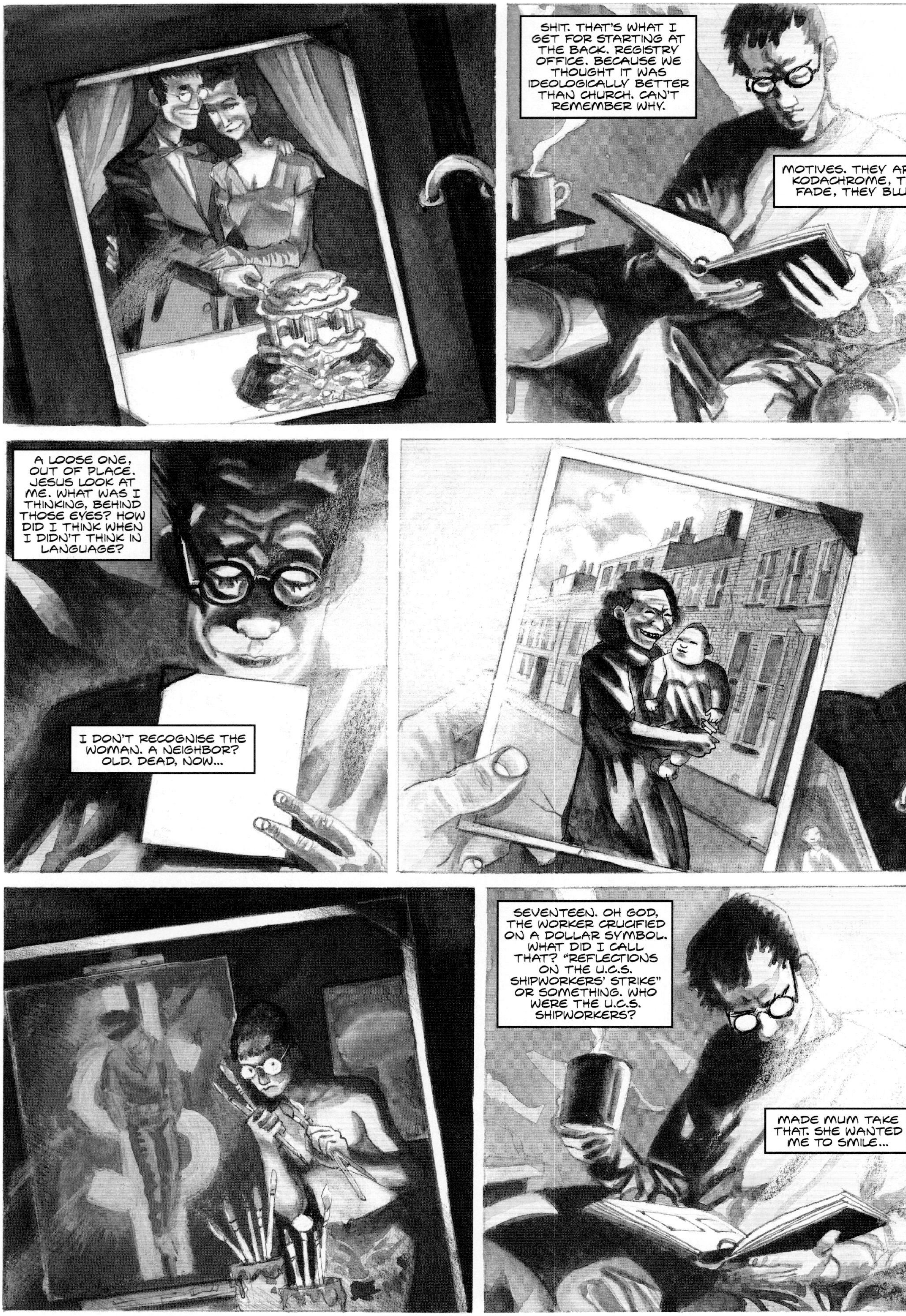
SHIT. THAT'S WHAT I GET FOR STARTING AT THE BACK. REGISTRY OFFICE. BECAUSE WE THOUGHT IT WAS IDEOLOGICALLY BETTER THAN CHURCH. CAN'T REMEMBER WHY.
MOTIVES. THEY AREN'T KODACHROME, THEY FADE, THEY BLUR...
A LOOSE ONE, OUT OF PLACE. JESUS LOOK AT ME. WHAT WAS I THINKING, BEHIND THOSE EYES? HOW DID I THINK WHEN I DIDN'T THINK IN LANGUAGE?
I DON'T RECOGNISE THE WOMAN. A NEIGHBOR? OLD. DEAD, NOW...
SEVENTEEN. OH GOD, THE WORKER CRUCIFIED ON A DOLLAR SYMBOL. WHAT DID I CALL THAT? "REFLECTIONS ON THE U.C.S. SHIPWORKERS' STRIKE" OR SOMETHING. WHO WERE THE U.C.S. SHIPWORKERS?
MADE MUM TAKE THAT. SHE WANTED ME TO SMILE...

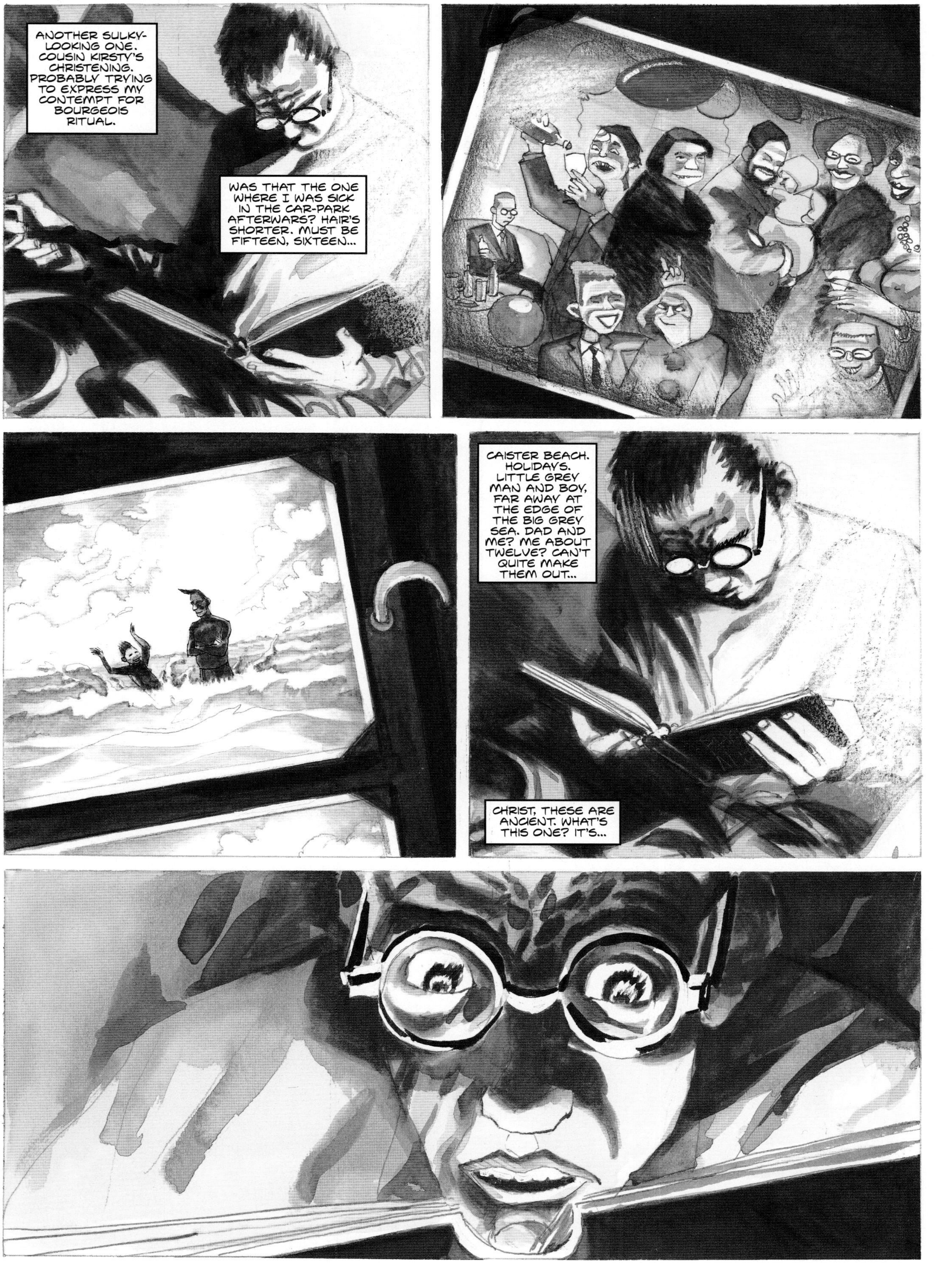
ANOTHER SULKY-LOOKING ONE. COUSIN KIRSTY'S CHRISTENING. PROBABLY TRYING TO EXPRESS MY CONTEMPT FOR BOURGEOIS RITUAL.
WAS THAT THE ONE WHERE I WAS SICK IN THE CAR-PARK AFTERWARS? HAIR'S SHORTER. MUST BE FIFTEEN, SIXTEEN...
CAISTER BEACH. HOLIDAYS. LITTLE GREY MAN AND BOY, FAR AWAY AT THE EDGE OF THE BIG GREY SEA. DAD AND ME? ME ABOUT TWELVE? CAN'T QUITE MAKE THEM OUT...
CHRIST, THESE ARE ANCIENT. WHAT'S THIS ONE? IT'S...

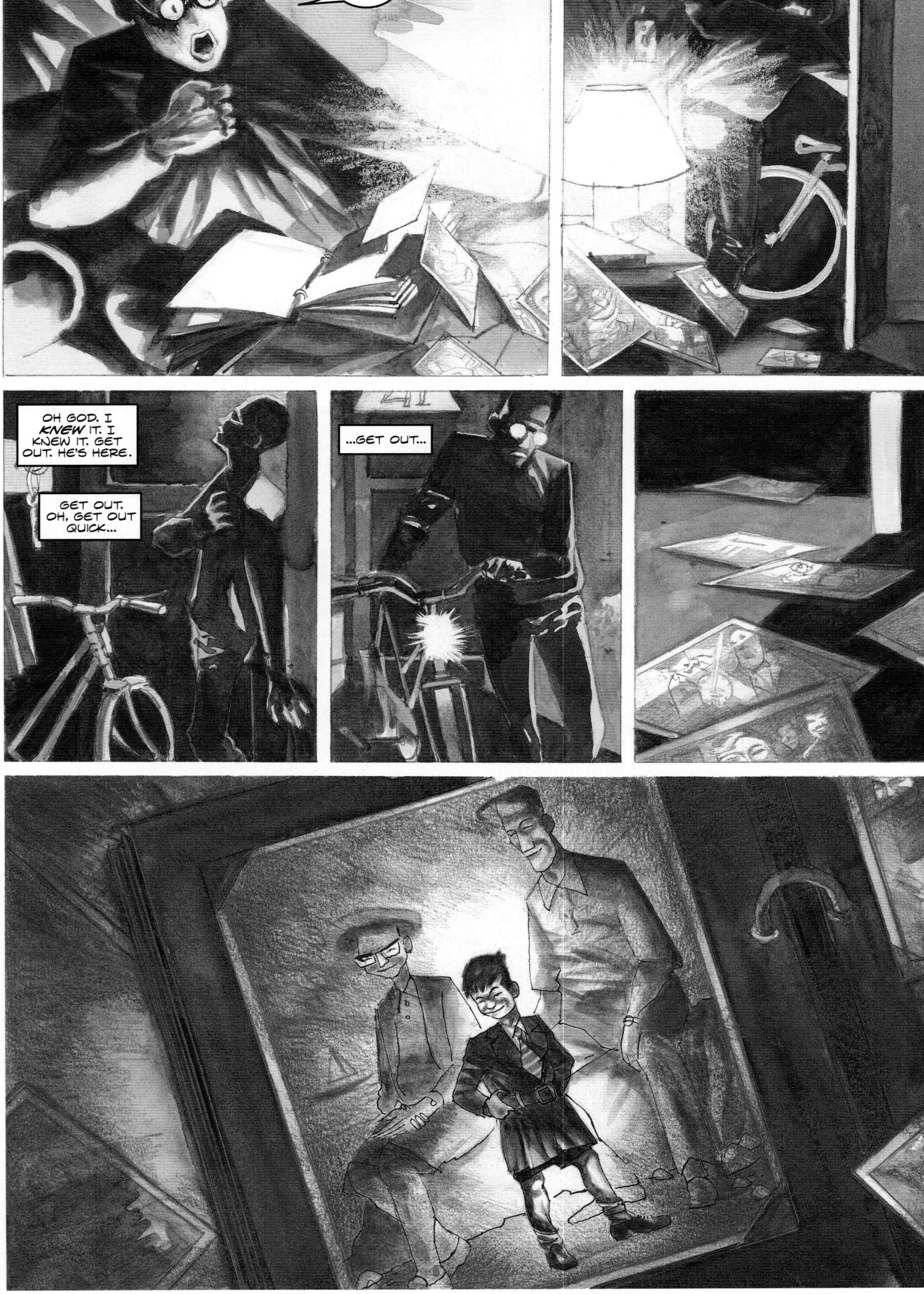
AAAA!
OH GOD. I KNEW IT. I KNEW IT. GET OUT. HE'S HERE.
GET OUT. OH, GET OUT QUICK...
...GET OUT...

THE MURDERER.

HE'S HERE.

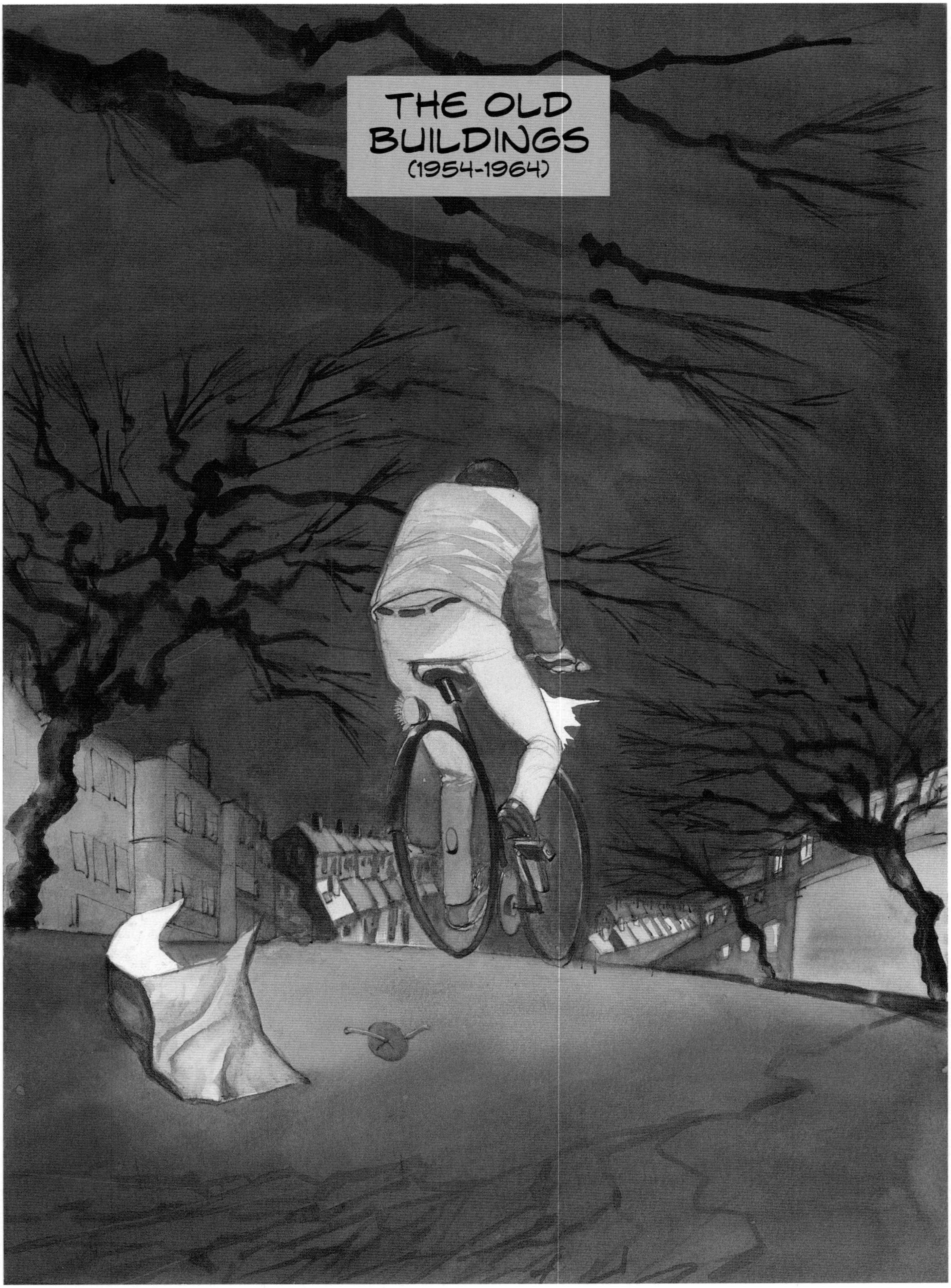
THE OLD BUILDINGS
(1954-1964)

...CHASING THIS PUDDLE OF PISS-COLOURED LIGHT AS IT SKIMS BETWEEN FLATS PAINTED POST-WAR AUSTERITY MUSTARD AND MAISONETTES BRICK-BUILT IN SCABBY-KNEE BURGUNDY DURING THE MACMILLAN YEARS...

THROUGH THESE STREETS; THROUGH THIS SCRAPYARD OF CLAPPED-OUT UTOPIAS; FAILED SOCIAL VISIONS THAT CAME HERE TO DIE JUST LIKE ME, JUST LIKE ME...

HOW ON EARTH DID I COME TO BE HERE?

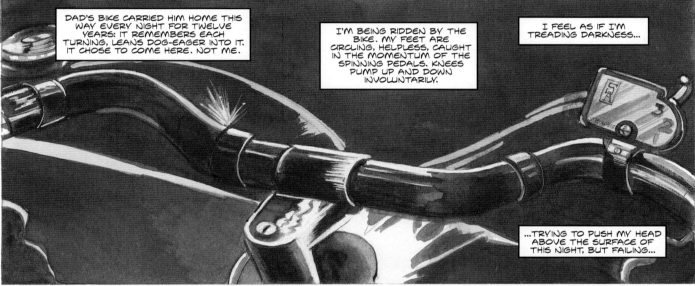

DAD'S BIKE CARRIED HIM HOME THIS WAY EVERY NIGHT FOR TWELVE YEARS: IT REMEMBERS EACH TURNING, LEANS DOG-EAGER INTO IT. IT CHOSE TO COME HERE. NOT ME.

I'M BEING RIDDEN BY THE BIKE. MY FEET ARE CIRCLING, HELPLESS, CAUGHT IN THE MOMENTUM OF THE SPINNING PEDALS. KNEES PUMP UP AND DOWN INVOLUNTARILY.

I FEEL AS IF I'M TREADING DARKNESS...

...TRYING TO PUSH MY HEAD ABOVE THE SURFACE OF THIS NIGHT, BUT FAILING...

...GOING DOWN...

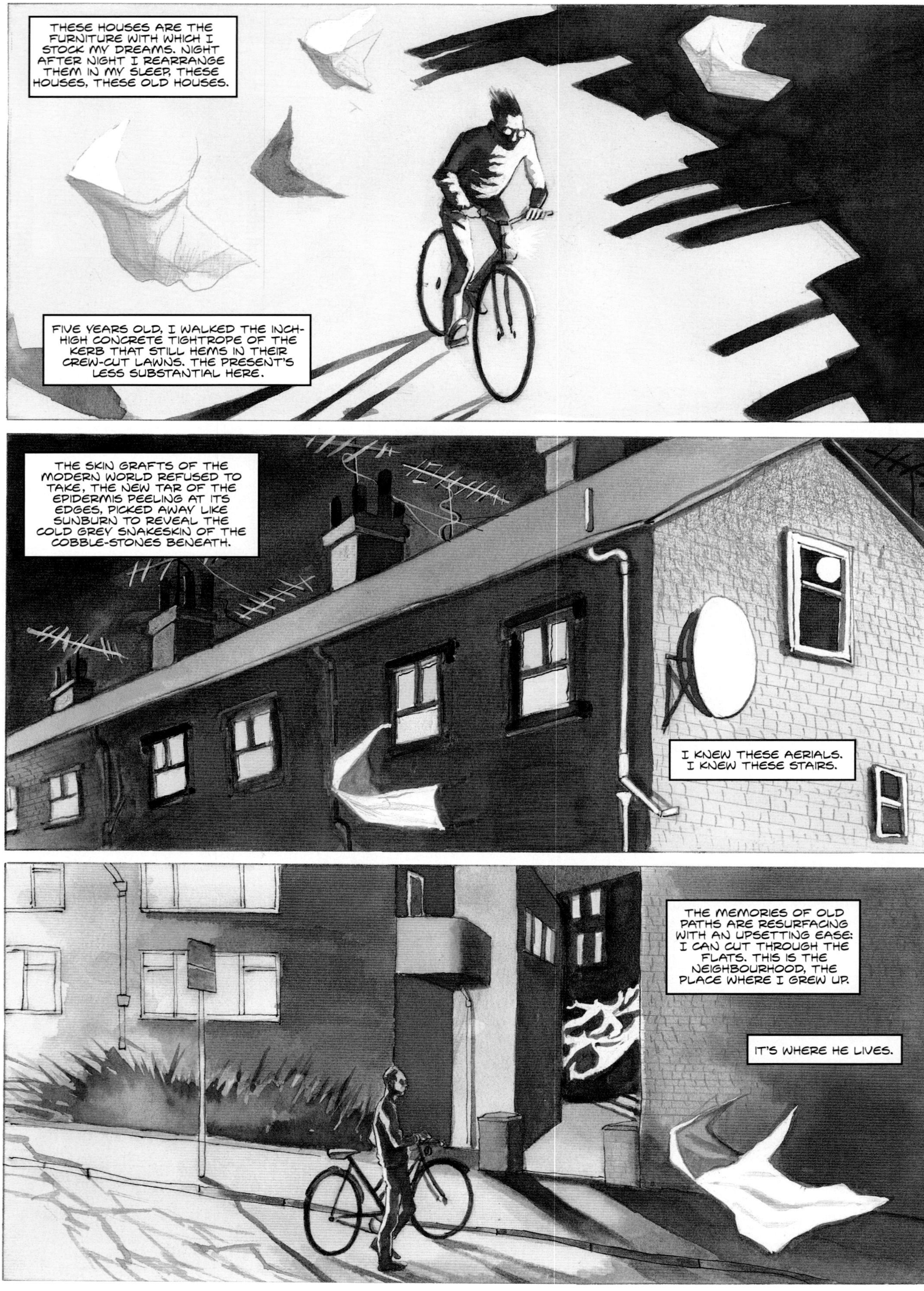
THESE HOUSES ARE THE FURNITURE WITH WHICH I STOCK MY DREAMS. NIGHT AFTER NIGHT I REARRANGE THEM IN MY SLEEP, THESE HOUSES, THESE OLD HOUSES.
FIVE YEARS OLD, I WALKED THE INCH-HIGH CONCRETE TIGHTROPE OF THE KERB THAT STILL HEMS IN THEIR CREW-CUT LAWNS. THE PRESENT'S LESS SUBSTANTIAL HERE.
THE SKIN GRAFTS OF THE MODERN WORLD REFUSED TO TAKE, THE NEW TAR OF THE EPIDERMIS PEELING AT ITS EDGES, PICKED AWAY LIKE SUNBURN TO REVEAL THE COLD GREY SNAKESKIN OF THE COBBLE-STONES BENEATH.
I KNEW THESE AERIALS. I KNEW THESE STAIRS.
THE MEMORIES OF OLD PATHS ARE RESURFACING WITH AN UPSETTING EASE: I CAN CUT THROUGH THE FLATS. THIS IS THE NEIGHBOURHOOD, THE PLACE WHERE I GREW UP.
IT'S WHERE HE LIVES.

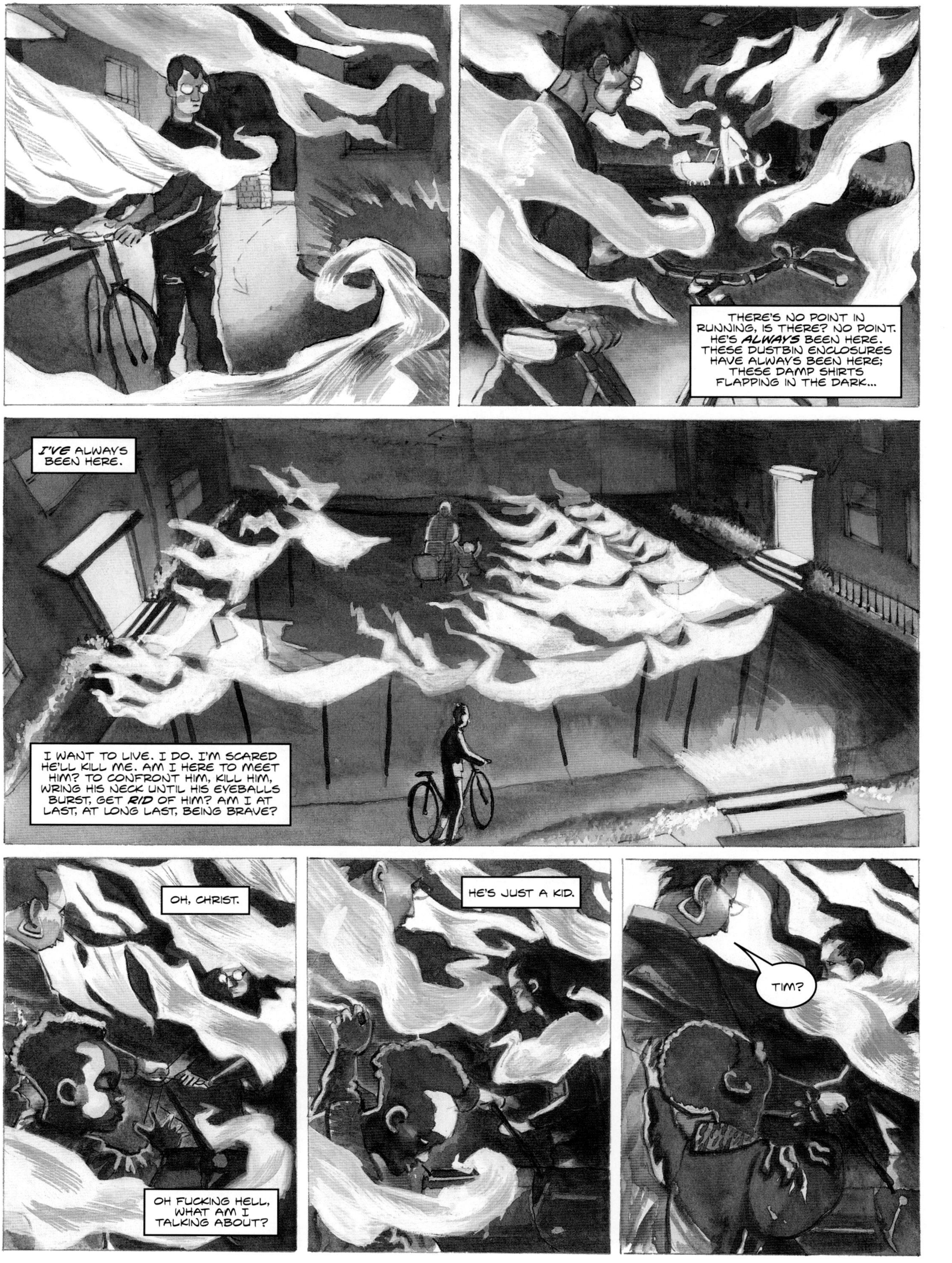
THERE'S NO POINT IN RUNNING, IS THERE? NO POINT. HE'S ALWAYS BEEN HERE. THESE DUSTBIN ENCLOSURES HAVE ALWAYS BEEN HERE; THESE DAMP SHIRTS FLAPPING IN THE DARK...
I'VE ALWAYS BEEN HERE.
I WANT TO LIVE. I DO. I'M SCARED HE'LL KILL ME. AM I HERE TO MEET HIM? TO CONFRONT HIM, KILL HIM, WRING HIS NECK UNTIL HIS EYEBALLS BURST, GET RID OF HIM? AM I AT LAST, AT LONG LAST, BEING BRAVE?
OH, CHRIST.
OH FUCKING HELL, WHAT AM I TALKING ABOUT?
HE'S JUST A KID.
TIM?

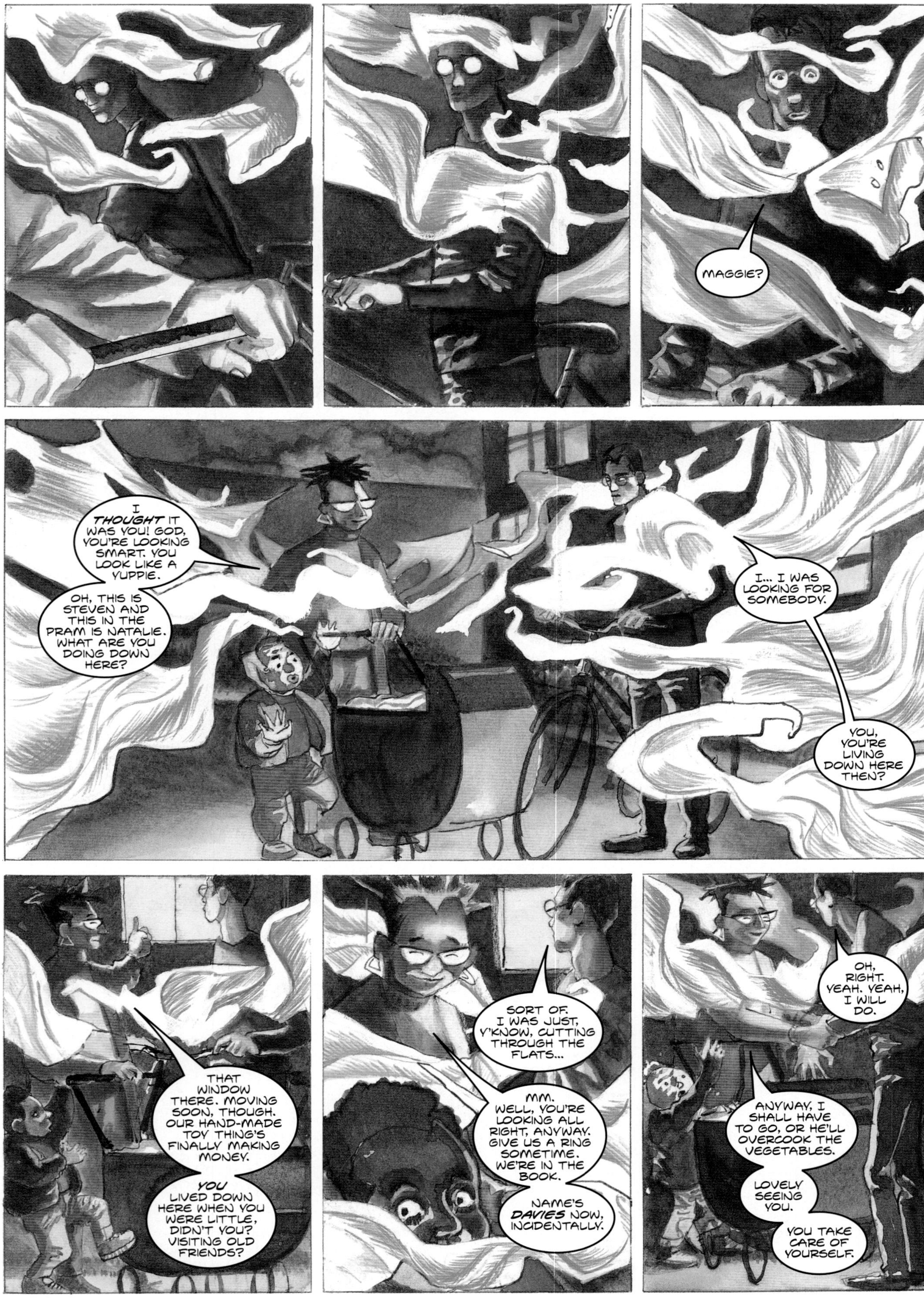
MAGGIE?
I *THOUGHT* IT WAS YOU! GOD, YOU'RE LOOKING SMART. YOU LOOK LIKE A YUPPIE.
OH, THIS IS STEVEN AND THIS IN THE PRAM IS NATALIE. WHAT ARE YOU DOING DOWN HERE?
I... I WAS LOOKING FOR SOMEBODY.
YOU, YOU'RE LIVING DOWN HERE THEN?
THAT WINDOW THERE. MOVING SOON, THOUGH. OUR HAND-MADE TOY THING'S FINALLY MAKING MONEY.
YOU LIVED DOWN HERE WHEN YOU WERE LITTLE, DIDN'T YOU? VISITING OLD FRIENDS?
SORT OF. I WAS JUST, Y'KNOW, CUTTING THROUGH THE FLATS...
MM. WELL, YOU'RE LOOKING ALL RIGHT, ANYWAY. GIVE US A RING SOMETIME. WE'RE IN THE BOOK.
NAME'S *DAVIES* NOW, INCIDENTALLY.
OH, RIGHT. YEAH. YEAH, I WILL DO.
ANYWAY, I SHALL HAVE TO GO, OR HE'LL OVERCOOK THE VEGETABLES.
LOVELY SEEING YOU.
YOU TAKE CARE OF YOURSELF.

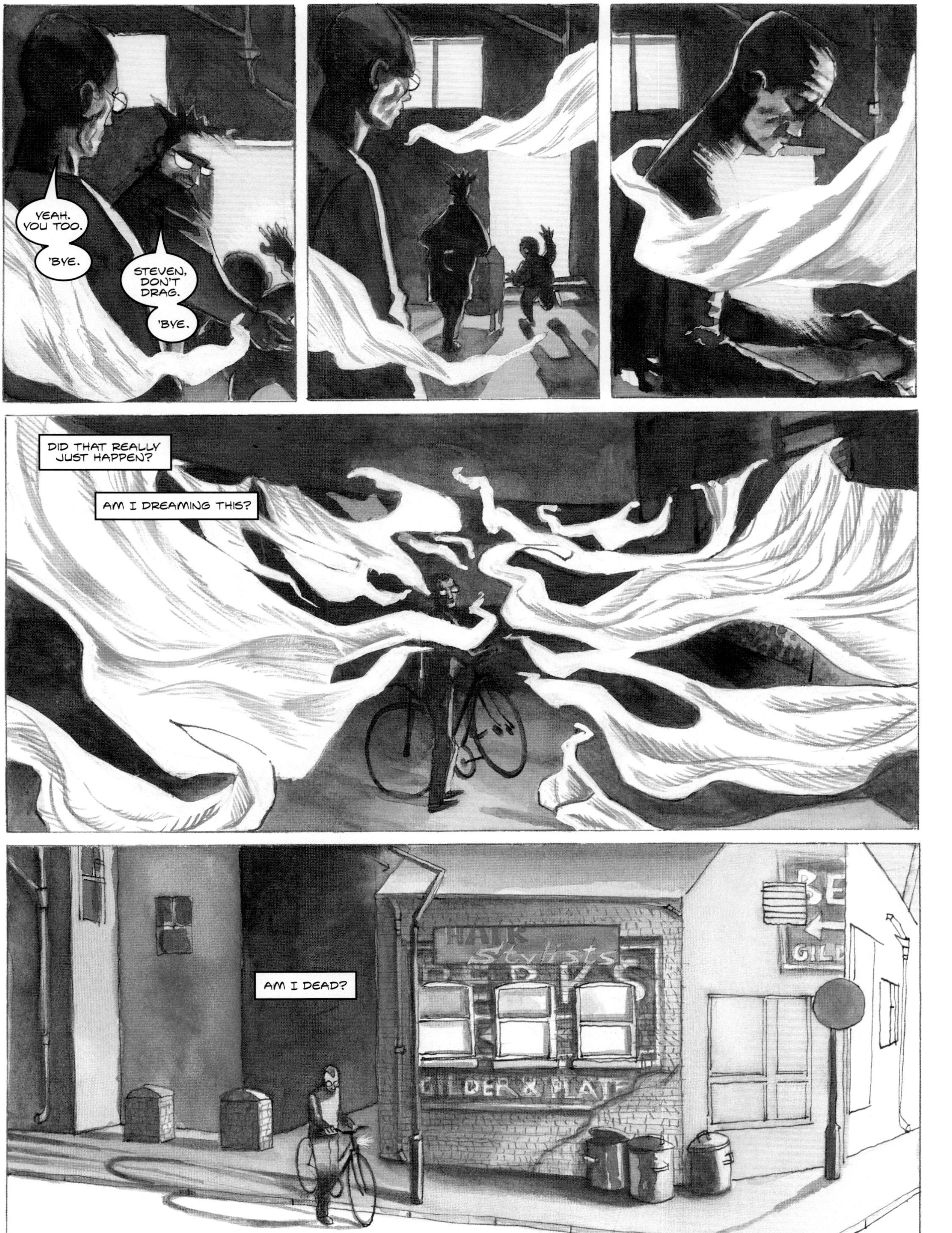
YEAH. YOU TOO.
'BYE.
STEVEN, DON'T DRAG.
'BYE.
DID THAT REALLY JUST HAPPEN?
AM I DREAMING THIS?
AM I DEAD?
Stylists
GILDER & PLATE

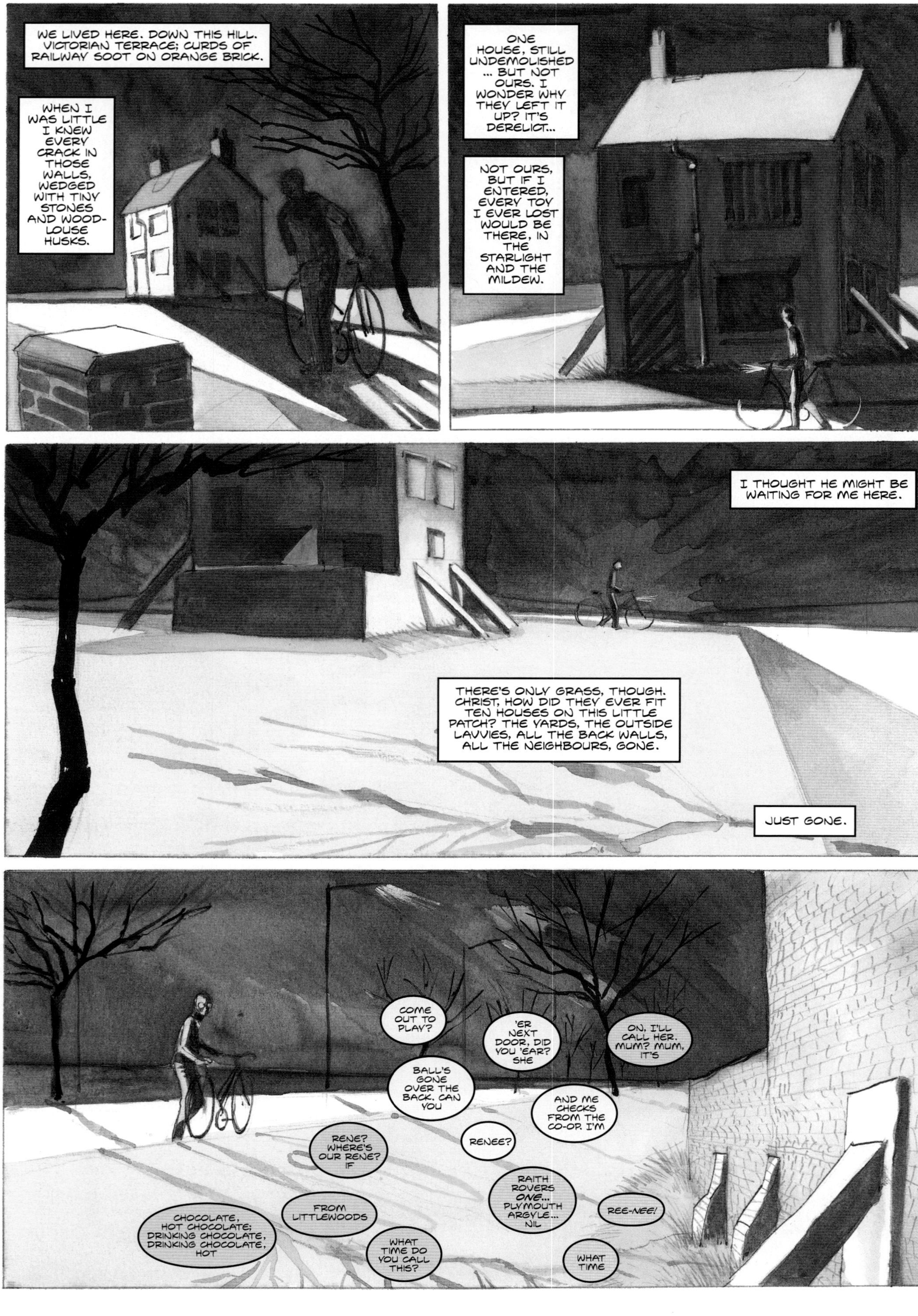

WE LIVED HERE. DOWN THIS HILL. VICTORIAN TERRACE; CURDS OF RAILWAY SOOT ON ORANGE BRICK.
WHEN I WAS LITTLE I KNEW EVERY CRACK IN THOSE WALLS, WEDGED WITH TINY STONES AND WOOD-LOUSE HUSKS.
ONE HOUSE, STILL UNDEMOLISHED ... BUT NOT OURS. I WONDER WHY THEY LEFT IT UP? IT'S DERELICT...
NOT OURS, BUT IF I ENTERED, EVERY TOY I EVER LOST WOULD BE THERE, IN THE STARLIGHT AND THE MILDEW.
I THOUGHT HE MIGHT BE WAITING FOR ME HERE.
THERE'S ONLY GRASS, THOUGH. CHRIST, HOW DID THEY EVER FIT TEN HOUSES ON THIS LITTLE PATCH? THE YARDS, THE OUTSIDE LAVVIES, ALL THE BACK WALLS, ALL THE NEIGHBOURS, GONE.
JUST GONE.
COME OUT TO PLAY?
'ER NEXT DOOR, DID YOU 'EAR? SHE
ON, I'LL CALL HER. MUM? MUM, IT'S
BALL'S GONE OVER THE BACK. CAN YOU
AND ME CHECKS FROM THE CO-OP. I'M
RENE? WHERE'S OUR RENE? IF
RENEE?
RAITH ROVERS *ONE*... PLYMOUTH ARGYLE... NIL
REE-NEE!
CHOCOLATE, HOT CHOCOLATE; DRINKING CHOCOLATE, DRINKING CHOCOLATE, HOT
FROM LITTLEWOODS
WHAT TIME DO YOU CALL THIS?
WHAT TIME

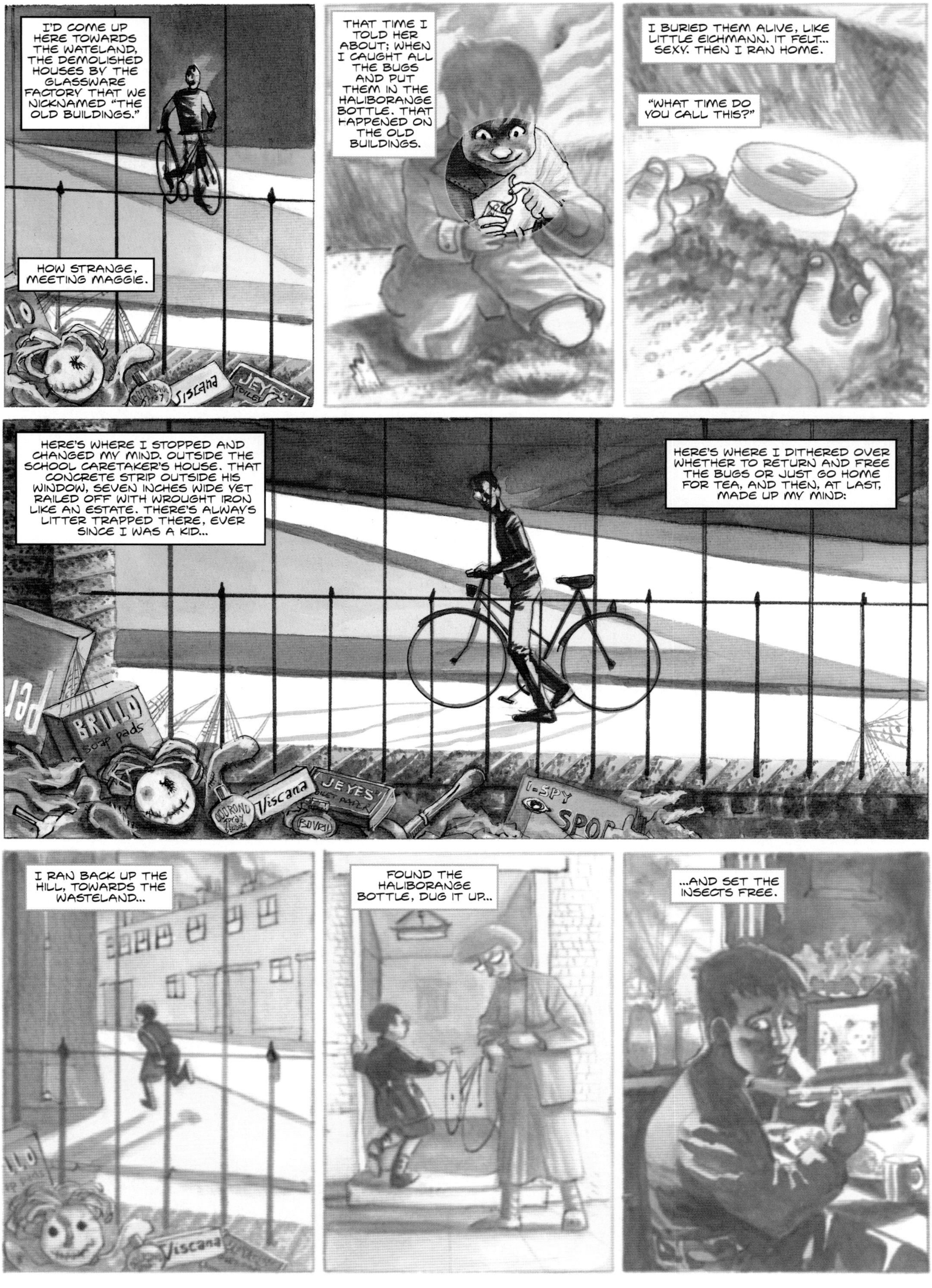
I'D COME UP HERE TOWARDS THE WATELAND, THE DEMOLISHED HOUSES BY THE GLASSWARE FACTORY THAT WE NICKNAMED "THE OLD BUILDINGS."
HOW STRANGE, MEETING MAGGIE.
Viscana
JEYES
THAT TIME I TOLD HER ABOUT; WHEN I CAUGHT ALL THE BUGS AND PUT THEM IN THE HALIBORANGE BOTTLE. THAT HAPPENED ON THE OLD BUILDINGS.
I BURIED THEM ALIVE, LIKE LITTLE EICHMANN. IT FELT... SEXY. THEN I RAN HOME.
"WHAT TIME DO YOU CALL THIS?"
HERE'S WHERE I STOPPED AND CHANGED MY MIND. OUTSIDE THE SCHOOL CARETAKER'S HOUSE. THAT CONCRETE STRIP OUTSIDE HIS WINDOW, SEVEN INCHES WIDE YET RAILED OFF WITH WROUGHT IRON LIKE AN ESTATE. THERE'S ALWAYS LITTER TRAPPED THERE, EVER SINCE I WAS A KID...
HERE'S WHERE I DITHERED OVER WHETHER TO RETURN AND FREE THE BUGS OR JUST GO HOME FOR TEA, AND THEN, AT LAST, MADE UP MY MIND:
BRILLO
soap pads
Viscana
JEYES
TOILET PAPER
BOVRIL
I-SPY
I RAN BACK UP THE HILL, TOWARDS THE WASTELAND...
Viscana
FOUND THE HALIBORANGE BOTTLE, DUG IT UP...
...AND SET THE INSECTS FREE.

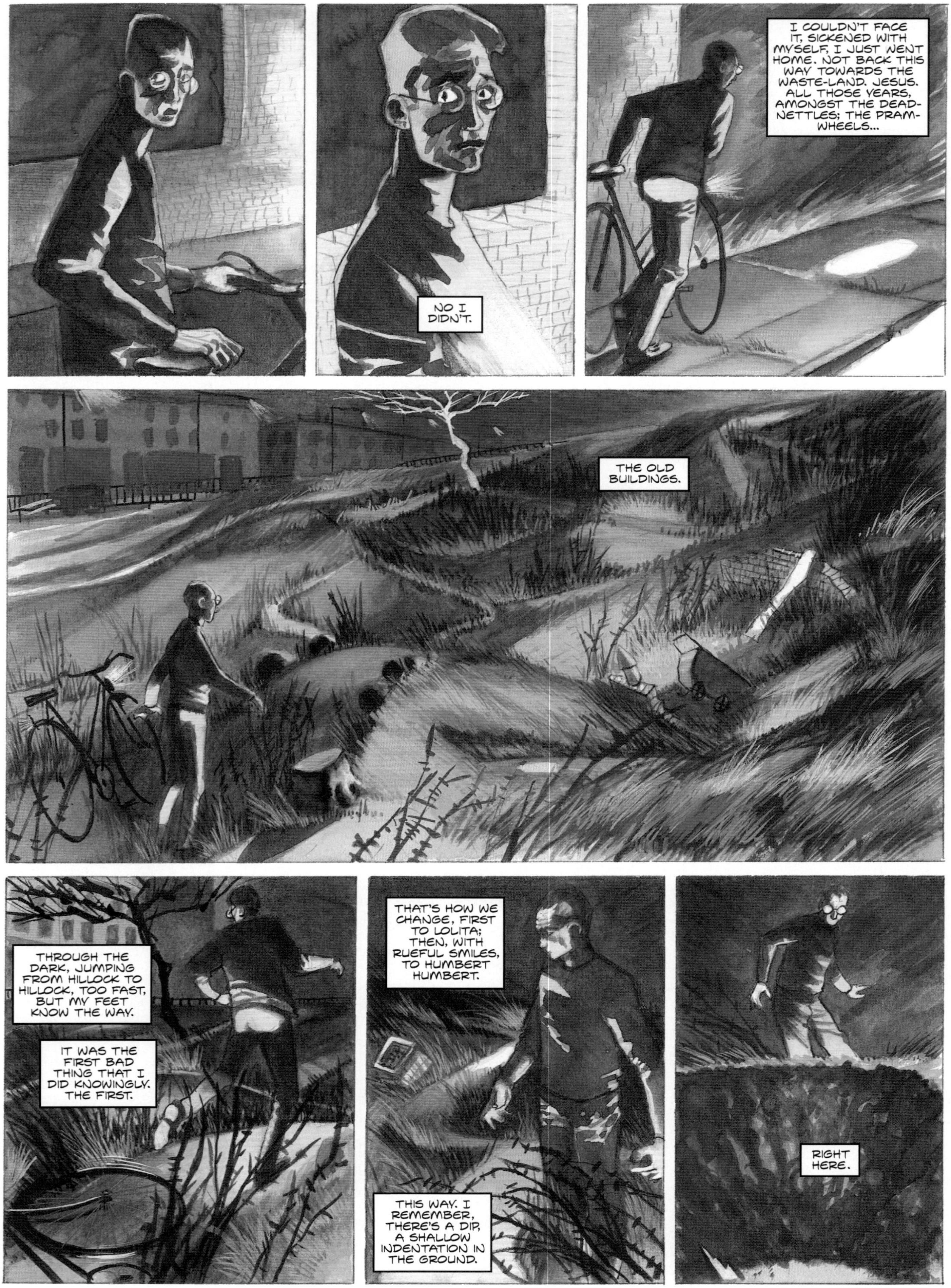
NO I DIDN'T.
I COULDN'T FACE IT, SICKENED WITH MYSELF, I JUST WENT HOME. NOT BACK THIS WAY TOWARDS THE WASTE-LAND. JESUS. ALL THOSE YEARS, AMONGST THE DEAD-NETTLES; THE PRAM-WHEELS...
THE OLD BUILDINGS.
THROUGH THE DARK, JUMPING FROM HILLOCK TO HILLOCK, TOO FAST, BUT MY FEET KNOW THE WAY.
IT WAS THE FIRST BAD THING THAT I DID KNOWINGLY. THE FIRST.
THAT'S HOW WE CHANGE, FIRST TO LOLITA; THEN, WITH RUEFUL SMILES, TO HUMBERT HUMBERT.
THIS WAY. I REMEMBER, THERE'S A DIP, A SHALLOW INDENTATION IN THE GROUND.
RIGHT HERE.

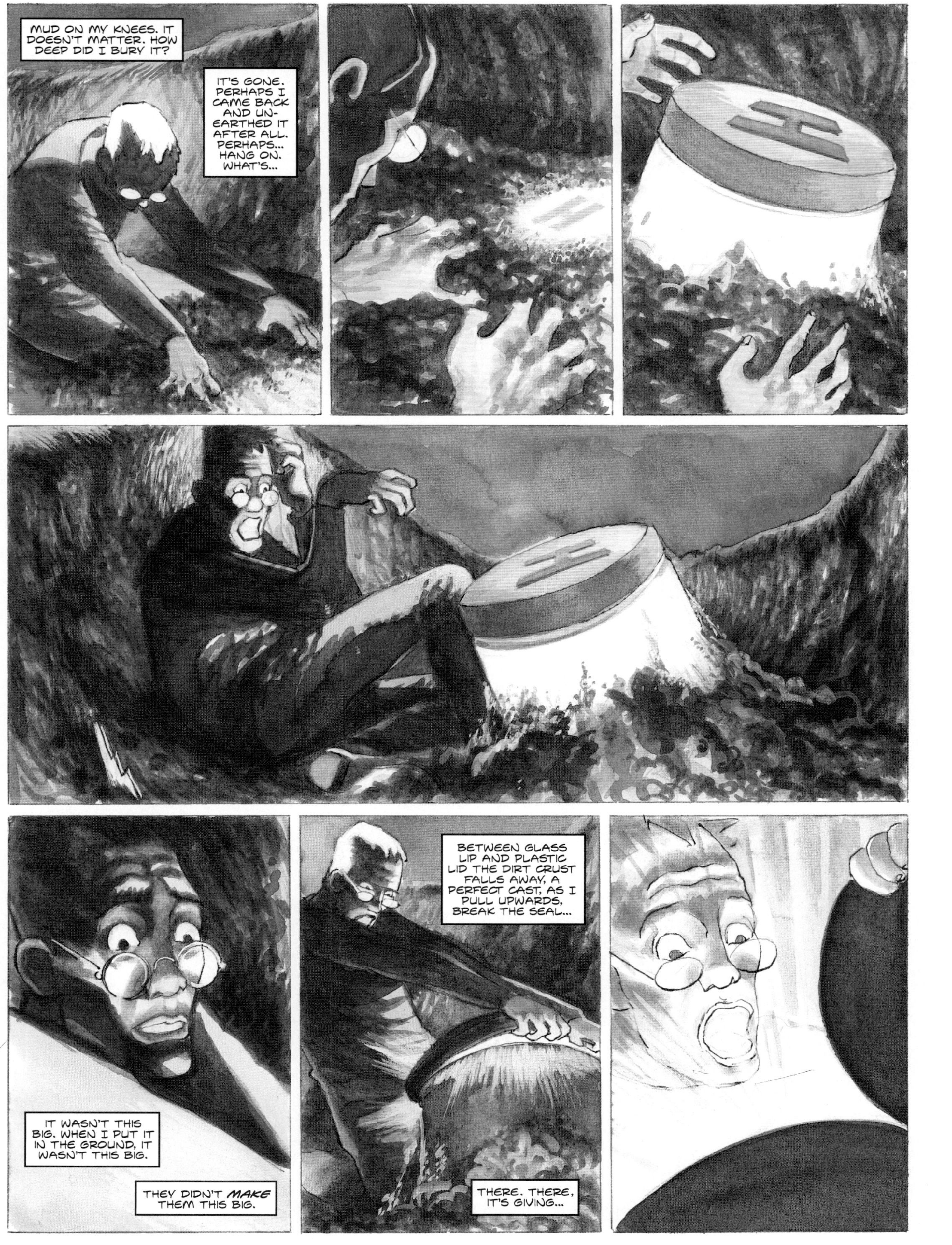
MUD ON MY KNEES. IT DOESN'T MATTER. HOW DEEP DID I BURY IT?
IT'S GONE. PERHAPS I CAME BACK AND UN-EARTHED IT AFTER ALL. PERHAPS... HANG ON. WHAT'S...
IT WASN'T THIS BIG. WHEN I PUT IT IN THE GROUND, IT WASN'T THIS BIG.
THEY DIDN'T MAKE THEM THIS BIG.
BETWEEN GLASS LIP AND PLASTIC LID THE DIRT CRUST FALLS AWAY, A PERFECT CAST, AS I PULL UPWARDS, BREAK THE SEAL...
THERE. THERE, IT'S GIVING...

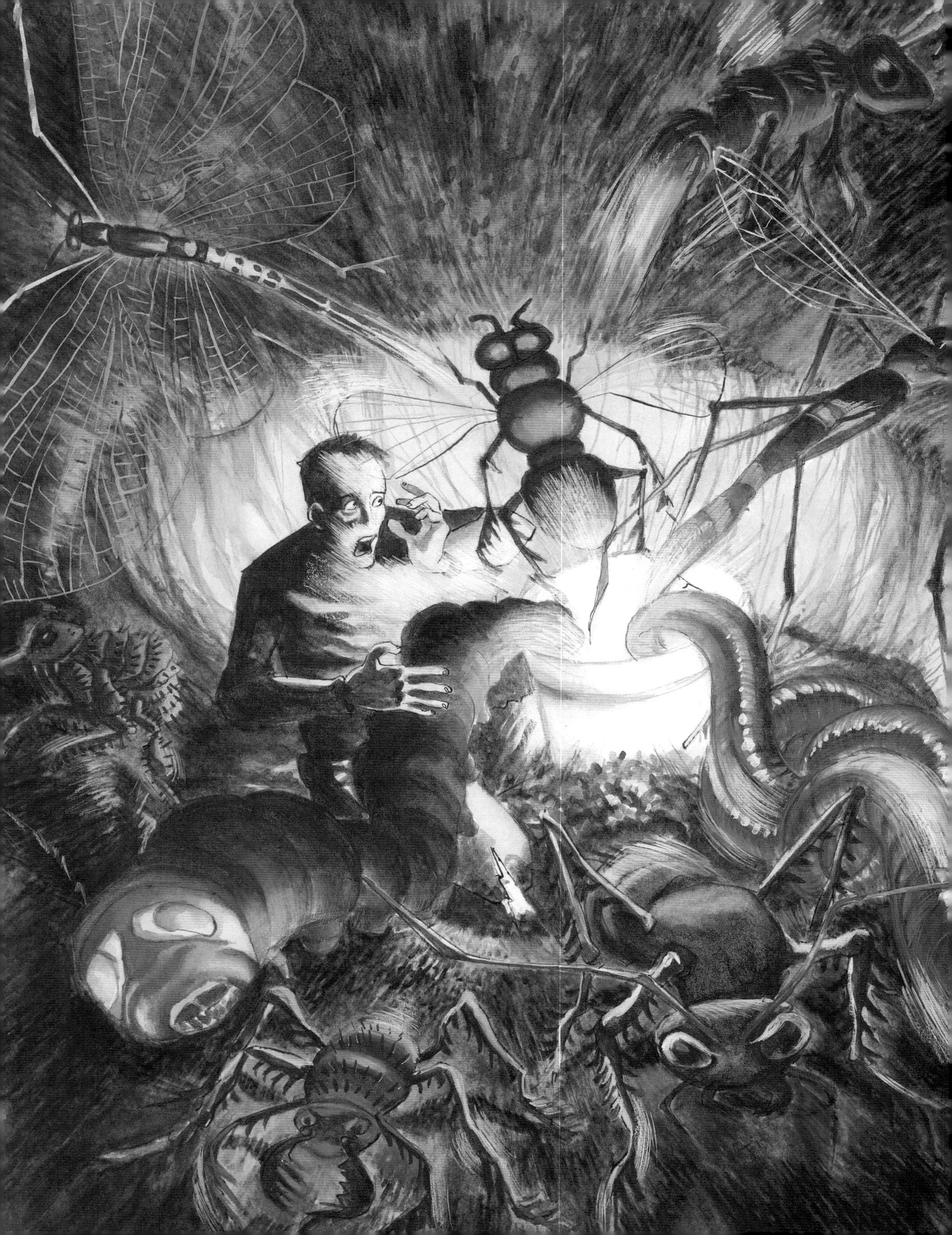

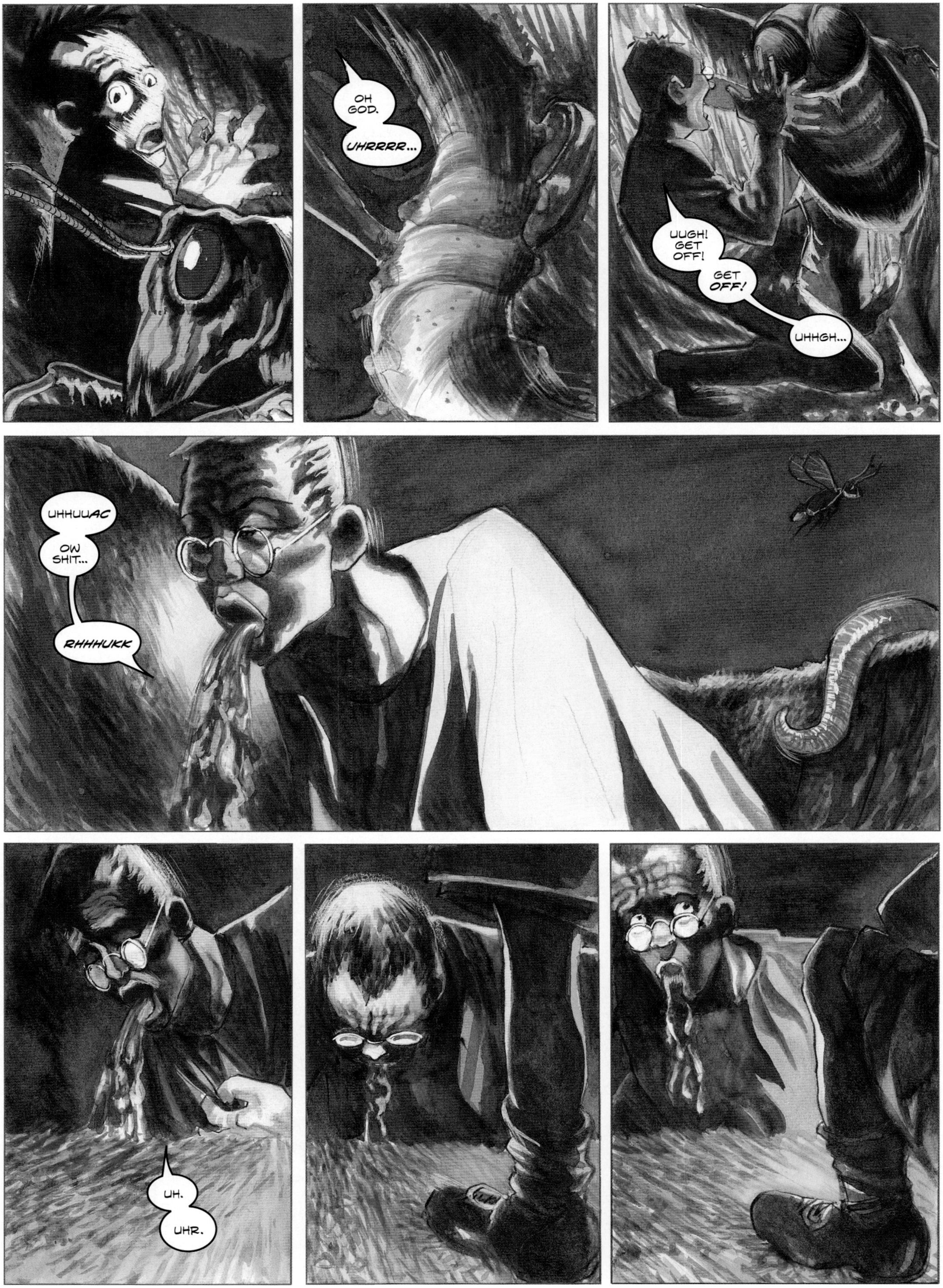
OH GOD.
UHRRRR...
UUGH! GET OFF!
GET OFF!
UHHGH...
UHHUUAC
OW SHIT...
RHHHUKK
UH.
UHR.

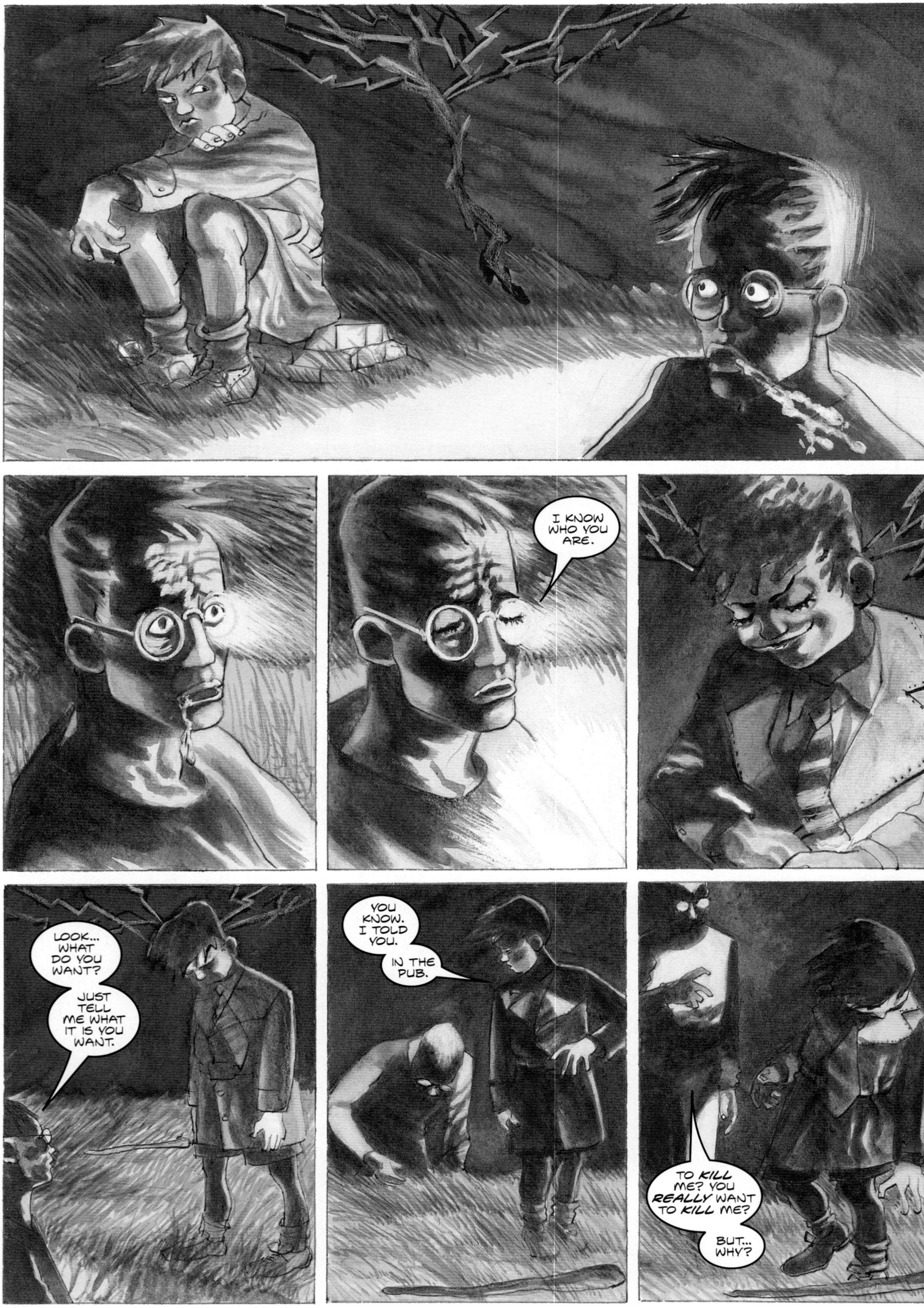
I KNOW WHO YOU ARE.
LOOK... WHAT DO YOU WANT?
JUST TELL ME WHAT IT IS YOU WANT.
YOU KNOW. I TOLD YOU.
IN THE PUB.
TO KILL ME? YOU REALLY WANT TO KILL ME?
BUT... WHY?

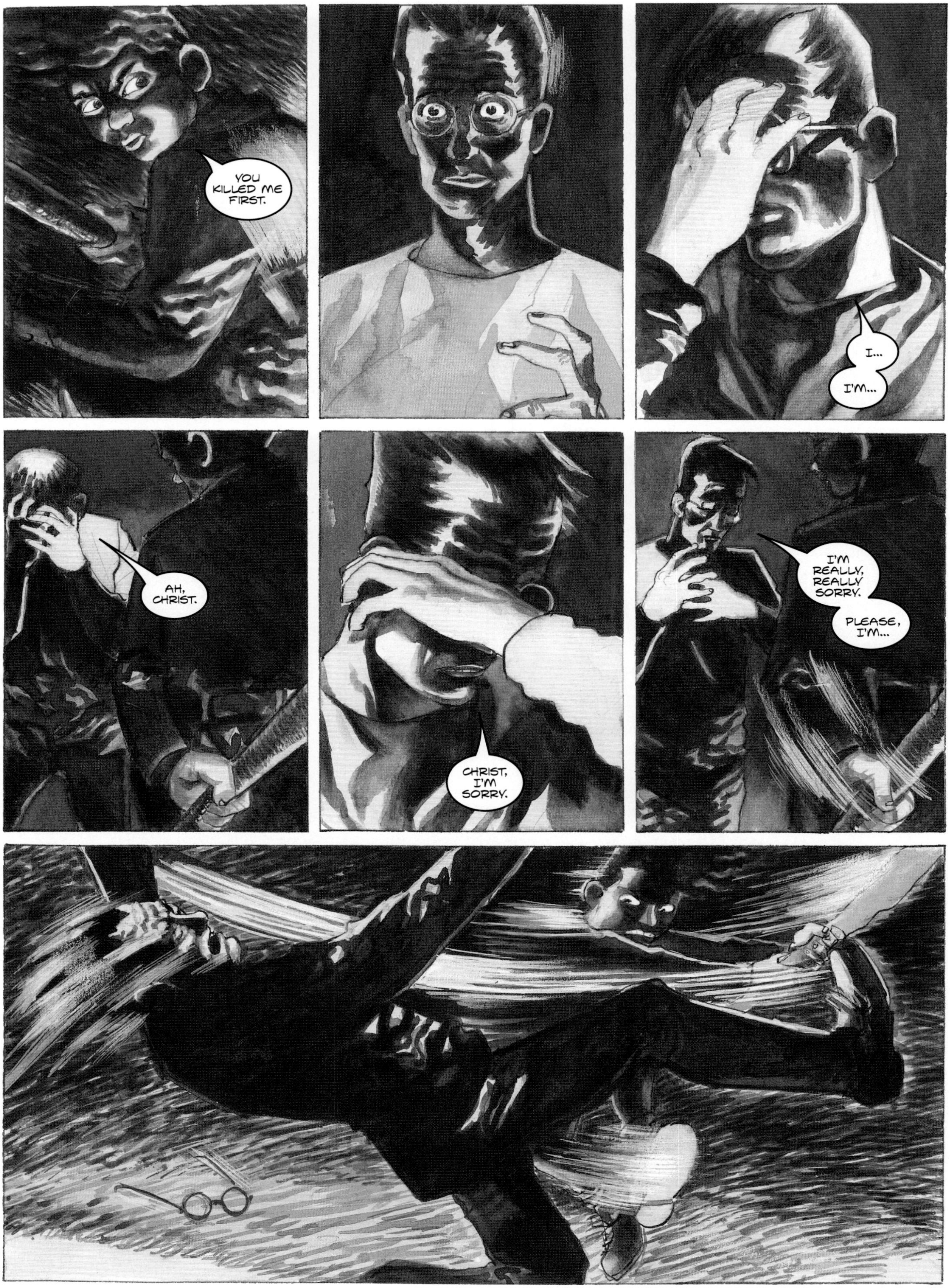
YOU KILLED ME FIRST.
I...
I'M...
AH, CHRIST.
CHRIST, I'M SORRY.
I'M REALLY, REALLY SORRY.
PLEASE, I'M...

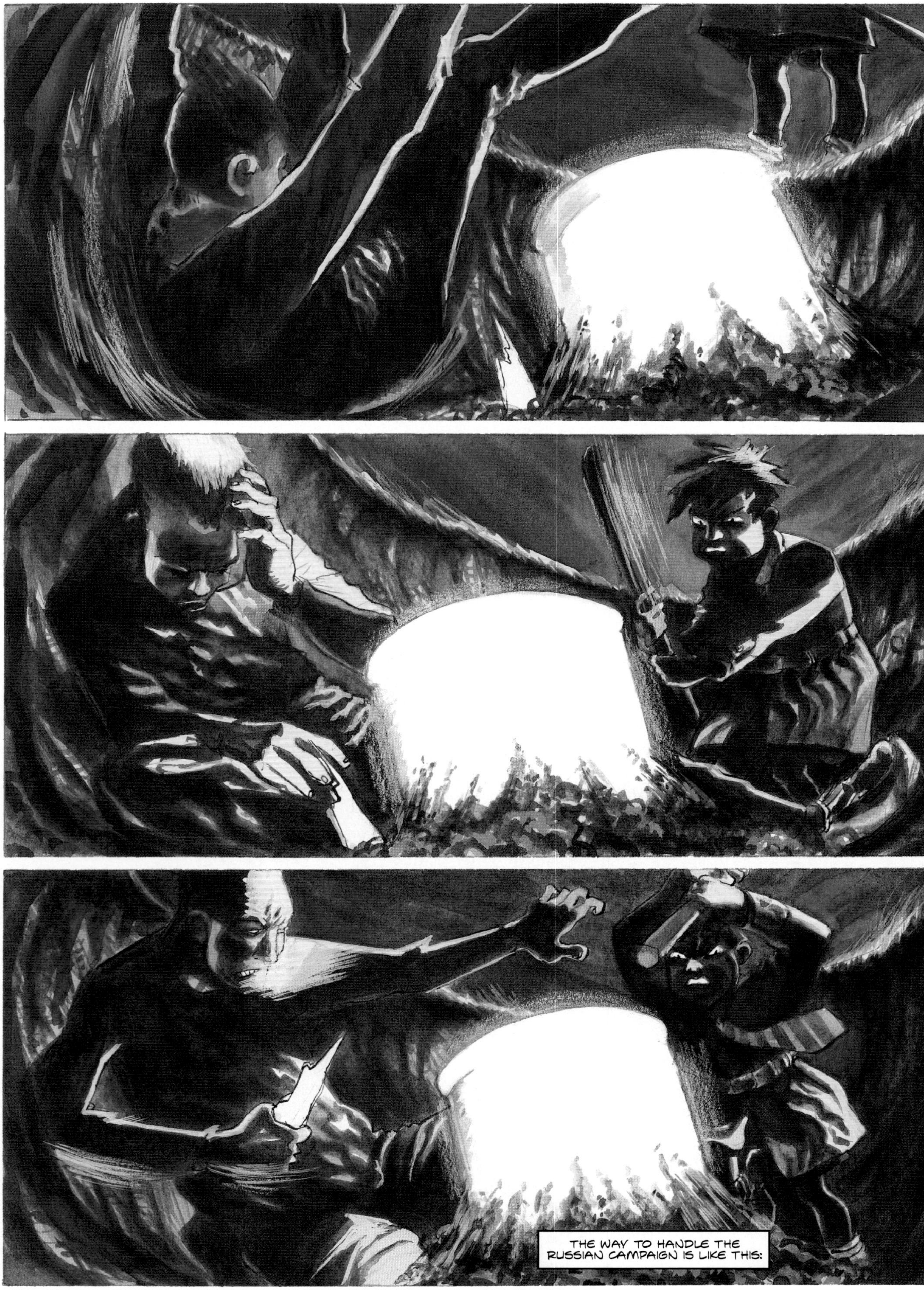
THE WAY TO HANDLE THE RUSSIAN CAMPAIGN IS LIKE THIS:

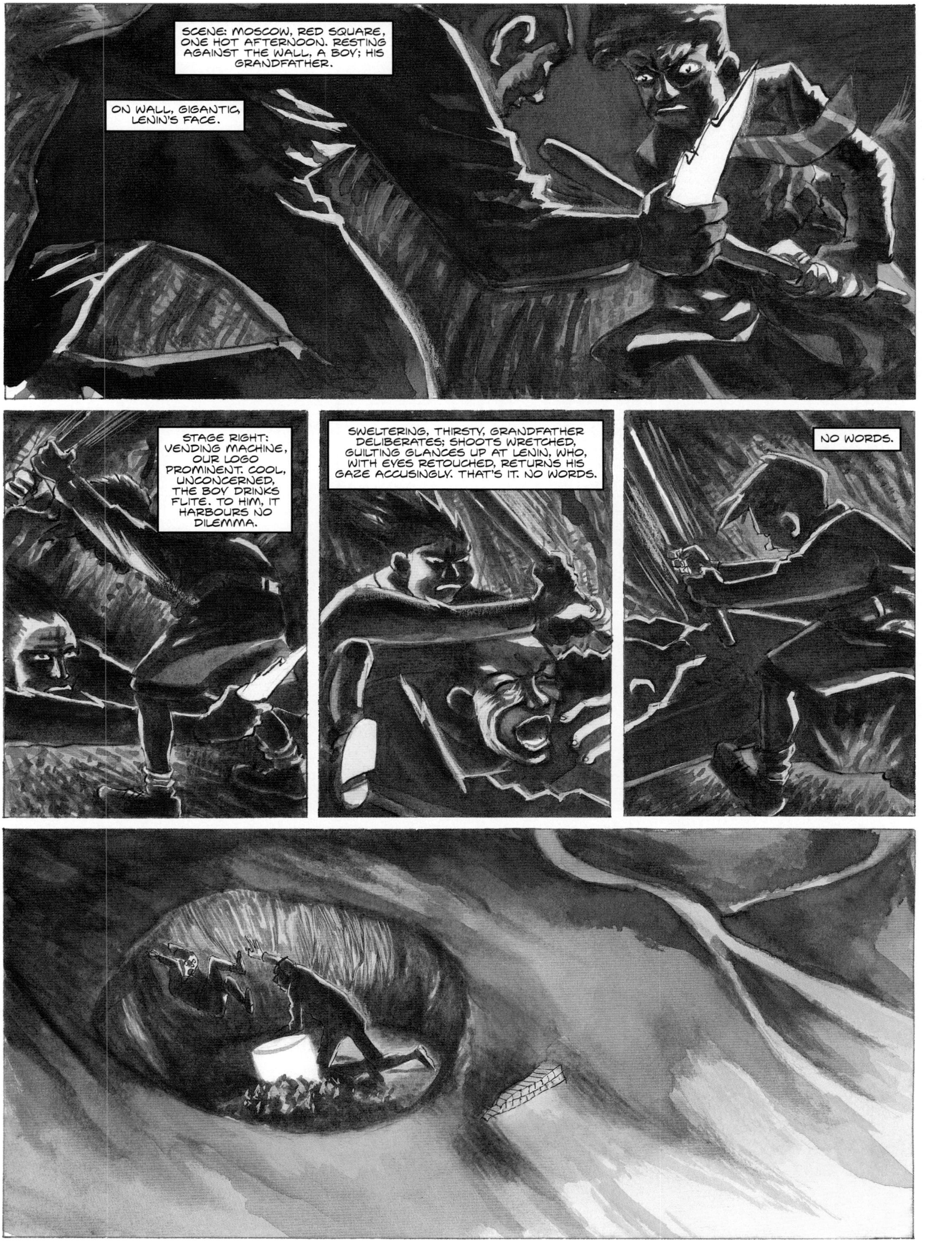
SCENE: MOSCOW, RED SQUARE, ONE HOT AFTERNOON. RESTING AGAINST THE WALL, A BOY; HIS GRANDFATHER.
ON WALL, GIGANTIC, LENIN'S FACE.
STAGE RIGHT: VENDING MACHINE, OUR LOGO PROMINENT. COOL, UNCONCERNED, THE BOY DRINKS FLITE. TO HIM, IT HARBOURS NO DILEMMA.
SWELTERING, THIRSTY, GRANDFATHER DELIBERATES; SHOOTS WRETCHED, GUILTING GLANCES UP AT LENIN, WHO, WITH EYES RETOUCHED, RETURNS HIS GAZE ACCUSINGLY. THAT'S IT. NO WORDS.
NO WORDS.

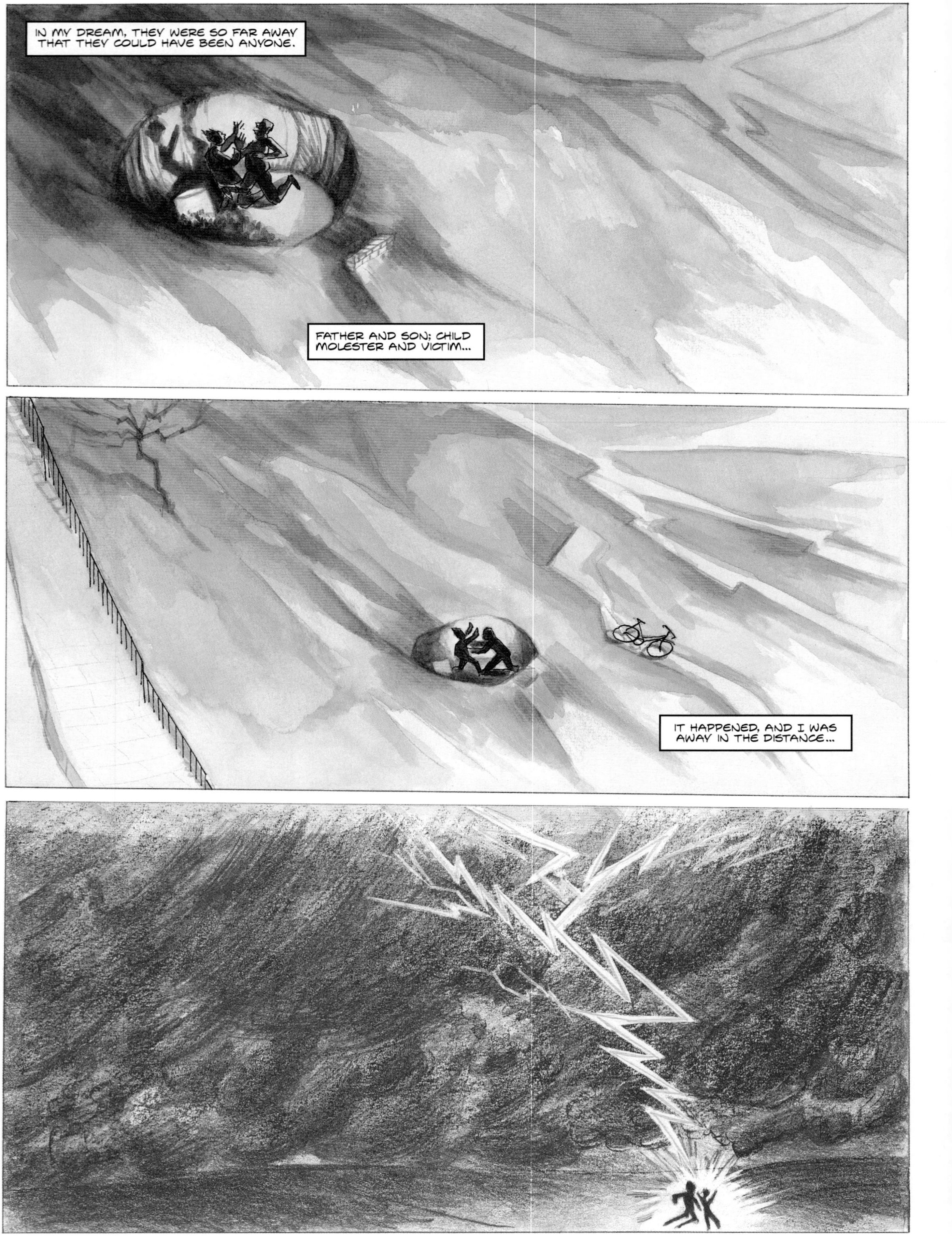
IN MY DREAM, THEY WERE SO FAR AWAY THAT THEY COULD HAVE BEEN ANYONE.
FATHER AND SON; CHILD MOLESTER AND VICTIM...
IT HAPPENED, AND I WAS AWAY IN THE DISTANCE...

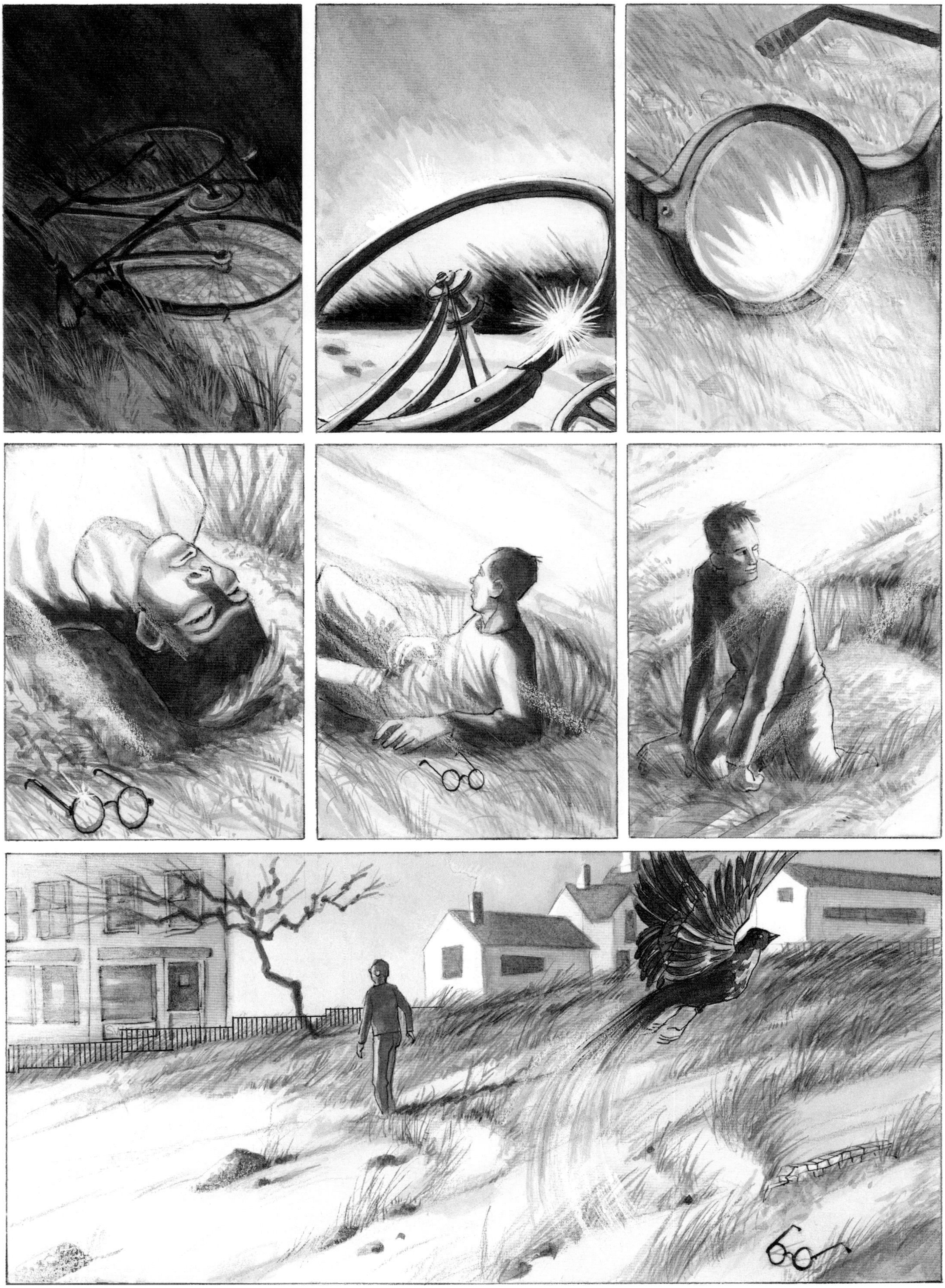

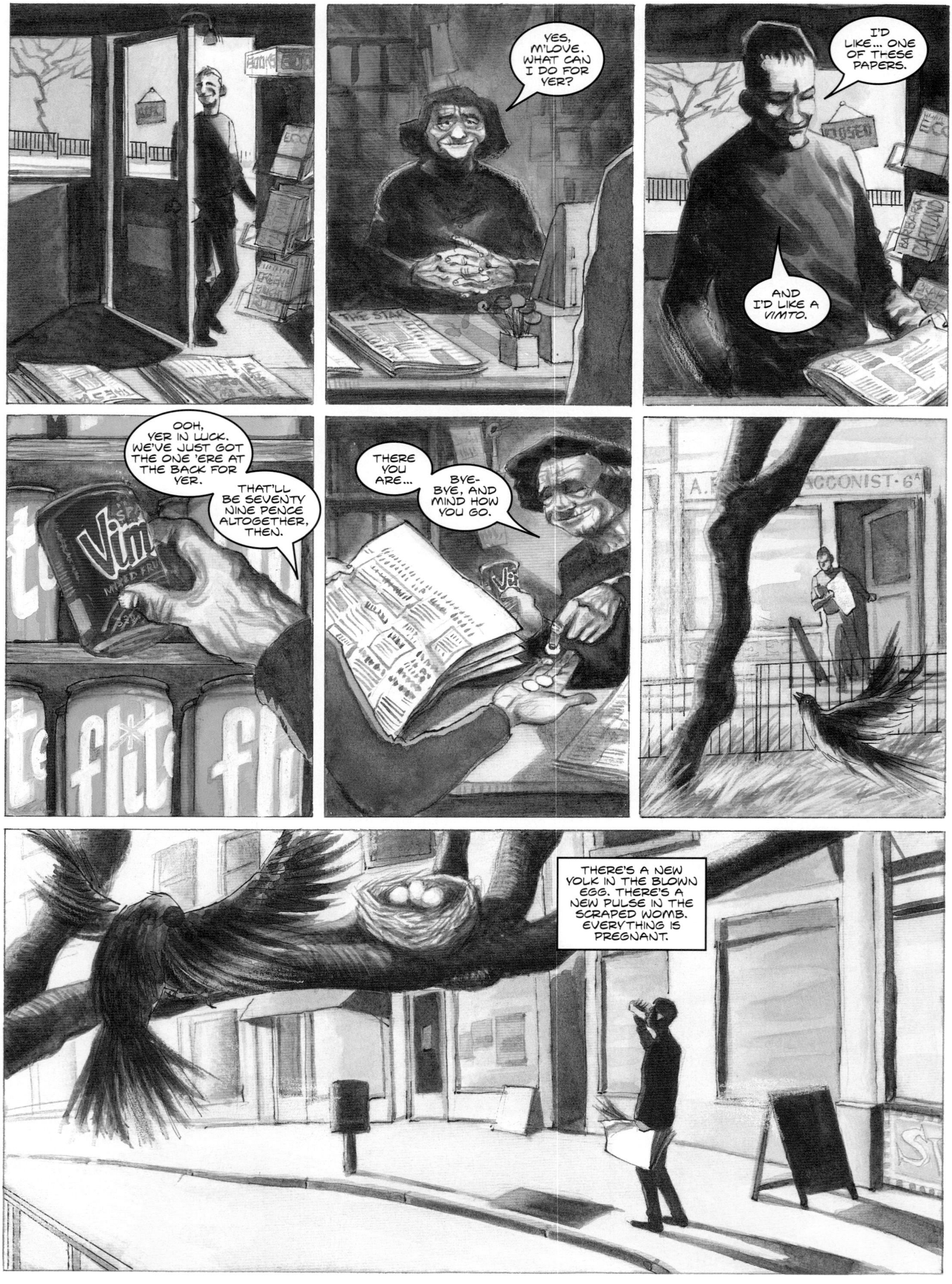
YES, M'LOVE. WHAT CAN I DO FOR YER?
I'D LIKE... ONE OF THESE PAPERS.
AND I'D LIKE A VIMTO.
OOH, YER IN LUCK. WE'VE JUST GOT THE ONE 'ERE AT THE BACK FOR YER.
THAT'LL BE SEVENTY NINE PENCE ALTOGETHER, THEN.
THERE YOU ARE...
BYE-BYE, AND MIND HOW YOU GO.
THERE'S A NEW YOLK IN THE BLOWN EGG. THERE'S A NEW PULSE IN THE SCRAPED WOMB. EVERYTHING IS PREGNANT.

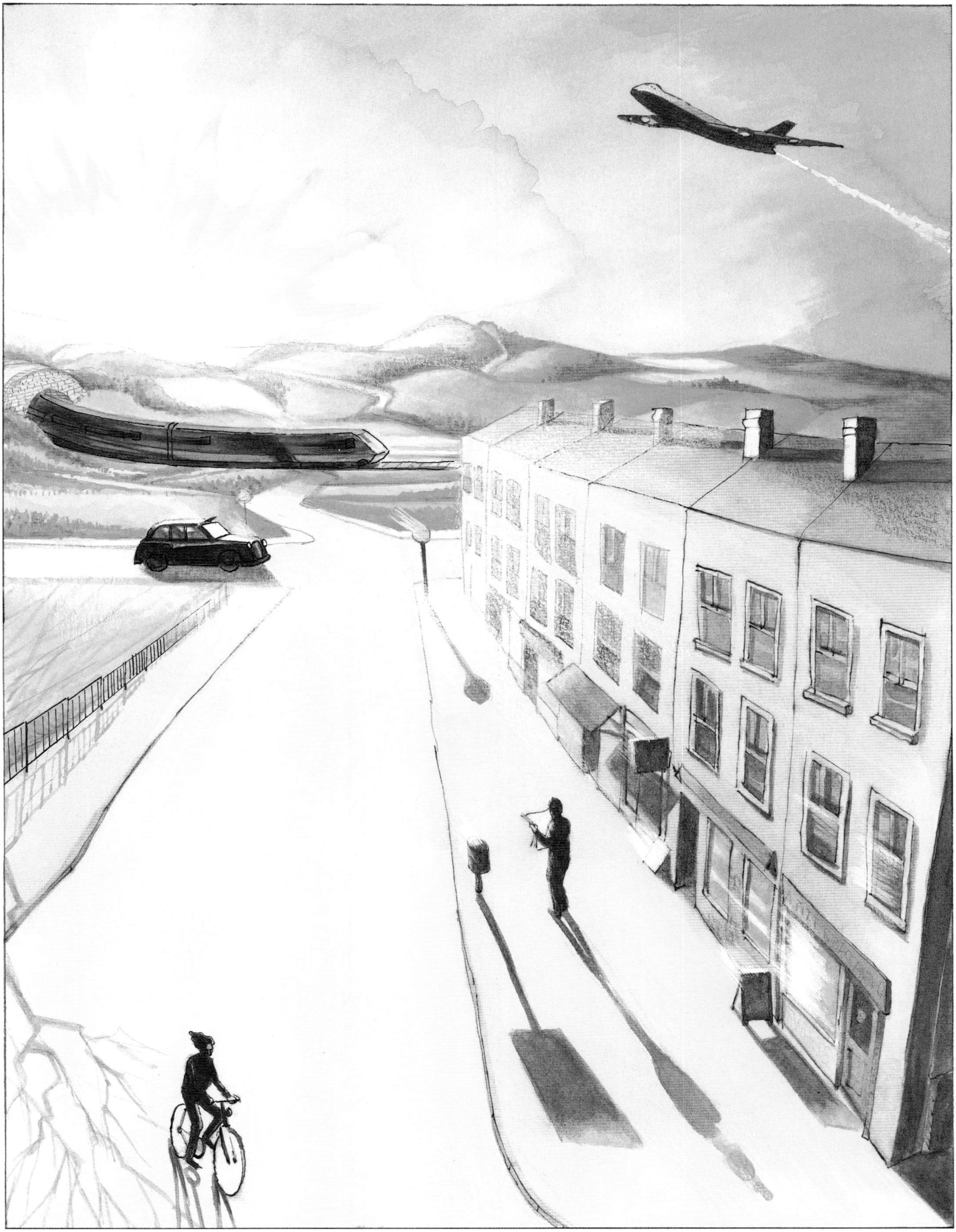
INTO THE MORNING, UNNOTICED, I SLIP FROM THE SCENE OF THE CRIME.

ANATOMY OF A KILLING

Alan Moore and Oscar Zarate talk about the concepts, aims and process behind *A Small Killing*

A Small Killing is a work of firsts. It was the first time Alan Moore had tackled a complete graphic novel without superhero trappings, the first time Oscar Zarate's work was seen by most of the British/American comics audience, and the first time either creator had worked in such a unique collaborative manner.

As coda to a story which exposes the inherent unreliability of memory, it's perhaps appropriate that more than a decade after its publication Moore and Zarate have differing recollections of how *A Small Killing* first came to light.

Zarate remembers that he met Moore, "As you meet anyone. In this case, it happened at a party. I knew a little bit of his work and he knew some of my work, and there was a mutual interest in each other's creations. He had seen a book of mine already published and the idea just sprang up of doing something together, in spite of coming from different styles of doing comics. He used to create superheroes and I had nothing to do with superheroes.

"But we shared a curiosity: He wanted to innovate, to move in some other way. After that enormous thing he did, *Watchmen*, he wanted to talk about other things and it seems that our encounter happened at the right time. We spoke a while about what we could do together, we had several encounters and I proposed to him something that I really wanted to do. And he said, 'Yes, I can join you.' And from then on, we began working together in a very leisurely way."

Moore, recalls their initial encounter as less coincidental, with a certain caveat: "I think the first time I saw Oscar was somewhere in London. My memories are cloudier than Oscar's, and he probably recalls it all better than me.

"From what I remember, Oscar had already made a contribution in an anthology called *Aargh!* [*Artists Against Rampant Government*

Homophobia - Ed], a book we published as a protest against proposed Conservative government legislation against homosexuality. We got in touch with Oscar and Alexei Sayle, who'd recently collaborated on *Geoffrey the Tube Train and the Fat Comedian*, which is a very funny book, and we asked them if they wanted to take part in the anthology with a page of their own. And possibly that was the first time I talked with Oscar, in relation with *Aargh!*.

"Oscar told me an idea he had, about an adult who was pursued by a child. It intrigued me, because it was a way of working that I'd never used before. I'd never taken on other people's ideas before, because I usually have plenty of ideas of my own. But I liked Oscar very much and I was very fond of his work. His proposal intrigued me. I wanted to know if I was flexible enough to work with an artist like Oscar.

"And I began to think about it. I remembered a dream I had as a teenager. In that dream I met myself, as I was, when I was a very little boy. And the boy was complaining about what I had become as an adult. And I remember it as a dream that affected me deeply. So I began thinking about it in the way Oscar suggested: an adult chased by a boy. I realized later that the adult and the child were both the same person, and that notion was the idea that grew into *A Small Killing*."

FORM AND STRUCTURE

The lines are further blurred by Zarate's input into the story's structure and catalyzing moments: "The narrative timing is mine. This was my first approach to Alan: I touch your back, you turn and there's no one there. I touch your back again, you look down and you see a little boy: 'How do you do? Do you want something?' He says 'No.' Until you say, 'Who are you?' And he says "I am you when you were ten years old. And I came to kill you.' 'Why?' 'Because you betrayed me.'

"So I also told Alan, "He has to work back through different means of locomotion: a plane, a train, a car, a bicycle and two legs." I was very involved in the fact that each chapter should be presented in this way. From then on, Alan began to do his new things. The structure starts from the fact that the story has to go backwards.

"But what I care more about are the undertones, the moments. And therefore, that's why I like the kind of analysis he does. I like it because he understood it, not because he agreed with me. When you say, 'Ah yes! That's what I intended all along.' And suddenly, the identity of the little boy is irrelevant. You read two pages and you know who he is. It's not important. It's a tiny detail you just put in there. These are things one includes to explain what is important to oneself, as much as anything.

"Besides, Alan is a great listener. With him, you get to a point in which you don't know where one person's ideas start and the other's finish. For example, he often uses things that I didn't say and that, nevertheless, I thought they should be in the story."

Moore elaborates on the collaborative nature of the book's genesis: "We threw ideas to each other. It was a long, organic process. We began to define what was going to happen, how the main character should be. We decided to begin the story in the then-present-day 1980s and from there go backwards in time. We knew that the character, in some way, should represent the sum and synthesis of the culture that surrounded us in those times, the end of the eighties."

AUTOBIOGRAPHY AND FICTION

Such surrounding cultures inevitably have their influence on artists and their works. But despite some reviewer's claims to the contrary, Moore insists *A Small Killing* is not autobiographical.

"I suppose that precisely because the book has such a personal feel," he says, "There were people who assumed 'Ah, this has to be about the fact that Alan Moore was so successful that he went to his home town, and felt guilty about his past, and therefore came to this conclusion.'

"No, the truth is that I am a writer, and writers create fictions. This doesn't mean that any of my characters haven't included fragments of myself, but the fact that Timothy Hole works in advertising seemed to me to be emblematic of the culture of the eighties. Actually, back then I didn't realize that Oscar had indeed worked in advertising. On the other hand, when I wrote the background dialogues of the party in the first part of the book... I've read some reviews of the book written by people who've worked in advertising, who said the dialogues sounded as if they were written by someone who'd worked in that profession. But I didn't even ask Oscar for help. I simply invented it.

"I put myself in the same situation, the same role, the same time, the same way of thinking, and then I thought my way into the world of advertising. And the main idea in advertising at that time was taking an emblematic image and putting it together with your client's brand, the one you were representing. From there we took the sequence of the Odessa steps with the baby carriage and the Kiddiecare brand on the side. It was obvious that was the way in which advertisers think. I simply deduced it and Oscar informed me I was right. When I showed it to him, he told me I had hit the nail on the head.

"There are also things that Oscar drew, like Timothy Hole's hometown... That's supposed to be Sheffield, when in fact it's Northampton's landscape with small changes. But many of these sequences: the old houses, the overgrown wasteland, the piece of grass with a house resting

against a piece of wood... that patch of grass is the actual area on which my house used to stand when I was a boy. That was Oscar's idea, because he realized that I could write better about a place to which I was linked with an emotional contact, and therefore he decided to use aspects of Northampton to portray Sheffield. The greater part of the visual decisions came from Oscar, and he tried to imagine the story in a way in which I could get emotionally involved.

"The bugs Timothy Hole buried... That is the only truly autobiographical element in *A Small Killing*. When I was a boy, I remember having caught a bunch of bugs like a spider, a centipede and things like that. I put them inside an empty vitamin tablet jar, closed it and buried it. Going home I began feeling so guilty and ashamed that I went back, dug them up and set them free.

"That's how I recall it. I can't swear it happened exactly that way. Maybe I didn't go back and dig up the jar. I believe I did, I remember that moment, but maybe it's just a memory I made up to cover my guilt at having condemned a bunch of living creatures to that horrible death. But I do believe I let them free. If I search the depths of my conscience I'd swear that finally I freed them. But what if I didn't?

"Then I understood that the whole thing could turn into a symbol for all the little unknown secret, buried, nasty things that I could have done in my life. And I thought it could serve as a very potent metaphor. Not because of the real feelings I had when burying the bugs, but because I could understand someone's intentions in doing it."

LANDSCAPE AND MEMORY

One synergistic aspect of the collaboration was how much both creators relied entirely on their memories.

"Alan doesn't take notes," explains Zarate, "And neither do I. He has an amazing memory. When we were doing *A Small Killing*, we passed through a neighborhood that I later used for the scene with the washing lines. I made a stray comment while talking about other things, and then six years later he told me that my forgotten remark had interested him very much. I had forgot and he made me remember. His memory is so powerful, it's scary. A Small Killing was like that, chatting about a lot of things and saying, 'I want this to be in the story.'

"Later Alan managed to work these things into the book, and we began talking again. There are certain things that I needed to be included there. Then Alan has his own need to tell something and I am curious about that. Alan describes the idea and I don't necessarily relate with it, but trust him in how he's going to express it. In this particular case, I had an idea of how to approach things, because

we had been talking about it. Its structure was not difficult to conceive. Like, say, the structure of a plane... inside that framework, the story was going to move.

"And he had no influence in my work. He made no comments. Alan is capable of giving that space to me, we're both adults. He had seen my things, he was confident, and curious about a situation in which he'd never been before. He made not a single remark regarding my work. I think he was satisfied with it. There is a lot of his stuff there, not in the mechanical part of the formal structure but in mumbling, in which he was interested."

When Zarate received the final script, Moore's memory would impress him again: "I was really happy when I got it, vainly happy, because suddenly I saw that he'd noticed ideas of mine that he'd appeared not to notice!"

TRUST AND SYNTHESIS

Zarate continues, "Suddenly the script began being mine. There was no discussion there. Alan agreed. Alan ended the first chapter and the book was mine. He had nothing to do with it, there was no explanations, checking or notes done by him. My own mark, my signature was there.

"It wasn't a question of Alan's stuff not being interesting, but I had a different kind of information to convey, a visual feeling, picturing it all. It was my way of feeling that the story was also mine. I must feel this story is mine because if I don't feel so, I cannot do it. I am a frustrated writer because I don't know how to write. I like how Alan deals with the structure, because that is not what calls the attention. I like the strings he touches, the characters and a way of worldly observation that is absolutely his.

"Besides, he treated issues that were happening in England at that time. That's what I felt. In that time we had Thatcher defining a great part of the world. England is not and will never be again what it was. And the world has changed, turning into something a lot more reactionary and cruel. You need a machete to go on with life in these times. I feel we share certain feelings and a

certain aversion for what is happening around this kind of acute mediocrity we are suffering. It is putting us aside and marginalizing us more and more, we are having less and less space."

Moore emphasizes how much their collaboration relied on trust: "It may be that Oscar would have a strong idea that things should work in one way or another. I could change things sometimes to make them as Oscar wanted, because his view of it was the best. Maybe other times I told him, 'Look, I really think this should work like this.' But we never had a problem. Both of us were very attentive to the other's opinion, as well as to the aesthetic of the work as a whole.

"It's one of the things that always made me feel so proud as a writer. I mean, I'm very proud of the style of my prose, I'm proud of my skills with dialogue, I'm very good with plots, etc. But what makes me the proudest is my capacity for cooperating with other people. One of the nicest things about my working process lies in changing the way in which I write to make it more appropriate to the way in which someone draws, to adjust it to their favorite way of working.

"When that really works, it should appear to be a work done by a single person. That's the best compliment you can pay to a comic made in collaboration. And I think that Oscar and I accomplished this throughout the whole creation of *A Small Killing*. At times we discussed, or

rather we debated, aspects related to the character. Some ideas were purely Oscar's. For instance, when he suggested that the character's ex-girlfriend would send him the pickled fetus in a jar, I resisted the idea. It seemed to be too shocking to me. I don't know if it seemed to me to be too extreme or too unreal, but after thinking it over, I thought it was acceptable and that it would work.

"There were some other things where it took me days, even weeks to understand what we both wanted and what would be the better solution, but generally speaking it wasn't so hard. We never really needed to debate too much.

"The most surprising consequence and benefit of deciding, all of a sudden, to do something that I'd never done before up to that point, was actually working with Oscar. It meant working with the germ of his idea and discovering that the way of working would be absolutely different from my regular way of working. In fact, the main reason I decided to do it was because of my curiosity. I wanted to see what would happen.

"So I followed this seemingly hazardous course and it turned out to be inspirational. I wanted to see what could happen if I worked in a different way with an artist. And yes, I suppose it is one of my most literary works. It is one of the most important works for me as a writer, because I was entering a new territory. I felt that I was attempting an unmistakably adult work, after all the superheroes I'd written before."

EMPIRES AND DENIAL

Both creators emphasize how much they wanted *A Small Killing* to reflect and comment on the larger issues of the time in which it was created.

Says Zarate, "In those times I was worried about what was happening in the world. There were rumors of a possible collapse of the East. Therefore, for better or worse, the world in which I was born had not become any quieter. There were parallel forces struggling with one another. But one manipulated the other and eventually subdued everyone. It is the United States, the new empire.

"And that was one of the issues we raised in *A*

Small Killing, that the identities of all those little countries would disappear. This was one of my worries, related to the world in which I live and think. Another concern was a kind of inner voice, a concern that Alan shared. It is about how when you are a kid, you think, 'When I'm a grownup, I'll plant twenty trees.' And when you come to that age, and you are a grownup and look how many trees you planted, you notice you didn't plant twenty trees. Maybe you only planted two. Then there comes a moment of crisis in which you ask yourself: 'What happened? Why didn't I plant twenty trees?'

"And all these issues were linked to our other idea related to the exterior world, and you think, well, if you are twenty and don't call for social change because you don't agree with what you inherited, then you don't have a heart. And if from thirty to forty you go on thinking the same way, it's because you don't have a head.

"This is more or less the main element of Timothy Hole's profile. I mean, we all have constant dilemmas, we betray friends without wanting to, because all of us are imperfect, and so we beg for pardon, and sometimes we don't say 'sorry' and the friendship ends. The character is so. He's countenanced such a big betrayal that he loses himself. He goes back to the place where he was born looking for something of what he used to be. He is like a wounded animal who comes back to an elephant's graveyard. I wanted that to be Sheffield because inside England's context, it is a socialist town. Sheffield is the red town. And Timothy had rejected all this and said, 'All of you who are here are stupid morons.'

"To reinforce his own transformation, he eliminates everything: 'I'm going away to hell, but I will not go alone, many are coming with me.' That's Timothy. He is looking for a way to justify himself, as happens with the abortion. That gives you a measure of who he is. He has a kind of catatonic emotional state. The girl tells him, 'I don't want you to make the decision for me. I want to know what you think and what you feel,' and he doesn't say anything, because he can't. On the other page he is with the friend who helped him and inspired him, the old man with whom he has a fatherly relation, and to whom he gives a kick in the ass without saying, 'Excuse me, but such is life.' He tries to make thing easier because he cannot do that.

"Finally in the book, a redemption takes place. It's a book about redemption. When I told the story to Alan, he said, 'I want this story to have a happy ending.' That was great because I haven't thought about how I wanted it to end. I suppose that had much to do with him, because he was coming from a very apocalyptic thing like *Watchmen*. It seemed all right for me, because nowadays to do a happy ending you have to work in order not to do a Hollywood ending. It's an ending that I agree and accept, which breaks with people's expectations.

"Timothy Hole is a very accommodating person, as all human beings are, because at any moment there's a sense of things going all right or all wrong with this man. He is a human being who has made a lot of mistakes. In his case, he chooses to blame the rest of the world. And he forgets things because it is better for him to forget. He prefers to move on a certain unconscious level because then he is not so guilty about his own behavior.

"From the moment he accepts that he did things that have harmed people, he takes personal responsibility and therefore he has the chance of getting to a certain space with an opportunity for freedom. Because up to that moment he is not free

at all. This is a very important moment in the life of a person."

Moore elaborates on the ending, and Timothy Hole's salvation: "I wanted some kind of redemption to take place, because it didn't seem enough for me to just paint the picture of a heartless doomed man. It's too simplistic to describe a character as being only that, and it doesn't add much resonance to the story. I wanted to say that even a person like that has the chance to redeem himself if he faces his past.

"And I also wanted to suggest that, in a more general sense, in the same way an individual may face his past and redeem himself, maybe the same thing could be applied to a whole culture. Maybe if the great world powers, like the USA, and in a much lesser measure Great Britain, could admit the things we have done to get where we are now, if we could only look our own dark history in the eye, maybe we would have a chance to leave it behind and advance to the future, to progress.

"But if we refuse to accept or examine our history, we will carry it on our backs forever. And ghosts will haunt us, we will always be exposed to resentment. It isn't simply that I wanted to finish with a note of optimism, as a palliative. I wanted to suggest that there exists the possibility of facing these things, even if it is not a nice thing to do, even if it means facing a jar full of bugs and centipedes. We should be able of open it up and see what's inside.

"As I see it, the final battle between the two parts of his personality comes on that wasteland in his hometown. That's the moment in which he understands the perfect way to handle the Flite campaign that worried him so much all through the whole book. At the end of this battle he is a different person. He has fused these two parts of himself into a whole, integrated person. Consequently, he no longer cares about the advertising for Flite. He is going to look for a new job, and to see what he wants to do with his life. Yes, he has solved the problem that tortured him all through the book, but he has done it in such a way that the original problem turned into something totally irrelevant to the new person that he'd become. If he'd been an entirely soulless

character, that central conflict wouldn't happen.

"I mean, in this case the character, as was true of many eighties yuppies, probably had a past in which he was a left-winger during his youth. Most of the yuppies had been hippies ten or fifteen years before. So we had Timothy Hole selling an American soft drink to Russia, as a symbolic betrayal of a lot of things. And it could be that all the unresolved guilt was the reason for this little boy coming from his past.

"He's getting to a point at which the main decisions he has to take sit less and less comfortably with the person he'd once been. And it is at that moment when there appears a kind of demon of his past that casts an unfamiliar and unpleasant light upon his present life."

Of course, such denial is hardly limited to Timothy Hole, or even just people. As Moore points out, such actions are also endemic to governments, and he believes people recognize it when they see it.

"About, for example, the disputed sinking of the Argentinean warship Belgrano during the Falklands war... I think people will understand it, will understand the context, will know what we are talking about. Even if they don't remember the Falklands War or if they don't remember about the Belgrano, I think they may understand the context in which we are talking. Because of course, there is a parallelism between the acts of a person and

the acts of the whole culture. The way in which politicians and media paper over the past has a lot of similarities with the mindset of Timothy Hole. All of them block their past, deny the nasty part of their story, the buried crimes, the forgotten sins, the archived atrocities.

"As a nation, we are in a constant state of denial. That's as true of the USA as it is of England. Great Britain has passed the times of its Empire. We lost it fifty or sixty years ago, and everybody—well, except for Tony Blair—has noticed that we are no longer a major world power. We have become a strange kind of parasite of the USA.

"The USA is now living through its Imperial phase, and has probably not yet arrived at the conclusion that sooner or later the end will come to their empire too, because empires don't last forever. However, the fact of having had one makes everybody else despise you for ages. We are in a post-empire phase and we still have to learn what the Romans already learned, what everybody else learned: Empires may only survive if they forget.

"They can only live with themselves if, concerning the moment when they committed the massacre or invaded another country and suppressed its citizen's rights, they decide to forget all that, rewrite the history and say, 'This never happened, it was a long time ago, and it doesn't matter now, because things were different and people didn't know the things they know now.' Bullshit. Be it as individuals or as a culture, we cannot make a step forward into a viable future as long as we are not capable of bearing the overwhelming weight of the dark side of our past.

"I don't know if facing that darkness is possible, but I know it is necessary. I mean, it is possible when it concerns a sole individual, a single person. I truly believe that is so, because I have seen people bound straight for Hell and seemingly incapable of arresting their descent, and I also have known people redeemed in an almost miraculous way, become able to recognize how they were before and genuinely want to improve and make progress. I mean, at least in the personal area, a positive change is possible.

"Based on my anarchist dislike for any kind of government, I tend to suspect that government itself is a creature so strange that it cannot be compared with a human being. I would say that government, as an entity, is perhaps irredeemable. I find it hard to imagine any good political leader, except for... I don't know... Maybe in the Netherlands, which seems to be an oddly benevolent country. There aren't many countries like it.

"Apparently, there were Dutch troops in Rwanda, who were supposed to protect the people that were confined in a refugee camp, but were distracted while local paramilitaries massacred them. The curious thing is that the official Dutch government spokesman said, 'It was our fault. We had assumed that we were the most liberal people in the world and that we would never allow something like that. Yet, we let it happen.' I cannot imagine any country in the world, except for The Netherlands, that would say, 'Yes, we were wrong. Blame us for those killings.' But I believe that if the Dutch could do that, it shows us that it is possible to do it.

"I don't know... Maybe in fifty years, could be earlier, could be later, our various nations might be able to acknowledge their faults, recognize them, and then we'll all be able to progress to something better."

Original interviews conducted by Jaime Rodriguez in June and September 2002. This version modified from Moore's corrections and amendments by Antony Johnston, May 2003.